W9-BON-476

The Complete Idiot's Reference Card

Right Royal Records

- Longest-reigning monarch: Queen Victoria (63 years, 216 days).
- Shortest-reigning monarch: Jane Grey (9 days).
- Oldest monarch: Queen Victoria (81 years, 243 days).
- Youngest monarch: Henry VI (38 weeks, 3 days).
- Monarch with most legitimate children: Edward I and James II (19 each).
- Monarch with most illegitimate children: Henry I (21)
- Monarch with most children (combined): Henry I and James II (25 each)
- Monarch with most husbands or wives: Henry VIII (6 wives).
- Adult monarch with the youngest spouse: Richard II (who was 29 years old when he married 8-year-old Isabella of France).

Royal Places of Interest

- **Balmoral**   In Scotland, the favorite holiday residence of Queen Elizabeth II and her family.
- **Bleinheim Palace**   Built by Queen Anne for the Duke of Wellington, it is now the most lavish of Britain's non-royal homes.
- **Brighton Pavilion**   Built as an opulent royal getaway for George IV when he was Prince Regent, it was later sold and is now open to the public.
- **Buckingham Palace**   London residence of the sovereign.
- **Holyroodhouse**   The famous seat of Scottish royal power, this Edinburgh residence is still used for ceremonial occasions.
- **Kensington Palace**   The London residence of the late Princess Diana and also home to Princess Margaret.
- **Sandringham**   The Norfolk estate of Queen Elizabeth II, it is frequently used by the monarch and her family at Christmas, and open to the public at other times of the year.
- **St. James's Palace**   London residence of the sovereign in the days before Buckingham Palace had been purchased by George III. It is now where Prince Charles stays when he is in London.
- **The Tower of London**   Formerly a royal residence as well as a jail and place of torture, murder, and execution. It currently houses the Crown Jewels.
- **Westminster Abbey**   England's most famous church, this is the scene of royal weddings, coronations, and funerals, and the resting place of many monarchs and men of letters.
- **Windsor Castle**   A favorite weekend residence in Berkshire.

British Monarchs with the Most Illegitimate Children

- Henry I (21)
- Charles II (14)
- William IV (11)
- John (8)
- James II (6)
- George I (4)
- Stephen (3)
- Henry II (2)
- Edward IV (2)
- George IV (2)
- Richard I (1)
- Henry VIII (1)
- Edward I (1)
- Edward II (1)
- Edward III (1)

alpha
books

Principal Princess Diana Dates

- July 1, 1961: The Honourable Diana Frances Spencer born to Viscount and Viscountess Althorp at Park House on the Royal Sandringham estate.
- April 1969: Diana's parents, Frances and Johnnie, are divorced.
- November 1977: Prince Charles and Lady Diana Spencer meet for the first time, during a pheasant shoot on the Royal Sandringham estate.
- February 24, 1981: Announcement of the engagement between the Prince of Wales and Lady Diana Spencer.
- July 29, 1981: Charles and Diana marry at St. Paul's Cathedral, London.
- June 21, 1982: Diana gives birth to Prince William Arthur Philip Louis.
- September 15, 1984: Diana gives birth to Prince Henry Charles Albert David.
- December 1992: Charles and Diana agree to a separation.
- August 28, 1996: Charles and Diana are divorced.
- August 31, 1997: Diana, Princess of Wales, is killed in a Paris auto crash.
- September 6, 1997: The funeral service of Princess Diana at Westminster Abbey is watched live around the world.

Some Right Royal Slip Ups

- Princess Diana wrongly addressed Charles as "Philip Charles Arthur George" during their wedding ceremony, prompting Prince Andrew to quip that she had just married his father.
- During the same ceremony Charles generously vowed "all *thy* goods with thee I share," instead of "all *my* worldly goods with thee I share." Princess Anne muttered, "*That* was no mistake."
- At the funeral of Princess Charlotte, the pallbearers got stinking drunk.
- At the coronation of Queen Victoria the aptly named Lord Rolle slipped from the grasp of two peers who were holding him up and rolled down the steps of Westminster Abbey.
- During Victoria's coronation the Archbishop placed the Queen's ring on the wrong finger.
- The myopic writer, E.M. Forster, bowed to the cake at a wedding reception when he mistook it for Queen Mary, wife of George V.
- Near-sighted Queen Olga of the Hellenes mistook a naked statuette of Lady Godiva for Queen Victoria. (!)
- During William I's coronation a guard panicked and set fire to the building, after he mistook the cheers of French guests for an attack on the King. The crowd fled, leaving the clergy alone with a petrified monarch.
- At the coronation of George III someone forgot to bring the chairs for the King and Queen to sit on.
- At the Royal Ascot horserace meeting one year, Queen Mary ordered a sporting peeress to be ejected from the Royal Enclosure for wearing a sailor's cap with the legend in gold lettering, *HMS Good Ship Venus*.
- William IV chatted loudly throughout the funeral of his brother, George IV, and then left early.
- Throughout the funeral of William IV, "mourners" gossiped, joked, and laughed out loud.

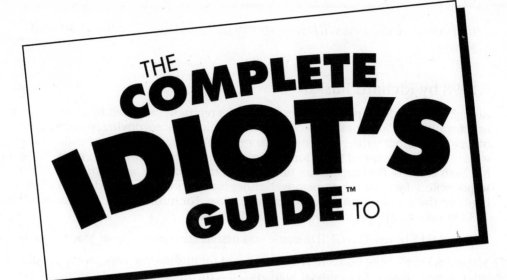

THE COMPLETE IDIOT'S GUIDE™ TO

British Royalty

by Richard Buskin

alpha books

A Division of Macmillan Reference USA
A Simon and Schuster Macmillan Company
1633 Broadway, New York, NY 10019-6785

This book is dedicated with love to my own royals, Dorothy-Jean and Melanie.

©1998 by Richard Buskin

THE COMPLETE IDIOT'S GUIDE name and design are trademarks of Macmillan, Inc.

Macmillan Publishing books may be purchased for business or sales promotional use. For information please write: Special Markets Department, Macmillan Publishing USA, 1633 Broadway, New York, NY 10019.

International Standard Book Number: 0-02862346-0

2000 99 98   4 3 2 1

Interpretation of the printing code: The rightmost number of the first series of numbers is the year of the book's printing; the rightmost number of the second series of numbers is the number of the book's printing. For example, a printing code of 98-1 shows that the first printing occurred in 1998.

Printed in the United States of America

Alpha Development Team

Brand Manager
Kathy Nebenhaus

Executive Editor
Gary M. Krebs

Managing Editor
Bob Shuman

Senior Editor
Nancy Mikhail

Development Editor
Jennifer Perillo
Amy Zavatto

Editorial Assistant
Maureen Horn

Production Team

Development Editor
Nancy D. Warner

Production Editor
Cindy Kitchel

Illustrator
Judd Winick

Designer
Glenn Larsen

Cover Designer
Mike Freeland

Indexer
Chris Barrick

Production Team
Angela Calvert

Contents at a Glance

Contents

Foreword

This is a unique reference book about the ancient and modern British Royal Family and all the extraordinary trappings and quaint customs that surround it. Everybody who has an interest in monarchy should read it.

Queen Elizabeth II was under attack by the media and the public more than ever following the tragic death of Diana, Princess of Wales. She didn't expect this. Her family had been under constant fire for the past five years, yet the criticism of Her Majesty had never been so personal. Caught on the defensive, she had to consult with her royal courtiers before taking the unprecedented step of addressing the British people in a live television broadcast. The world watched while the monarchy adhered to public opinion. It was a landmark event, yet only one of many during 12 centuries of royal rule.

This deeply researched book does not just look at the royals within a modern timeframe. Readers are taken back into the mists of time, certainly more than one thousand years. We learn about how the Anglo-Saxons battled the Great Danes, how the Crusades began and ended, the vile things that took place in medieval times, and why the English and the French learned to loathe and distrust one another—a condition that began some five hundred years ago and still exists today!

We are gently and expertly guided through Tudor times (learn what *really* went on in the "Star Chamber"!) and how good old King Henry VIII neatly solved the problem of divorce without having to pay out exorbitant sums of alimony.

In the days when Henry ruled the land, he also owned much of it. Today, it is easy to look at "BP" (as the Queen refers to Buckingham Palace, her official London residence) and at "KP" (Kensington Palace, where Princess Diana lived following her split from Charles) and think the royals are privileged beyond belief. With other homes such as Balmoral Castle in Scotland, Holyrood Palace in Edinburgh, Sandringham House in Norfolk, and, of course, Windsor Castle—the Queen's favorite official residence—they never have to travel far to put a roof over their heads. But the number of royal homes is quite modest today when compared to centuries gone by.

Elizabeth I had 14 palaces and castles in regular use. Her ancestor Edward I had many more. William the Conqueror had at least a couple dozen. He would not have been even vaguely impressed at the current sovereign's three official palaces!

But then again, Williams' actions and behavior were never queried in the insolent way that happens today.

While the men ruled alone for a very long time, there have also been several good female monarchs over the years. Queen Victoria, who lived beyond the age of 80 and set an example of family values that would carry down to future generations, reigned over an Empire on which, literally, the sun never set. But possibly the greatest of all sovereigns was Queen Elizabeth I. Her fame, thanks to her great sailors and explorers, spread far and wide—even as far as the Americas.

The Hanoverians—the early Georges and William IV—are explained in this guide before we reach the horrors that face the contemporary queen and her largely dysfunctional family.

Elizabeth II may still be respected and even revered in some quarters, but many people wonder if subsequent generations of royal children will have a kingdom to reign over when their time comes. There are a number of people who are certain they won't. Others who are happy with the status quo say, "Give us Prince William as our next sovereign, not the discredited Prince Charles." These are troubling times indeed for the House of Windsor.

As a full-time observer of the British Royal Family for the past 30 years and the author of four books about them, I confess to being an admirer of many of their goings-on. But I have never been an uncritical one and my printed views speak for themselves.

This book addresses the subject of how "the tabloid press" has impacted the Royal Family and in many ways has forced it to change. A great deal has happened these last few decades; the Queen now pays tax, for goodness sakes!

Richard Buskin's *Complete Idiot's Guide to British Royalty* is not for idiots at all. Fools would not be able to properly comprehend such depth of knowledge. This book is compulsive reading for anybody studying the history of the Royal Family, planning a visit to the "Mother Country," or simply wanting to impress. The Brits could learn from it, too.

—James Whitaker

James Whitaker is the royal correspondent and columnist for *The Mirror* newspaper in London, England. Whitaker, the journalist who first broke the story to the public that Charles and Diana were an item, has been reporting on the British Royal Family since 1968.

Introduction

Okay, so you've heard about the House of Windsor and inhabitants such as Queen Elizabeth II, Prince Charles, and the late Princess Di. You may also be familiar with names like William the Conqueror, Richard the Lionheart, Henry VIII, Elizabeth I, and Queen Victoria, but do you really know very much about them? In fact, do you know *anything* about them? As a child growing up in England, I certainly didn't.

Studying history at school was, for me, a real bore. It was all about memorizing facts and dates that I had absolutely no interest in because I couldn't relate to them: "The Battle of Bosworth Field took place on August 22, 1485," or "King John sealed the Magna Carta on June 15, 1215," or even "During the late ninth century King Alfred burnt the cakes." That's how the information seemed to fly at me; "Alright, today we're going to learn about King Alfred..." *Why? Who cared?* Not me.

Later on, however, after I'd finished my school education and emerged none the wiser about the long and elaborate history of my country, I started to do some reading of my own on the subject. To my amazement, what I quickly discovered was that the topic wasn't boring; only the presentation was boring. Indeed, when everything is put in its proper context, condensed in order to include only the most important details, and assembled in chronological order, it makes for an absolutely fantastic story.

This book is full of juicy tales about heroism, treachery, lust, greed, glamor, deception, aggression, and ingenuity, and the one constant throughout is the English (and later British) monarchy. British history is largely defined by its kings and queens, and the anecdotes involving them range from the funny and the ridiculous to the sad and the downright disgusting. It's sometimes difficult to believe what many of them got up to, and even more incredible when you realize that, in relation to the history of the world, such episodes took place fairly recently. All of this goes to prove that the current generation of Brit royals really are pretty well behaved in comparison to their illustrious predecessors.

This book takes you on an incident-filled journey from the beginnings of the monarchy to the present day, with barely a pause for breath between the lies, schemes, scandals, and chivalry. I hope you enjoy reading it at least half as much as I've enjoyed writing it.

What You'll Learn in This Book

The Complete Idiot's Guide to British Royalty is divided into six parts that tell you all that there is to know about the kings and queens of England—which in recent centuries became the head of the United Kingdom and Great Britain. You'll learn how the monarchy started, how it evolved, how its role has changed, and the purpose and tradition behind the various customs and ceremonies.

Part 1, "By Royal Command," describes America's fascination with the Royal Family and how the Queen and her relatives fit in with the rigid British class system. A brief explanation of how the monarchy started and evolved is followed by a description of royal traditions, trappings, and honors. In addition, I tell you about some of the more notable or notorious slip-ups down the years. Lastly, I compare the "fashion" sense of Princess Diana with that of the recent Royals, and I explore Diana's colorful ancestry, troubled childhood, and social impact.

Part 2, "Divide and Conquer (802-1216)," commences the historical journey with King Alfred the Great. He and his successors were in constant conflict with vicious Vikings over who should have possession of the English throne. Then, just when that dispute appeared to have been settled, William the Conqueror came along and took the spoils for the French. In this part of the book, you'll see how the Conqueror's kids squabbled among themselves, how one king was responsible for the murder of an Archbishop, and how Richard the Lionheart spent far more time in his native France than he ever did in England. Finally, for his bad behavior, we have King John agreeing to the Magna Carta, a charter that *attempted* to limit royal power.

Part 3, "Medieval Mischief (1216-1485)," kicks off with the Plantaganet dynasty, which endured the gruesome murder of one monarch, the abdication of another, a plague that wiped out a third of the English population, battles with the French, and some revolting peasants. After all that excitement I tell you about the House of Lancaster and characters such as Henry V and Joan of Arc—people who precede two dynasties going head-to-head in a struggle for the throne. The end is a dramatic one, with a young king and his brother murdered in the Bloody Tower. Was Richard III responsible or innocent of all charges?

Part 4, "Soft Beds, Hard Battles (1485-1625)," is an action-packed section in which the House of Tudor reigns supreme and women come to the fore. The monarchs are all powerful, most notably Henry VIII, a tyrant who executes those he disagrees with, including some of his six wives; Mary I, whose retributions against non-Catholics earned her the nickname Bloody Mary; and Elizabeth I, whose iron will helped see the defeat of the Spanish Armada. I'll finish by telling you about a Scottish king ascending to the English throne, a plot to blow him up as well as Parliament, and the English settlements in North America.

Part 5, "Anarchy in the U.K.—Monarchy Under Siege (1625-1837)," starts with the monarchy getting itself into a mess and being replaced by a republic headed by Oliver Cromwell. When the throne was restored, it was with much less power, Parliament now pulling most of the strings. I also tell you about the romantic escapades of Charles II, the frustrated ambitions of his immediate successors, and the formal merging of the royal families of England and Scotland. Last but certainly not least, you'll read about the misadventures of a largely disinterested German dynasty, as well as poor George III, who suffered mental problems in addition to the loss of the American colonies.

Part 6, "A Bunch of Posers—The Figurehead Monarchy (Since 1837)," starts with the story of Queen Victoria, whose death at the dawn of the 20th century heralds an age when the monarchs are rulers in title only. Nevertheless, they're a fairly colorful bunch, ranging from the playboy Edward VII to the traitorous Edward VIII. I'll also tell you all about the present-day Royals—who they are and what they do—including the background of Prince Charles, a potted history of Windsor scandals, and the marriage of Charles and Di. The section ends with Diana's death and funeral, and a look at the future heirs to the throne. Finally, there's a chronological list of all the monarchs in Appendix A, a collection of Royal Family trees in Appendix B, a selection of recommended books in Appendix C, a list of famous battles in Appendix D, a trip to royal residences in Appendix E, a look at the Royals in film in Appendix F, and the answers to the quizzes in Appendix G.

Royal Regalia

In addition to the main text, I've also included other tidbits to inform and entertain you throughout this book. These appear in separate boxes (or *sidebars*), which can be recognized by the following symbols and names:

Hear Ye, Hear Ye
The kings and queens in their own words or those of others. Look out for some unforgettable quotes.

Palace Parlance
To understand uniquely royal or archaic English terms, check out these definitions sidebars.

Royal Rebuttal
I'll put the lie to those myths, rumors, fabrications, and misunderstandings that could prevent you from becoming a royal expert.

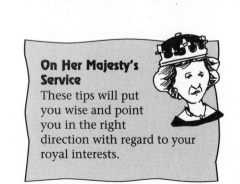

On Her Majesty's Service
These tips will put you wise and point you in the right direction with regard to your royal interests.

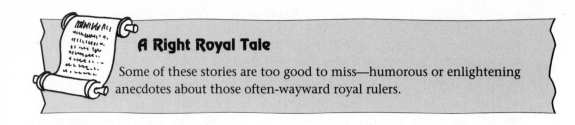

A Right Royal Tale

Some of these stories are too good to miss—humorous or enlightening anecdotes about those often-wayward royal rulers.

Acknowledgments

The author would like to thank the following people for their assistance on this project:

Allen J. Wiener for his selfless and invaluable research work, which included being around at (nearly) all hours to answer my questions. I couldn't have done this without you, Allen!

Cindy Kitchel and Nancy Warner for their editorial expertise and commendable ability to see the humor in my jokes.

Gary M. Krebs for being on top of this project right from the start and for his willingness to always go that extra yard to make things happen. (And there were *plenty* of extra yards.)

Phil Kitchel for his capacity to turn his hand to more than one thing at a time while making sure that all of the loose ends were tied up.

Jack Bennett and Pari Esfandiari for their help with additional research.

And last, but not least, Dorothy-Jean and Melanie for putting up with a frequently preoccupied and bleary-eyed partner and father.

Part 1
By Royal Command

Those British sovereigns. Ah, where would we be without them? Or, more to the point, where would they *be without us? After all, there are quite a few royal families still in existence around the world today, but none of them evoke anywhere near as much interest, excitement, and sheer controversy as the British version.*

Up until the early 1980s, things were bubbling along at their usual steady pace for the Queen and her imperial cohorts. Then a certain Lady Di entered onto the scene and nothing would ever be the same again. In this first part of your Idiot's Guide *we'll therefore familiarize ourselves with the British monarchy; its image at home and abroad, and its rules and traditions, not to mention the rejuvenating and disruptive contributions of "The People's Princess." This is a family saga that easily surpasses* Dallas, Dynasty, *and all of the other TV "super-soaps" of the 1980s and 1990s. So, let's not hang around a moment longer—Their Royal Highnesses are ready and it's extremely poor form to keep them waiting!*

Chapter 1

British Reserve—
Her Majesty & Co.

In This Chapter

➤ The Royal Family's bumpy ride through recent times

➤ Why Americans are so captivated by the British monarchy

➤ How the queen and her relatives are viewed in their home country

➤ The question regarding the monarchy's survival

While there's an undeniable fascination with today's Royal Family, that interest varies sharply from one side of the Atlantic to the other. For Americans, the lives of the queen and those around her encompass many of the most dramatic aspects of a TV mini-series, while also representing the kind of historic grandeur that many associate with Britain's elite. For the British, on the other hand, the monarchy is very much a way of life; not reflective of how "common" citizens live, but nevertheless ingrained in the nation's psyche. While Americans are either enthralled with or indifferent to the royals and their activities, for the Brits it's largely a case of adoring or just tolerating them: There's little in between. In this chapter, then, I get the ball rolling by describing how Elizabeth II's reign has prompted such sharply contrasting emotions.

As the millennium draws to a close and the queen prepares for her sixth decade on the throne, the fate of her successors is far from certain. (That's another hot topic that we take a look at in the next few pages.) Because your ignorance on the subject of British royalty is nothing to boast about, I think I'll start off by throwing you straight in at the deep end.

For Better or for Worse: A 20th-Century Soap Opera

Scandal is hardly new to the British monarchy. Ever since their beginnings during the ninth century AD, the nation's sovereigns and their relations have consistently been embroiled in one form of transgression or another: murder, rape, pillage, adultery, you name it. In fact, given some of the iniquities of past centuries, the members of recent royal households have led fairly tame lives. I mean, what's a spot of physical fun among friends? At least it isn't among relatives, which couldn't be said with respect to every monarch.

No, the 20th-century Brit Royals certainly haven't been as badly behaved as many of their predecessors. Yet, they have often suffered far more for their sins—largely due to the advent of radio, television, and the tabloid press. Before these modern mediums came along, royal peccadilloes may have been discussed in private circles and whispered along the public grapevine, but they never garnered the kind of mass attention accorded to current true or rumored indiscretions.

A Right Royal Tale

King Charles II, who reigned from 1660 to 1685, wasn't known as "The Merry Monarch" for nothing. He had a long list of lovers gathered from all walks of life, prompting George Villiers, son of the first Duke of Buckingham, to remark, "A king is supposed to be the father of his people, and Charles certainly was father to a good many of them." Still, although Charles' mistresses bore him many children, his wife never did. When he died, therefore, his brother, James II, succeeded him on the throne. William IV suffered the same fate in the 19th century, fathering 10 children with actress girlfriend Dorothea Jordan but remaining heirless. He was succeeded by his niece, Queen Victoria.

Furthermore, only during very recent times has an attitude of "anything goes" overtaken the popular press. Certainly there were royal controversies earlier in this century. At that time, however, the public was never afforded "inside information" about what went on in the bedrooms of, say, Edward and Mrs. Simpson (who you'll read about in Chapter 22) or Princess Margaret and her beau, Peter Townsend (who make an appearance later in that same chapter). That's not to say that so-called "friends" or "sources" close to those people wouldn't have been willing to sell their stories. It's just that newspaper, magazine, and book editors were not willing to publish them. Now, however, the situation has changed drastically; Kitty Kelly's recent title *The Royals* illustrates the new willingness to tattle on the royals.

Constituents of the royal household were once revered characters who made occasional public sorties but generally hid behind a protective cloak of well-respected privacy. Today they're more like the cast of a glitzy, up-market soap opera, which is a shame. For while the flawed, warts-and-all image makes them more human and more accessible, it is the mystery, the magic, and the fantasy that really comprise the life-blood of the current monarchy. Strip away these characteristics and, with no real political power to speak of, the sovereign is left looking a bit too ordinary.

Still, who am I to argue with the consensus of public opinion? People have their own perceptions as to what the Royal Family represents, and so, for that matter, do the members of the Royal Family.

On the surface there doesn't appear to be too much dissension among the ranks within the House of Windsor. The current monarch, Elizabeth II, her husband, and their children all fully believe in the monarchy's position at the top of British society and their respective roles within it, as do the queen's mother, her sister, and her numerous cousins, nephews, nieces, and grandchildren.

If serious questions are raised in this respect, it's nearly always behind closed doors, where the ever-present royal advisors usually have their say and ensure that everybody falls into line. During the 20th century, however, some notable exceptions to this rule have emerged: Edward VIII, Sarah Ferguson, and Lady Diana Spencer.

> **Palace Parlance**
> **Windsor** is the surname of the current Royal Family. Down the centuries there have been 10 formal dynasties and no fewer than 67 different kings and queens. I'll deal with them soon, so be patient and don't start skipping pages!

> **Hear Ye, Hear Ye**
> "It's a fabulous story for a musical."
> —*Composer Jonathan Segal, September 1997, after he had "put some initial concepts together" for a Broadway show about the life and death of Princess Diana*

Edward VIII abdicated from the throne in order to marry the twice-divorced woman he loved. Sarah Ferguson and Lady Diana married into the Royal Family but evidently never felt comfortable with some of its more stuffy formalities. Consequently, when their relationships with Princes Andrew and Charles came apart, they both aired their grievances publicly. Of course, all of this provided juicy material for sensational tabloid headlines and, yes, TV dramatizations. So did the jet-set lifestyles Fergie and Di pursued, mixing with assorted members of the glitterati in a variety of exotic locales while the paparazzi kept a watchful eye on their doings.

On one hand, all of this media attention has popularized the Royal Family; on the other, it has helped to underline just how much its image is in need of an overhaul. Whether the royals will change their image remains to be seen. In the meantime, there will be plenty of speculation because, as I've already told you, it's the world's longest-running soap opera.

Fantasy and Glamour: America's Fascination

Although the Windsors were rivaling *The Colbys* and numerous other TV-soap families for America's attention back in the 1980s, it hadn't always been that way. The centuries-old pomp and ceremony that surrounds the monarchy has always held a certain attraction for many non-Brits, especially those whose country has a relatively short history and no royalty. The colorful costumes, glittering jewels, and pageantry of a special occasion make for eye-catching entertainment, but the royals do more than provide pomp. They also help fulfill a need in people to make a connection with a supposedly more innocent time: a time when England's green and pleasant land wasn't populated with tall buildings, fast cars, and multi-lane highways, and when those who led the nation carried with them an air of mystique.

There, however, the attraction basically ends. It comprises a fantasy that can brighten a dull day or a spectacle that will liven up a holiday trip to the U.K. On the whole, however, royalty isn't something that most Americans (or many Brits, for that matter) can readily identify with.

Nor could the public identify with some of the major cast members of "Palace Dallas," as the royal household came to be known during the 1980s: the predictably staid-looking queen, the sweet little old Queen Mother, crusty Prince Philip, stuffy Prince Charles, and the unsmiling Princess Anne. Princess Margaret did, at least, help lighten the mood for a while during the 1970s by way of her amorous flings with younger men, but even she got her act together after a while. No, for many Americans the plots were predictable and the characters fairly boring. Then came Diana.

Initially dubbed "Shy Di" in the early-1980s because of her quiet, reserved demeanor, everyone's favorite Princess quickly evolved into "Dynasty Di," the sharp-looking, highly fashionable wife of Britain's future King. For a while, through American eyes, the couple was one of the most glamorous in the world, and following fast on their heels were Fergie and "Randy Andy" (the name accorded Prince Andrew during his freewheeling bachelor days). During an era when America's royalty consisted of discredited Kennedys and high-profile music and movie celebrities, these young Brits were royal superstars. Unlike their predecessors, they—including Charles for a time—appeared to be in tune with the modern world, while making the whole idea of the monarchy interesting and appealing.

Suddenly more people than usual were flocking to the U.K. to take in the royal sites and get a flavor of the country that Britain's foremost ambassadors were promoting. At the same time, when Charles and Di visited the United States in 1985; they created a sensation. Their attendance at a charity dinner in Palm Beach, Florida, was considered by many of the wealthy attendees to be the "social event of the season."

Snow business like royal business—Di and Fergie share a laugh on the ski slopes in Klosters, Switzerland. (Photo courtesy of Reuters/Corbis-Bettmann)

A Right Royal Tale

During their five-day trip to Washington, D.C., and Palm Beach, Florida, in November 1985, Charles and Diana were guests of honor at a White House banquet thrown by Ronald and Nancy Reagan. That night the stars turned out, with Clint Eastwood, Neil Diamond, Tom Selleck, Mikhail Baryshnikov, and opera singer Leontyne Price being among those who gravitated toward the royal couple. John Travolta made a splash when he and the Princess danced to "You're The One That I Want," yet perhaps the highlights of that unforgettable evening were Nancy Reagan singing "I Concentrate On You" and the President making a speech in which he referred to Diana as "Princess David."

American interest in Britain's Royal Family had reached new heights. It would diminish in the wake of the scandals that subsequently rocked the House of Windsor (which you'll learn all about in the last chapter of this book), only to experience a resurgence as a result of Diana's tragic death. By then, however, the admiration and sympathy that had once been the exclusive domain of Princess Di would be passed on to her two sons, the Princes William and Harry. To most Americans, the other members of the royal household were now just objects of intense curiosity.

That Touch of Class: The British Perspective

Americans may have lost respect for the Royal Family in light of the controversies of recent years, but on the whole, royal naughtiness has little effect on American life. The British, on the other hand, have an altogether different take on royal events; after all, the British public financially supports the Windsors by way of their taxes. In return, they expect the Royals to keep their noses out of political affairs while serving as goodwill ambassadors abroad. Therein, however, lies a conflict. You see, outside India and its caste system, Britain is one of the most class-conscious societies on earth. In fact, among many citizens is an underlying belief that, while you can take the person out of the social class, you can't take the social class out of the person. In other words, you are what you were born into.

The majority of the population consists of the working and middle classes, while the remainder comprises the affluent upper class (millionaire businessmen, for example), and, of course, the aristocracy (such as the Princess of Wales in the days when she was Lady Diana Spencer). Some people even choose to break down these categories further by having a lower-middle and upper-middle class. Whatever the validity of that argument, one thing is indisputable: No one, be they British citizen or political ruler, can aspire to the heights of the monarchy, which is so unique that it's virtually "class less." This, however, is where the conflict has arisen, especially during the past 15 or so years.

On Her Majesty's Service

If you're interested in learning more about British society and its class system, here are some books worth reading: *Inside British Society: Continuity, Challenge and Change* by Gordon A. Causer (St. Martin's Press, 1987), *State and Society: British Political and Social History 1870-1992* by Martin Pugh (St. Martin's Press, 1994), and *Social Class in America and Britain* by Fiona Devine (Edinburgh University Press, 1997).

Being "class less" also largely amounts to appearing aloof, boring, and out of touch with the real world. This has been a common criticism of the Royal Family. Yet, when new members such as Fergie and Di instilled a little glamour and excitement into the proceedings, jet-setting their way around the world's top holiday resorts or, as in the case of Diana, spending a fortune on clothes and beauty care, there was considerable resentment. This was especially true during the late 1980s and early 1990s, when many people felt that they were paying for the royals to enjoy the high life while the rest of the country was suffering through a crippling economic recession.

Add some well-publicized shenanigans—such as Fergie and Di poking a friend's behind with their umbrellas during a horse-race meeting at Ascot—and the Windsors were in severe danger of no longer being viewed as "class less." Instead they were being branded as "upper class twits," with Fergie and Diana also earning the title of "Throne Rangers."

Obviously, Fergie and Di were just behaving like ordinary people, but evidently many of the queen's *subjects* (meaning citizens of Britain and the Commonwealth) were less than happy with their conduct. The monarchy should behave with dignity and decorum. This kind of carrying on in public was embarrassing and...well, just not royal!

Now Diana is gone, Fergie is pursuing her own life, and people are once again criticizing the Windsors for being, that's right, aloof and boring. So, what is the solution? Right now, it's anyone's guess.

Palace Parlance
The queen's **subjects** refers to the citizens of Great Britain as well as the British Commonwealth. These even include the members of the Royal Family. The only exception is the sovereign herself.

God Save the Queen? The Struggle for Survival

Will the British monarchy make it through to the 21st century and beyond? Well, if precedence is anything to go by it has already survived wars, murders, treachery, and all forms of scandal down the years, so why not these latest setbacks? People power is the answer.

If the monarchy is to play a part in the new millenium, it will do so by listening to the views expressed by large sections of the British public—or at least by the tabloid newspapers who invariably take their lead from the direction of popular opinion. Diana certainly had her critics, not least among royal circles, but in the wake of her death, the general message has been for the Windsors to clean up their act and, in line with the princess' much-appreciated warmth and affability, try to act more like a Royal Family of the people instead of the stoical, apparently cold-hearted residents of the various London palaces.

For one thing, the nation—if not the world—is telling Prince Charles and the queen that they had better take tender, loving care of the young Princes William and Harry, who enjoyed great warmth and affection in the hands of their mother. It would do the father and grandmother no harm if they were to—Shock! Horror!—hug the kids in public; the question is whether they can bring themselves to do so.

"Don't let those corgis near the water!"—Princes Philip, Edward, Charles, and Andrew, together with the queen, grandson Peter Phillips, and Princess Anne in Balmoral, 1979. (Photo courtesy of UPI/Corbis-Bettmann)

It may be difficult to change the habits of several lifetimes. Nevertheless, considering the many concessions to public opinion that have been made following Diana's death (which you'll read about in Chapters 3 and 25), the Palace has shown that, when it's up against the ropes, it isn't above changing in the name of survival.

Still, besides acting as the model father, it isn't yet clear how Charles, the future monarch, should proceed from here. After all, let's face it, the self-confessed philandering former husband of the late, lamented Princess of Wales isn't exactly Mr. Popular right now. Amid talk that maybe he should step down as heir to the throne in favor of his extremely popular eldest son William (who benefits from having the attractive looks of his mother), there is an even touchier issue to resolve: namely, Charles' relationship with his longtime mistress, Camilla Parker-Bowles.

Again, we'll take a look at that hot little topic in a later chapter (number 25, to be precise), but suffice it to say that she isn't exactly Madam Popular with the people of Britain, either. Before Diana's death there was talk that Charles and Camilla might marry. That is now out of the question for the foreseeable future—unless he wants to relinquish his right to succession—as is any idea of there being a Queen Camilla. Don't even try to imagine the outrage that would be stirred up by *that* move.

No, for now they have been confined to a lovers' state of limbo, while Charles must wait to see whether Elizabeth II lives to the same age as that of the old Queen Mum. Remember, his whole life has been geared toward becoming king, and he must certainly want to fulfill his destiny. If, on the other hand, he should step aside and make way for William, the move may prove to be very popular...or completely disastrous. Indeed, it could provoke a division of opinion in the U.K. that would spell the end of the monarchy.

Still, in my humble but—being that I'm the author of this book—vital opinion, ending the monarchy is unlikely. For all of their displeasure with the current Royal Family, the British don't appear to be hankering after a republic. All that they want is for the monarchy to change and stay on.

Now, that shouldn't be too difficult, should it?

The Least You Need to Know

➤ The behavior of the current generation of royals is not nearly as bad as that of many of their predecessors.

➤ The entry of Princess Diana into the royal household really boosted American interest in the Windsors.

➤ Britain is one of the most class-conscious societies in the world, yet the Royal Family should remain "class less."

➤ The British monarchy will have to change and align with public opinion if it wishes to survive.

Chapter 2

All in the Family

In This Chapter

➤ The roots of the British monarchy

➤ A run-down of the different royal families and foreign influences

➤ A comprehensive list of who is currently in line to the throne

➤ Details of how royal power has changed through the ages

The British monarchy has been around for so long that you might be forgiven for thinking that it dates back to the Garden of Eden. Well, it doesn't go back quite that far, but it has actually been around for more than 1,100 years now, so it's quite an institution. In fact, it's the oldest institution of government.

What isn't so well established is the Royal Family itself. There have been a good number of them, each dividing up into separate "houses" and some deriving from places outside the British Isles. In this chapter, I provide an overview of how everything started, as well as how the monarchy has evolved from many different sources to become the unified Crown of the United Kingdom. Along the way, you'll see how the power of the sovereigns has diminished with the passing of time. And thanks to the "line of succession" that I provide, you'll be relieved to discover that, no matter what disaster befalls the royals, there's always another heir to the throne waiting in the wings.

Beginnings: A Need for Leadership and a Desire to Rule

To begin, you should know that the United Kingdom, consisting of Great Britain (England, Scotland, and Wales) and Northern Ireland is only a tiny spot of land compared to the United States. In fact, England itself is only slightly bigger in size than the state of New York, yet the democratic ideals and system of justice formulated there provided the foundation for the laws of free nations around the world.

Stretching back as far as 12,000 BC, people from the European mainland started settling in what is now known as Britain. In fact, it was a group of Celts from Western Europe, known as Britons, who lent their name to the citizenship that exists today. They landed in England and Wales during the 700s BC (we've just taken a shortcut across several millenniums to get here), and by the first century BC, these Britons had developed a proper farming society complete with log housing, horse transportation, and the weapons of war.

Unfortunately, however, said weapons weren't enough to defend themselves against the might of the burgeoning Roman Empire.

In 55 and 54 BC, having already invaded what is now known as France, Julius Caesar led his army across the English Channel and landed in Britain. Still, while the Brits may have lost the battle, they hadn't entirely lost the war. They kept scrapping with the Romans until 43 AD, when the Emperor Claudius decided that enough was enough and once and for all established Roman rule…well, for 400 years, at least.

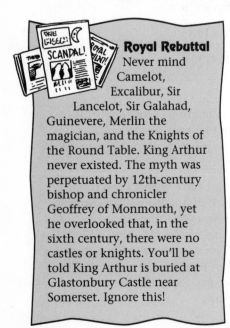

Royal Rebuttal
Never mind Camelot, Excalibur, Sir Lancelot, Sir Galahad, Guinevere, Merlin the magician, and the Knights of the Round Table. King Arthur never existed. The myth was perpetuated by 12th-century bishop and chronicler Geoffrey of Monmouth, yet he overlooked that, in the sixth century, there were no castles or knights. You'll be told King Arthur is buried at Glastonbury Castle near Somerset. Ignore this!

These Romans were very sophisticated. The Brits had their own transportation, but they didn't have roads. The Romans built roads, as well as forts to defend themselves against the aggressive Scottish and Welsh tribesmen. In fact, the most northerly boundary of the Roman Empire was Hadrian's Wall, built along the border with Scotland in 128 AD in order to protect people who were living by the philosophy of "When in Rome (or in this case England, annexed to Rome) do as the Romans." They inhabited modern towns, paid taxes, and went to the Christian churches that started springing up during the fourth century AD. Just over a hundred years later, however, the status quo changed once again as the Roman Empire shrank and the invaders withdrew, only to be replaced by others from north of Hadrian's Wall as well as a whole slew of Germanic invaders.

Those poor Brits! No wonder they would one day wreak revenge by ruling much of the world! The Germanic invaders were known as Angles, Saxons, and Jutes, and it was at this point, in or around the 500s AD, that England got its name, evolving from "Angle-land." Again, the Britons didn't give up without a fight, and, according to legend, one of those who led them into battle was none other than King Arthur of Camelot.

Whatever the origins of the Arthurian story, Arthur didn't help with the invasion. The Anglo-Saxons took over, dispensed with the Roman traditions, and instigated their own rules and regulations. Pagans when they first arrived in England, the Anglo-Saxons eventually converted to Christianity as a result of Pope Gregory I sending missionary Saint Augustine to see King Ethelbert of Kent.

Kent is presently a county of England, but until the ninth century there was no one leader ruling over the entire country. Instead, at the beginning of the eighth century, there were no fewer than seven kingdoms in England: East Anglia, Essex, Sussex, Wessex, Kent, Mercia, and Northumbria. Each of these was, naturally, ruled by a king, whose warriors meted out justice and whose representatives, known as *earldormen* (later *earls*), were given land that helped earn more money for their leader.

This setup was all very nice, except that in the mid-to-late ninth century some nasty Norwegians and Danes decided to spoil the party by burning English monasteries, murdering the monks, and stealing prized treasures. For a time, it looked as if the marauders would take over completely. Then along came Alfred the Great to restore a little sanity to the proceedings…

Foreign Ties and Family Changes

Later in this book I tell you about the reigns of the various kings and queens of England. For now, however, having already described how the Romans and the Anglo-Saxons each decided that they were well-suited to rule the Britons, I'll fill you in on some other overseas influences who had their day and their say.

The Royal Dynasties Since 802

Date	Dynasty
802-1066	Anglo-Saxons *(no dynasty)*
1066-1154	House of Normandy
1154-1216	House of Angevin
1216-1399	House of Plantagenet
1399-1461	House of Lancaster
1461-1470	House of York
1470-1471	House of Lancaster
1471-1485	House of York
1485-1603	House of Tudor
1603-1649	House of Stuart

continues

continued

Date	Dynasty
1649-1660	Interregnum (between reigns)—*No monarchy*
1660-1714	House of Stuart
1714-1901	House of Hanover
1901-1910	House of Saxe-Coburg and Gotha
1910-present	House of Windsor

Basically, after King Alfred of Wessex managed to defeat the Danish leader Guthrum during the late-ninth century, he generously agreed to share the spoils (knowing that he didn't have the forces to rule over the entire country). Alfred took control of England's southwest region, while Guthrum presided over the northeast, renamed Danelaw for obvious reasons. Danelaw would eventually be reconquered by subsequent English kings, meaning that the Danes then had to invade all over again. Such an inconvenience! In 1013, England actually became part of the kingdom of Denmark, and it stayed that way for just under 20 years, when the English returned to the throne.

The Saxon rule came to an end in 1066 when William, Duke of Normandy (in what is now France), took over. This was an important date in more ways than one: To date England has not been invaded again.

English rulers resumed power at the start of the 1200s, and while future centuries would see further foreign rulers on the throne, on those occasions they would be responding to invitations rather than forcing themselves on unwilling subjects.

A Right Royal Tale

When a king ascends to the British throne, his wife becomes the queen, even though she is not the monarch. Conversely, when a queen ascends to the throne, her husband is not named king, but instead remains a royal prince. There has been one exception to this rule, however, and that was when two monarchs presided at the same time. No, they weren't fighting each other, they were married to each other (then again, maybe they were fighting). He was the Dutchman, William III ("William of Orange"), who reigned from 1689 to 1702, and she was Mary II, who co-reigned until 1694. Dying childless, William was succeeded by his sister-in-law, Anne.

The current Royal Family is directly descended from German ancestry in the form of the Hanovers, whose British reign ended with Queen Victoria. Unlike her Hanoverian predecessors, Victoria wasn't allowed to rule simultaneously in Germany. The British lineage therefore had to change, and so her son, Edward VII, took his name from Victoria's husband, Prince Albert of Saxe-Coburg and Gotha.

In 1917, amid anti-German sentiment in Britain during the First World War, Edward's son, King George V, decided it might be wise to adapt a family name more closely attuned to the country he presided over. He therefore opted for *Windsor*, as in the castle of the same name and the town in which it is located.

And so Windsor it has remained. However, you and your fellow royal-watchers can now ponder the fact that, if it hadn't been for the outbreak of war between England and Germany, we might be discussing the recent scandals that have rocked the House of Saxe-Coburg and Gotha. That doesn't roll off the tongue quite so easily, though, does it?

As Time Goes By: The Ups and Downs of Royal Power

The British monarchy's evolution from a position of all-consuming power to that of a mere figurehead establishment has taken place over the course of many centuries. As you work your way through this book, you'll be able to chart each stage of that journey. To help summarize some of the major twists and turns of royal power, however, I provide you here with a brief overview.

At the start and end of the 13th century, two changes took place—one imposed on the monarchy, the other instigated by it—that would subsequently result in redressing the balance between the rulers and those under them. The first of these was the Magna Carta, a charter that King John was forced to sign in 1215, giving rights to the nobles that would eventually be passed on to the rest of society. Then, in 1295, King Edward I called together an assembly of town representatives, nobles, and church leaders that came to be known as the "Model Parliament" because of the way in which it served as a blueprint for future Parliaments.

Hear Ye, Hear Ye
"I am born of a rank which recognizes no superior but God."
—*King Richard I ("the Lionheart") to the Holy Roman Emperor*

Meanwhile, on the religious front, Henry VIII threw a monkey wrench in the works when, in retaliation for the Pope refusing to grant him a divorce from his first wife, he initiated the Protestant Reform. That was in 1529, and five years later he ensured that Parliament passed a law naming him, not the pontiff, as supreme head of the Church of England. Clearly, Henry wasn't a man who hesitated to wield the full force of his magisterial powers, and during the next century several other monarchs followed his lead.

In fact, Charles I was so power-mad that he didn't even allow Parliament to meet from 1629 to 1640. Then, when he did, Parliament couldn't fix the situation. Civil war broke out, and, after Charles lost his head (quite literally) in 1649, England became a "Protectorate" under the command of its new "Protector," Oliver Cromwell. The monarchy returned with Charles II in 1660, but then his successor, James II, got big ideas about restoring Catholicism to England, resulting in the country's leading politicians inviting the Dutch ruler, William of Orange, to "invade." In 1688, James fled to France.

The following year, on becoming England's joint rulers, William and his wife Mary agreed to the Bill of Rights, which granted basic civil rights to ordinary citizens and reduced the power of the monarchy. From now on, this would be the trend, even though the reigning sovereign ruled over England, Scotland, and Wales after 1707, when the Act of Union created the Kingdom of Great Britain.

In 1714, Queen Anne's successor was her German cousin, George I, who didn't speak much English and therefore relied on his chief minister, Sir Robert Walpole, to largely run matters. Walpole presided over a council of ministers, which in effect made him Britain's first prime minister. The Cabinet style of government was here to stay.

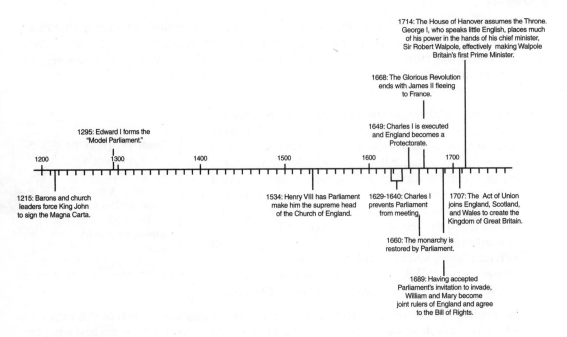

Changes in the balance of Royal power.

Today the roles of the Royal Family are largely ceremonial. The queen opens Parliament and invites a newly elected prime minister to form a government, but in truth she has no *real* political power. In fact, she can't even dismiss the government or punish its leader.

Nevertheless, some constitutional powers are at her disposal, such as, along with the prime minister, being able to pass legislation instantly during wartime. What you won't see her do, however, is actually declare war.

Who's on First: The Line of Succession

Kings initially either forced their way onto the British throne as powerful leaders of men or they were chosen from a family descending from such a leader. As time passed, however, the whole idea of hereditary successions became much more firmly established.

The principle of *primogeniture* resulted in a number of continuous dynasties, some of which took a left turn when a particular monarch wasn't able to have children (or at least have legitimate children). Still, this principle has its drawbacks, the most notable one being that because an heir doesn't succeed to the throne on the basis of how capable he or she is, there's no saying what the results might be.

Down the years the outcome has been a mixed bag. Some successors were useless, while others were far more talented than their pathetic predecessors. You can make up your own mind about those who are currently listed in the line of succession to Queen Elizabeth II's throne, but one thing's for sure: As you'll see from the

> **Palace Parlance**
> **Primogeniture** refers to the right of succession or inheritance that belongs to either a first-born child or eldest son. This is why reigning monarchs are always desperate to sire offspring who will succeed them.

following list of the Top 35, correct as of 1996, the Royal Family ensures that there's no lack of likely successors. In fact, there are way more people on the full list, but I don't want to bore you. Besides, it's more than enough for you to memorize 35 potential successors in the right order. Oh yes, by the way, I should point out that this list could all change if the British government passes a proposed new law allowing the eldest daughter to succeed to the throne even if she has a younger brother!

The following is the line of succession to the British throne:

1. His Royal Highness Prince Charles, The Prince of Wales (b. 1948)

2. HRH Prince William of Wales, eldest son of Prince Charles (b. 1982)

3. HRH Prince Henry of Wales, younger son of Prince Charles (b. 1984)

4. HRH Prince Andrew, The Duke of York, second son of Her Majesty Queen Elizabeth II (b. 1960)

5. HRH Princess Beatrice of York, eldest daughter of Prince Andrew (b. 1988)

6. HRH Princess Eugenie of York, younger daughter of Prince Andrew (b. 1990)

7. HRH Prince Edward, youngest son of HM Queen Elizabeth II (b. 1964)

8. HRH Princess Anne, The Princess Royal, only daughter of HM Queen Elizabeth II (b. 1950)

9. Peter Phillips, son of Princess Anne (b. 1977)

10. Zara Phillips, daughter of Princess Anne (b. 1981)

11. HRH Princess Margaret, The Countess of Snowdon, younger sister of HM Queen Elizabeth II (b. 1930)

12. David Armstrong-Jones, Viscount Linley, son of Princess Margaret (b. 1961)

13. Lady Sarah Chatto, daughter of Princess Margaret (b. 1964)

14. Samuel Chatto (b. 1996)

15. HRH Prince Richard, The (2nd) Duke of Gloucester (b. 1944)

16. Alexander Windsor, Earl of Ulster (b. 1974)

17. Lady Davina Windsor (b. 1977)

18. Lady Rose Windsor (b. 1980)

19. HRH Prince Edward, Duke of Kent (b. 1935)

20. Edward Windsor, Baron Downpatrick (b. 1988)

21. Lady Marina Charlotte Windsor (b. 1992)

22. Lady Amelia Windsor (b. 1995)

23. Lord Nicholas Windsor (b. 1970)

24. Lady Helen Taylor (b. 1964)

25. Columbus Taylor (b. 1994)

26. Cassius Taylor (b. 1996)

27. Lord Frederick Windsor (b. 1979)

28. Lady Gabriella Windsor (b. 1981)

29. HRH Princess Alexandra, the Honorable Lady Ogilvy (b. 1936)

30. James Ogilvy (b. 1964)

31. Alexander Ogilvy (b. 1996)

32. Miss Flora Ogilvy (b. 1994)

33. Marina, Mrs. Paul Mowatt (b. 1966)

34. Christian Mowatt (b. 1993)

35. Miss Zenouska Mowatt (b. 1990)

The Act of Settlement of 1701 decreed that only Protestant descendants of Princess Sophia, Electress of Hanover and daughter of King James I would be eligible to succeed. Subsequent Acts have confirmed this, and so Prince Michael of Kent and the Earl of St. Andrews were both excluded from the succession after they married Roman Catholics.

If a monarch is under 18 years old when succeeding to the throne, or if he or she is totally incapacitated, there is a provision for a regent to be appointed in order to assume the royal functions.

The succession to the throne is known as the *accession*, and after this takes place there's a "convenient interval" of, say, a year or more, during which time he or she can settle into the new role. Then there is the coronation, which takes place at Westminster Abbey. This service is conducted by the Archbishop of Canterbury in the presence of representatives of the Houses of Parliament, the Church of England, and the State. Leaders from other nations are also invited to attend.

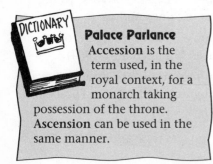

Palace Parlance
Accession is the term used, in the royal context, for a monarch taking possession of the throne. **Ascension** can be used in the same manner.

During the ceremony, the monarch swears an oath to rule according to the law of the land, and he or she is then anointed and crowned. The Archbishop of Canterbury and assorted senior peers pay their tributes, and then Holy Communion is celebrated.

Needless to say, the spectacular costumes, dazzling jewels, and colorful pageantry all make for eye-catching entertainment. In fact, when the present queen's coronation took place on June 2, 1953, there was a major boom in the sale of television sets in the U.K.

The boy who would be king? Prince William on the day of his mother's funeral. (Photo courtesy of AFP/Corbis-Bettmann)

The Least You Need to Know

➤ A group of Celts from Western Europe, known as Britons, landed in England and Wales during the 700s BC. England then got its name when the Angles, Saxons, and Jutes invaded in the sixth century AD.

➤ It wasn't until the ninth century that one leader ruled all of England.

➤ The Battle of Hastings in 1066 marked the last time that England suffered a hostile invasion.

➤ The monarchy started being divested of its power with the signing of the Magna Carta at the start of the 13th century.

➤ Only Protestant relatives of the monarch, and those who marry Protestants, are eligible for the line of succession.

Royal Customs, Regal Trappings

Chapter 3

In This Chapter

➤ How British royal tradition isn't all that it appears to be

➤ The lowdown on some royal practices and trappings such as the Crown Jewels

➤ Examples of royal mishaps and misunderstandings

➤ How recent times have seen some unprecedented behavior

Protocol, pageants, and tradition are what many people associate with the British monarchy. So are some less savory things that appear elsewhere in this book. However, just as the scandals have to be put into their proper historical perspective, so some of the royal customs should be properly explained, because they too are surrounded by a lot of false assumptions.

In this chapter, I explain how certain traditions are not nearly as ancient as you might think. Still, I describe some of the famous customs, as well as a number of amusing royal slip-ups through the years, and then I point out how in recent times Britain's first family has broken a number of well-established rules.

Oh yes, and just to show that the royals can outdo even the most diamond-encrusted of celebrities, I'll give you a brief description of some of the most priceless Crown Jewels. Tiffany's, eat your heart out!

Tradition! Real or Invented?

Okay, so we've already established that the British monarchy goes back a long way. However, you may be surprised to know that much of the pageantry associated with it doesn't date back to an early time at all. Instead, it has increased dramatically in recent years, amounting to a sort of "invented tradition."

Yes, I know that those glorious royal ceremonies, such as coronations, weddings, and funerals, are incredibly well organized, but this organization isn't the result of a millennium or more of practice. Not even a few hundred years of practice. What if I tell you that the royals didn't even start marrying in public until *1923*? That's right: All of those "traditional" proceedings that embellished the weddings of Princes Charles and Andrew to Diana and Fergie—the gilded carriage making its way through the heavily populated London streets, the parade of dignitaries, the wave to the people from the balcony of Buckingham Palace—only came into existence during the 20th century! All of the pomp and circumstance looks so convincing that, aside from a knowledgeable few—including you—no one, including the British, has a clue as to what is old and what is new. It's largely thanks to the infallible research of that nation's own historians that we now know better about these "centuries-old" traditions.

At the coronation of Queen Victoria in the early 19th century, no one burst into a rendition of the national anthem, "God Save the Queen" (which, incidentally, has the same tune as "My Country Tis Of Thee"). The clergymen presiding over the ceremony didn't wear those now-famous purple gowns, and the new sovereign didn't get to ride in a fancy carriage. She rode in a horse-drawn carriage, but it wasn't nearly so snazzy. Only during the reign of Edward VII did the monarchy obtain a nice gilded model.

Still, Victoria wasn't bothered. In fact, she wasn't very keen on immersing herself in the pageantry at all. At her Golden Jubilee in 1887 the stoic-faced queen turned out to be a party pooper when she actually refused to wear either her crown or her royal robes! But, then again, this was also the woman who passed up the chance to open Parliament for about 40 years of her reign.

Hear Ye, Hear Ye

"Why they got into the business of manufacturing traditions is easy to answer. They saw a need and filled it. Millions of people around the world find it reassuring to know that there are still a few human beings who get the opportunity every now and then to put on colorful stage costumes and ride around in horse-drawn carriages."
—*Richard Shenkman in* Legends, Lies & Cherished Myths of World History *(1993)*

Royal Rebuttal

As with the royal weddings, you may think that their funerals also conform to traditions that have remained constant for hundreds of years. Wrong! It wasn't until the 19th century that much attention was paid to the royal rite of passage. Before that, monarchs were buried in private; their corpses weren't open to public viewing until Edward VII was put on display in 1910.

So, you see, all is not as it appears to be. For, although the British evidently have an aptitude for combining tradition with excellence, as you'll learn later in this chapter, things haven't always been as they now are.

Regality: From Crown Jewels to the Changing of the Guard

Over the centuries ceremonies such as the coronation have become increasingly ritualized. Ancient traditions have been combined with more recent embellishments as the monarchy, divested of its powers, has sought to establish its importance in other ways. The all-important public perception is what counts, so as long as the supposedly time-honored rituals serve to emphasize the solemnity, grandeur, and continuity of the British monarchy, the objective is being achieved.

Let's now take a look at some of the customs and material goods that aid the Royal Family in its public image.

The Crown Jewels

The Crown Jewels, which originate from various eras and the rule of different royal houses, date back as far as the time of Edward the Confessor, who reigned from 1042 to 1066. When England became a short-lived republic after the execution of Charles I in 1649, Parliament took possession of the jewels and some of them were subsequently melted down or sold off! Others thankfully survived.

Here, as a way of starting, is a selection of the main items that are used during a coronation ceremony:

➤ **St. Edward's Crown**   This is made of solid gold, contains 440 semi-precious stones, and weighs just under five pounds. The original, which dated back to the time of Edward the Confessor (after whom it was named), was destroyed during the revolution of 1649, so this new crown was made when the monarchy was restored to the throne in 1660. It is believed that the gold it contains comes from the original.

➤ **The Royal Sceptre**   Held in the monarch's right hand during the coronation ceremony, this boasts at its head one of the world's largest diamonds, the Star of Africa, which weighs a whopping 530 carats. The sceptre is a symbol of regal power and justice.

➤ **The Sovereign's Orb**   The most sacred of all the coronation ornaments, this orb symbolizes the dominion of the Christian religion.

➤ **The Ampulla and Anointing Spoon**   The Ampulla is a vessel shaped like an eagle, and holy oil is poured through its beak into the Anointing Spoon. Then, in line with an ancient biblical tradition, the sovereign is anointed with the oil.

➤ **The Coronation Chair**   This was made in 1301 on the orders of King Edward I and has since been used for the coronations of all but two sovereigns. On the back are names carved into the wood: These belong to a group of 18th-century Westminster schoolboys!

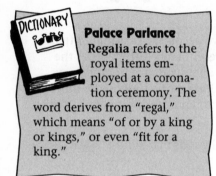

Palace Parlance
Regalia refers to the royal items employed at a coronation ceremony. The word derives from "regal," which means "of or by a king or kings," or even "fit for a king."

In addition to the aforementioned *regalia*, a coronation also requires the royal maces, three swords (representing mercy, spiritual justice, and temporal justice), the jeweled sword, the Great Sword of State, the golden spurs, and St. Edward's Staff. In addition, some of these regalia are used at other times, such as the State Opening of Parliament.

The Crown Jewels also include banqueting plates, orders, insignia, robes, and a unique collection of medals. Nevertheless, it is the crowns themselves, many of them donated by other sovereigns, that are the star attractions.

I've already told you about St. Edward's crown. Here are some others:

➤ **The Crown of Queen Elizabeth the Queen Mother**   The only crown to be mounted in platinum, this was made for Elizabeth II's mother when she was made Queen Consort in 1937. Among its more than 2,800 diamonds—most of which were taken from a circlet that once belonged to Queen Victoria—are the famous Koh-i-Noor and the Lahore.

➤ **The Imperial Crown of India**   Because English crowns can't leave the country, this was made for George V to be crowned King Emperor in India in 1911.

➤ **The Small Crown of Queen Victoria**   Choosing comfort over ostentation, Queen Victoria wore this crown instead of the Imperial State Crown whenever possible. Made in 1870 by Garrard (the Crown Jewelers), it weighs just five ounces, is set in silver and gold, and is studded with a mere 1,300 diamonds that were taken from a fringe necklace.

➤ **The Imperial State Crown**   Originally made for Queen Victoria's coronation in 1838, this contains the Second Star of Africa (which formed part of the Cullinan Diamond, the largest ever recorded). Weighing nearly three pounds, it is set with more than 3,000 precious stones! The queen wears this crown during the State Opening of Parliament, and it also comes into play following a coronation for the return from Westminster Abbey. After all, if celebrities can make costume changes, why shouldn't a monarch make a crown change?

A Right Royal Tale

Aside from the years of Oliver Cromwell's rule (1649-1660) and the Second World War (1939-1945, when they were hidden in a secret location), the Crown Jewels have been kept at the Tower of London ever since 1303. This placement followed a theft from Westminster Abbey, yet the most famous attempt at stealing the prized possessions occurred in 1671, courtesy of one Colonel Blood (not to be confused with Captain Blood, as portrayed by Errol Flynn in the film of the same name). Blood was caught at the Tower's East Gate, holding onto a sceptre, St. Edward's Crown, and the Sovereign's Orb.

Today, if you wish to see the Crown Jewels, you have to go to the specially designed Jewel House at the Tower of London. This house was opened by Queen Elizabeth II in 1994.

Royal Salutes

Royal gun salutes are fired on notable occasions such as the Coronation, the State Opening of Parliament, state visits, royal birthdays, and Trooping the Colour (which I'll tell you about in a few paragraphs).

A Right Royal Tale

The coronation of William I ("the Conqueror") was presided over by two prelates for the benefit of the English and French people attending the ceremony. Archbishop Ealdred of York spoke in English and Bishop Geoffrey of Coutences spoke in French, and each in turn asked his countrymen if they would accept William as their king. Both groups shouted enthusiastically that they would, yet when a guard posted outside heard the loud French response, he assumed a mob was threatening the new king. Acting quickly, he set fire to some of the buildings! Everyone fled, leaving behind a few members of the clergy and a king so frightened that he was visibly trembling!

On the day in question the guns are usually fired at midday in Central London's Hyde Park or Green Park by the King's Troop, Royal Horse Artillery, or at 1:00 p.m. at the Tower of London by the Honourable Artillery Company.

Now, while the basic royal salute consists of 21 rounds of gunshots, an extra 20 rounds are added when they are fired in Hyde Park, which is a royal park. Then, on actual royal anniversaries, a total of 62 rounds are fired at the Tower of London, consisting of the basic 21, a further 20 because the Tower is a royal palace and fortress, and yet another 21 for the City of London. Simple, eh?

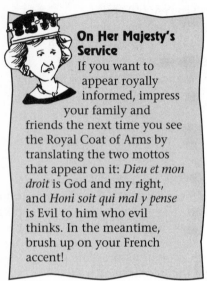

On Her Majesty's Service
If you want to appear royally informed, impress your family and friends the next time you see the Royal Coat of Arms by translating the two mottos that appear on it: *Dieu et mon droit* is God and my right, and *Honi soit qui mal y pense* is Evil to him who evil thinks. In the meantime, brush up on your French accent!

The Royal Coat of Arms

Identifying the sovereign as the Head of State, the Royal Coat of Arms contains symbols representing the history of the monarchy and of England, Scotland, and Ireland. (Wales is represented on the Arms of the Prince of Wales.) The Royal Coat of Arms appears on British money, in churches, on public buildings, and even on the products of companies that have been given the royal seal of approval (the Royal Warrant).

In addition, the sovereign also has a personal symbol (the royal cipher), consisting of the monarch's initials intermingled with a crown. This symbol appears on royal and official state documents, as well as on the famous red Royal Mail post boxes. Other members of the Royal Family also have ciphers designed for them by the College of Arms and approved by the queen.

Trooping the Colour

While we ordinary citizens only get to have one birthday a year (and not even that if you were born on February 29), that privileged individual, the British monarch, actually has two. This privilege isn't because a king or queen's birth is an unusually long process, but simply a result of the long-observed custom to publicly celebrate the sovereign's birthday on a nice summer day. Given the British weather, of course, there's no guarantee that a summer day will be nice. Therefore, while Queen Elizabeth II was born on April 21, 1926, the official celebration takes place every June. The hooplah is in the form of Trooping the Colour on London's Horse Guards Parade, featuring fully trained and operational troops from the Household Division.

In modern parlance "trooping the colour" literally means "carrying the flag," a throwback to the early 18th century when the battalion "colours" were "trooped" down the ranks of soldiers so that they could be seen by all. This parade has marked the sovereign's official birthday ever since 1748, but only after Edward VII acceded to the throne in 1901 did the monarch take the salute in person.

The Changing of the Guard

Following Oliver Cromwell's demise and the restoration of the monarchy in 1660 (which you'll read about in Chapters 17 and 18), it was thought wise to have Household Troops guarding King Charles II and his royal palaces. So wise, in fact, that they've been doing this for the reigning sovereigns ever since.

The Queen's Guard, which usually consists of foot guards wearing red tunics and furry busbys atop their heads, is based at St. James' Palace. There's also a detachment guarding her main home, Buckingham Palace, including the four sentries that you'll see at the front of the building when Her Majesty is in residence. Should the Queen's Guard have operational commitments to attend to, other units such as the brigade of Gurkhas are called in.

"Okay," I hear you say, "so what about the Changing of the Guard?" Well, if you want to catch the Changing of the Guard, stand outside Buckingham Palace from 11:30 a.m. to 12:15 p.m. every day in the summer—every other day in the winter—and you'll see the new Guard arriving in the palace forecourt from Wellington Barracks, accompanied by a Guards band. The old Guard hands over his duties during a ceremony in which the sentries switch places, with the ones being replaced returning to barracks. The new Guard then leaves the detachment at Buckingham Palace and marches to St. James' Palace.

All in all this is a pretty colorful event, so take your camera.

On Her Majesty's Service

Calling all Americans: Want to sound proper? Learn to pronounce certain English names the way the Brits do. Some examples: "Bucking-mm" (Buckingham Palace), "Tems" (River Thames), "Lester" (Leicester Square), "Barkley" (Berkeley Square), "Beaver" (Beauvoir Castle), and "Beech-mm" (Beauchamps Place). Strange? Well, who invented the language?

Mind Your Manners: Some Notable Mishaps

If you were among the billions of people around the world who tuned in their TV sets to watch the wedding of Prince Charles and Lady Diana Spencer on July 29, 1981, you may recall that, during the service, a nervous Di erroneously addressed her new husband as "Philip Charles Arthur George." This prompted Prince Andrew to quip that she had just married his father. At another point, instead of vowing "And all *my* worldly goods with thee I share," Charles generously promised "And all *thy* goods with thee I share." "*That* was no mistake," opined Princess Anne.

Still, as embarrassing as these little *faux pas* may have been, they were nothing in comparison to some of the major howlers that took place on other royal occasions. Take the 1760 coronation of George III—having started late, it was then discovered that there were no chairs for the king and queen to sit on! Someone had also forgotten to bring the Sword of State, and then there was a little problem to do with a horse. Basically, this poor animal had been trained to walk backwards so that, after having been shown to the king, it would back away and not insult the monarch by revealing its rear end. A brilliant idea, except that, on the big day, the confused nag actually entered the hall backward and reversed all the way to the king's table.

George III—His disastrous coronation may have been a sign of things to come: loss of the American colonies and mental illness. (Picture courtesy of Corbis-Bettmann)

Incredibly, by the time that George's son, George IV, acceded to the throne 60 years later, things hadn't gotten much better. His coronation costume was ridiculed for making him look fat, and, at George's own request, his wife Caroline was barred from entering

Westminster Abbey. This was the woman of whom he'd once said, "I had rather see toads and vipers crawling over my victuals than sit at the same table as her." (I should point out that victuals are food items.) Caroline died a few weeks after the coronation.

Oh well, even if the happy occasions created tears, at least the somber ones provided some laughs. When George IV died, his successor, William IV, was criticized for chattering constantly at his funeral and then leaving early.

However, when William passed on a mere seven years later, the "mourners" at his funeral reportedly gossiped, cracked jokes, and laughed out loud "within sight of the coffin." Still, at least they showed *some* restraint. At the funeral of Princess Charlotte in 1817, the undertakers actually managed to get stinking drunk! The only pity is that all of these incidents took place before movie cameras were invented. Afterwards, everyone would make *sure* that they were on their best behavior.

Out of the Past: Breaking with Convention

In a royal world full of etiquette and protocol, where the figureheads are addressed as "Your Royal Highness" and those highnesses are virtually programmed from birth to always keep their heads up and never show much emotion, Princess Diana broke many of the rules.

For one thing, she was never afraid to publicly show her emotions, whether, as a 20-year-old fiancée to the future king of England, she burst into tears while watching Charles play a polo match, or, as a mother of two, she showered her boys with hugs and kisses. Then there were the occasions when Di crossed the line of previously acceptable royal behavior, such as the spot of umbrella-poking that she indulged in with Fergie at Ascot in 1987. (For details, see Chapter 1.)

When her marriage was really faltering during the late 1980s, a number of the princess's public statements and actions caused anger within Buckingham Palace, and this turned to fury when Andrew Morton's biography, *Diana: Her True Story*, was published in 1992. Based on the disclosures of many of her own closest friends, as well as personal interviews with the princess that were only revealed after her death, the book was Di's barely disguised attempt to tell the story of her troubled marriage. Its publication eventually provoked Charles into giving his own all-revealing TV interview. Diana responded in kind.

Hear Ye, Hear Ye
"Oh no, it's not dogs I don't like; it's corgis. They get the blame for all the farts."
—*Princess Diana commenting on the Queen's favorite dogs*

Never before had any members of the Royal Family disclosed such personal secrets in such a public way, but then again Di was the instigator of many other breaks with convention. Not the least of these breaks was the way that she openly courted the press, as well as her insistence on allowing her sons to have as normal a childhood as is possible for two royal princes. In their mother's company, William and Harry wore jeans and baseball caps, ate at McDonald's, and took the unprecedented step of spending money out of their own pockets. (Not forgetting that said money had their grandmother's face printed on it.) Diana chose to buck the system during her years in the limelight, and even in death her influence in this respect has continued.

Amid the massive outpouring of grief surrounding her funeral and the public's condemnation of the Royal Family that had apparently shunned her, the queen, Prince Charles, and their advisors contrived to make concessions that were previously unheard of. For that matter, concessions of any kind on the part of the monarchy are largely unheard of.

In Chapter 25, I'll tell you all about Diana's "unique funeral," and of the way in which the Palace has continued to break new ground in order to both appease and adhere to public opinion. After all, one thing's for sure: Thanks to Diana and to people power, things on the royal front will never be the same again.

The Least You Need to Know

➤ Many apparently old British royal traditions have been created in recent times.

➤ The original Crown Jewels were largely destroyed during the rule of Oliver Cromwell. Today's collection is kept in the Jewel House at the Tower of London.

➤ Before the advent of movie cameras there were numerous slip-ups and instances of bad behavior at public royal occasions.

➤ Princess Diana was largely responsible for the many breaks with royal convention that have occurred in recent years.

Chapter 4

Down on One Knee, Decorated with Honor

In This Chapter

➤ How the royal honors system came about

➤ Details about the various honors and orders

➤ The way in which celebrity honors have become more acceptable

➤ A test of how much you've learned so far

No guide to British royalty, not even one for idiots, could be deemed complete without including a chapter on the honors system in the U.K.

Basically, it's quite unlike any other, and, of course, it's steeped in tradition, some ancient, some far more recent. The system is also pretty complicated, however, so I'm going to simplify matters and give you an outline of the process without going into *too* much minute detail.

To start off, we'll take a look at the origins of the various honors and orders, as well as the peerage. (If you don't understand these terms, don't worry; I explain them in a few moments.) Then I give a breakdown of the various titles that can either be inherited or conferred on people by the monarch, along with their background and what they mean. After that, I'll describe how, in recent times, more and more honors have been bestowed on celebrity figures (not all of them British), and how this trend has been condemned in some circles.

But that's not all. I hope that you've had an enjoyable read up to this point, but have you been taking all of the information in? Just to ensure that you've been doing your homework I placed some quizzes at strategic points in this book—and this chapter is one of those points. Now, I of course can't check on your responses to my questions, so I'll have to trust that you won't sneak a premature peek at the correct answers that await you in Appendix G.

Origins of the Honors System

To start, let me explain that Britain's honors system breaks down into three basic categories:

➤ **Decoration** The presentation of an emblem in return for "gallantry or long and valuable service"

➤ **Peerage** Dukes, marquesses, earls, viscounts, barons, and lords

➤ **Knighthood** Accorded to members of the higher grades of most Orders

Okay, so let's start with these Orders, which originated in medieval times with the Holy Orders, a fraternity comprising of monks and friars who lived according to a code of conduct that was set out for them by the Catholic Church. When the crusaders (who you'll read about in Part 3) decided to involve themselves with religion by battling to defend the Christian faith, the Orders took on a more military feel.

During the 14th century, when English kings began assuming power from the Church of Rome, they instituted their own Orders of *Chivalry* and modestly pronounced themselves Grand Masters. People who were deemed to be of "noble birth," and who vowed to do charitable work and give all of their support to the reigning monarch, were—surprise, surprise—eligible for membership.

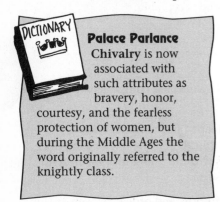

Palace Parlance

Chivalry is now associated with such attributes as bravery, honor, courtesy, and the fearless protection of women, but during the Middle Ages the word originally referred to the knightly class.

Eventually, however, the emphasis shifted from people who undertook to conform to a specific code and moved toward those who were being rewarded for the services they had already performed.

And so what were people given to signify that they were members of these chivalric orders? A membership card, perhaps? Well, no. They were presented with insignia such as gold chains—a favorite with the Kings Richard II (1377-1399) and his cousin Henry IV (1399-1413) and still in use today— as well as medallions, badges, and even weapons.

Recipients of the highest awards also often received a title and the right to bear a personal coat of arms, not to mention gifts of land that helped to boost the holder's social status and personal wealth. During those days, a lot of land was still available in Britain. As the royal dynasties (pronounced "dinasties") changed through the years, so did many of the titles and awards. Some were abolished and then revived, and others became obsolete due to changing circumstances. For example, there was the Order of the Indian Empire, which ceased existence when India left the British Empire in 1947, as well as the British Empire Medal, which isn't awarded anymore in the U.K. because there's no longer an Empire to speak of.

You'll shortly read about the old honors and orders that have survived, as well as those that have been instituted more recently. Before we get to that, however, let me give you some background about the Peerage. This originated during the Dark Ages of the Anglo-Saxon reign and Norman conquest. The reigning king used Peerage to administer and defend his territory.

After William the Conqueror invaded England in 1066, this Duke of Normandy introduced a number of titles that are now an established part of the Peerage. Basically, a *duke* comes immediately below a *prince* in rank, and this title is almost always conferred upon members of royalty. In fact, while Sir William de la Pole, Marquess of Suffolk's 1488 transformation into the Duke of Suffolk marked the first time a non-royal received a dukedom, the last people to do so were the dukes of Westminster and Fife in 1874 and 1900, respectively.

Royal Rebuttal
If you think that a Peerage entitles the holder to numerous privileges, think again. In addition to exemption from jury duty, the main privilege is being entitled to sit in the House of Lords which, along with the Commons, is one of two Houses of Parliament. What's more, years ago those lucky peers who were sentenced to death could choose to be beheaded rather than hanged!

On the next rung down the ladder below a duke is a *marquess*. In Norman Britain this title was given to an *earl* or *baron* who was responsible for guarding the border lands (or "marches") of Scotland and Wales. The title of earl, meanwhile, was established in Saxon England as the highest rank of nobility. Bestowed on the regal representatives who ran an earldom or a shire, it became a hereditary title during the Norman era for those who were in charge of a county. The title of the earl's deputy was *viscount*, while barons or lords, introduced during the Norman reign, were given land by the various kings in exchange for their military efforts.

Alright, so that's the background. Now let's take a closer look at some of the honors.

The Higher You Climb: Those Honors and Orders

In effect, practically anyone can be recommended for an honor and anyone can make the recommendation, including the person being recommended! Still, if you're thinking of trying it, don't hold your breath waiting for an approval.

Today, the awarding of British honors is based on merit, either for achievement or for service. The recipients are "selected" by the queen on the advice of the prime minister and other ministers, who often act on recommendations from the general public or their own departments. About a quarter of all the nominations are made directly to the prime minister's office by individuals, companies, and public organizations.

At the same time, honorary awards to foreigners are put forward by the Secretary of State for Foreign and Commonwealth Affairs, while the Ministry of Defence, as well as the Welsh and Scottish offices, can also make recommendations. As for the queen herself, she gets to personally select the recipients of the Order of the Garter, the Order of the Thistle, the Order of Merit, the Royal Victorian Order, the Royal Victorian Chain, the Royal Medals of Honor, and Medals for long service. All of the material from these various sources is collated at the Central Chancery, which was set up in 1904 with the approval of Edward VII.

Hear Ye, Hear Ye
"The object of presenting medals, stars, and ribbons is to give pride and pleasure to those who have deserved them."
—*Prime Minister Sir Winston Churchill in a speech to the House of Commons, 1944*

Each year a total of nearly 3,500 new names are eventually divided up into two lists, one of which is announced to tie in with the Queen's Official Birthday in June, and the other for New Year's Day. There are also special lists that coincide with a coronation and a Prime Minister leaving office.

Okay, so now you know about the selection process. Next, we get to the investitures and awards. Following the publication of an Honors List, there are investiture ceremonies at which the recipients are officially decorated.

Because of the numbers, there are normally 22 annual investitures, each of which are attended by about 130 recipients. Buckingham Palace is the main venue for these ceremonies, but they also take place at the Palace of Holyroodhouse in Edinburgh, Scotland; Cardiff Castle in Wales; and abroad during royal visits. Still, as you may have realized, 22 multiplied by 130 doesn't quite amount to the annual total of 3,500 recipients, so those who can't be included in one of the queen's investitures have to make do with receiving their awards from her official representative.

"So, what *are* the awards?" I hear you beg. Alright, here goes...

➤ **The Peerage**   This award comprises the titles of *duke* (whose wife is a *duchess*), *marquess* (whose wife is a *marchioness*), *earl* (whose wife is a *countess*), *viscount* (whose wife is a *viscountess*), and *baron* (whose wife is a *baroness*). All peers are addressed as "Lord" and their wives are called "Lady," with the exception of barons and baronesses (who are called "Sir" and "Lady"), and dukes and duchesses. Since the introduction of the Life Peerage Act in 1958, only a handful of hereditary peers have been created. Most are life peers, meaning that their titles only exist until they die and are not passed to their heirs. As of July 1995 there were 398 life peers, 65 of them women.

➤ **Knighthoods**   These derive from the days of medieval chivalry, when a soldier's proficiency was rewarded by the sovereign touching him on the shoulder with a flat sword (a ceremony known as "the accolade"). The *knight bachelor* (in line with his full title) doesn't rank as highly as the *knight,* who is a member of an Order of

Chivalry (which we'll get to in a moment), yet the knighthood is the most ancient of all the British honors, dating back to Saxon times.

All knighted men are addressed as "Sir" (except for clergymen, who don't receive the accolade), and their wives are called "Lady." Meanwhile, women who receive the honor don't get the sword on the shoulder, and they're addressed as "Dame." As for knighted members of the Order of Chivalry, they place initials after their names to denote the class of order that they've received. You see, unlike knight bachelors, usually only those who are awarded first or second class orders can become knights or dames.

➤ **Orders of Chivalry** Here are the principal orders listed in terms of importance, along with the initials that are placed after the recipient's name (male and then female):

Royal Rebuttal
Unlike the Hollywood legend, knights of old were often very poorly paid, lived in cold castles, had little food to eat, and rarely if ever rescued damsels in distress. As jousting tournaments didn't become popular until the late Middle Ages, the majority of knights never competed in them, and besides, most English ones didn't ride horses and couldn't afford those famous suits of shining armor.

➤ The Most Noble Order of the Garter, established in 1348. (KG or LG)

➤ The Most Ancient and Most Noble Order of the Thistle, revived in 1687. (KT)

➤ The Most Honourable Order of the Bath, established in 1725 and rewarded in both military and civil divisions for services to the Crown. This honor takes its name from the symbolic bathing that used to prepare a candidate for knighthood. The ranks in this order are Knight or Dame Grand Cross (CGB), Knight or Dame Commander (KCB or DCB), and Companion (CB).

➤ The Order of Merit, established in 1902 and awarded in recognition of services rendered in the armed forces or towards the advancement of art, literature, and science. (OM)

➤ The Most Distinguished Order of St. Michael and St. George, established in 1818 and awarded for service overseas or in connection with foreign or Commonwealth affairs. The ranks in this order are Knight or Dame Grand Cross (GCMG), Knight or Dame Commander (KCMG or DCMG), and Companion (CMG).

➤ The Royal Victorian Order, established in 1896 and awarded for services to the Royal Family. Ranks are Knight or Dame Grand Cross (GCVO), Knight or Dame Commander (KCVO or DCVO), Commander (CVO), Lieutenant (LVO), and Member (MVO).

➤ The Royal Victorian Chain, established in 1902, which counts among its 15 members the queen and Queen Mother.

➤ The Most Excellent Order of the British Empire, established in 1917 and awarded mainly to civilians and service personnel for public service or other distinctions. This order has military and civil divisions, and the ranks are Knight or Dame Grand Cross (GBE), Knight or Dame Commander (KBE or DBE), Commander (CBE), Officer (OBE), and Member (MBE).

➤ The Order of the Companions of Honour, established in 1917 and awarded for "service of conspicuous national importance." (CH)

➤ The Most Venerable Order of St. John of Jerusalem, established in 1888, usually known as the Order of St. John, and awarded for services rendered to the charitable works of the Order. Because this isn't a State Order, however, membership doesn't confer rank or title.

Finally, these medals are awarded to members of the armed services for outstanding acts of valor. Most are made from gold, silver-gilt, or pure silver, and some are even embellished with diamonds and precious stones. Here are several of the medals:

On Her Majesty's Service
Although some insignia of the Orders of Chivalry are returnable on death, many find their way into the hands of collectors. Prices vary according to the award and who it was conferred upon. For instance, the collar chain and badge ("The George") of the Order of the Garter can be worth more than 50,000 pounds ($75,000), and the price increases if the owner was famous.

➤ **Victoria Cross**   Established by Queen Victoria in 1856, this is still cast from a Russian cannon that was captured in the Crimean War. These medals are awarded either for gallantry or for distinguished service. (VC)

➤ **George Cross**   Established by King George VI in 1940, this is awarded for acts of bravery in times of peace. (GC)

➤ **Distinguished Service Order**   Established by Queen Victoria in 1886. (DSO)

➤ **Distinguished Service Cross**   Established by King Edward VII in 1901. (DSC)

➤ **Military Cross**   Established by King George V in 1914. (MC)

➤ **Distinguished Flying Cross**   Established by King George V in 1918. (DFC)

Non-Brits can be accorded honorary memberships of British orders. However, even though the appropriate letters are placed after their names, they don't get the pat on the shoulder with the sword and so they aren't addressed as "Sir" or "Lady." The following lists some recent American recipients of British honors:

➤ Former presidents Ronald Reagan and George Bush are Knights Grand Cross of the Most Honourable Order of the Bath.

➤ Generals Norman Schwarzkopf and Colin Powell are both Knights Commanders of the Most Honourable Order of the Bath.

➤ Caspar Weinberger is Knight Grand Cross of the Most Excellent Order of the British Empire.

➤ John Paul Getty II and Andre Previn are Knights Commanders of the Most Excellent Order of the British Empire.

The Celebrity Connection

In centuries gone by, royal honors were bestowed on men only. After all, it was the male of the species who ran the country at all levels the monarchy and government (and it was also he who waged all of the wars), so it was only natural that the awards should be handed out on the same fair basis.

"Arise Sir Francis Linnell," King George VI tells an air marshall as he confers a knighthood on him in June 1943. (Photo courtesy of Corbis-Bettmann)

39

By the 16th century, women at last acceded to the throne, but even then all others who shared the power and reaped the rewards were men. Furthermore, the honors were usually only accorded to guys who had fought the good fight or proved themselves to be outstanding supporters of the monarch, so things remained staid until relatively recently.

As the 20th century progressed it was no longer unusual for royal honors to be conferred on women or, for that matter, certain leading lights in the popular arts. In previous times, professions such as acting had been largely looked down upon by the upper echelons of British society, but now the word "celebrity" had an exciting ring to it and the powers that were started to recognize this trend.

Still, it was only the more "respectable" representatives of the "serious" arts who were accorded the honors; acclaimed orchestral conductors such as Sir Edward Elgar and Sir Thomas Beecham, for example, or famed thespians such as Sir Laurence Olivier and Sir John Gielgud. Then the "Swinging Sixties" arrived and all hell broke loose. In 1964, the forward-thinking, left-wing Labour Party came to power, replacing the stuffy old Conservatives who had led Britain for the previous 12 years.

The new prime minister was Harold Wilson, a canny politician who recognized the electoral value of associating with celebrities. This was the year that Liverpudlian pop group, The Beatles, took the world by storm, and fun-loving Harold instantly ensured that he appeared with them in front of the news cameras or was quoted in the press singing their praises. Still, as The Beatles' fame continued to flourish on an unprecedented scale, the popularity-seeking prime minister had yet another little trick up his sleeve.

When the Queen's Birthday's Honours List was released to the press on the night of June 11, 1965, the world learned that The Beatles were being awarded MBEs. Officially, this was for their "services to British export." Harold Wilson had made the recommendation to Her Majesty.

Hear Ye, Hear Ye
"She's lovely, great. She was very friendly. She was just like a mum to us."
—*Paul McCartney describing the Queen immediately after The Beatles received their MBEs, October 26, 1965*

Looking back, the award was fairly justified. The band, having popularized their country and their hometown of Liverpool around the world, had certainly inspired a boom in the purchase of suddenly trendy British goods and the number of tourists visiting the U.K. They also opened the way for British singers, actors, fashion designers, and so on to find success abroad. Many people saw the value in what The Beatles had achieved; however, others were not so appreciative, and a minor storm erupted around Buckingham Palace.

Among the main objectors were a few military figures and Royal Air Force heroes who had received their royal awards for outstanding service in the defense of their country. Evidently ignoring the fact that, for several decades, British sports heroes had also been rewarded with Orders of Chivalry, these dissenters asserted that conferring MBEs upon a pop group had cheapened the entire honors system. They therefore returned their medals to the queen.

One such character was Hector Dupuis, a member of the Canadian House of Commons, who complained that he'd been placed on the "same level as vulgar nincompoops!" The Beatles nevertheless received their honors and a new precedent was set. From now on, popular celebrities all over Britain and a fair few overseas would be accorded royal honors.

Today, it's practically impossible to count the number of celebrities who have received awards. Every time a new Honours List appears it contains a slew of them, from popular TV personalities to famous film stars and numerous others in between. As for The Beatles, in 1997, a sword on the shoulder transformed one of the four members into Sir Paul McCartney.

Are You a Complete Royal Idiot? Quiz #1

Okay, it's time to see just how much you've learned so far about British royalty. I'm only going to ask you about things that have appeared in the preceding pages (none of which you've skipped, of course), so try to answer them from memory. If that's a struggle you'll just have to brush up on what you don't know or can't remember.

1. Who was known as "The Merry Monarch"?

2. Which king abdicated in order to marry a twice-divorced woman?

3. How many different royal families have there been in Britain?

4. Who once referred to Diana as "Princess David"?

5. What nickname was given to Prince Andrew during his bachelor days?

6. How many kingdoms were there in England at the start of the eighth century?

7. Which king ruled one half of England while Danish leader Guthrum ruled the other during the late-ninth century?

8. In what year did William the Conqueror take over the throne?

9. Who were the only two national monarchs to reign at the same time?

10. From which dynasty do the present Royal Family derive their German heritage?

11. What does "interregnum" mean?

12. Who became England's Protector in 1649?

13. Which 1701 Act decreed that only Protestant descendants of Princess Sophia could accede to the throne?

14. In what year was Queen Elizabeth II's coronation?

15. Which king was the first to have his body put on public display following death?

16. What is the name of the Royal Sceptre's massive heart-shaped diamond?

17. What is the precise name of the location where the Crown Jewels are kept?

18. What is the date of Queen Elizabeth II's actual birthday?

19. What is the name of the parade that marks the sovereign's official birthday?

20. What are the three basic categories of the British honors system?

21. Where is all of the material relating to honors collated?

22. On what two occasions are the Honors Lists announced?

23. How many investitures take place each year?

24. From where is the metal that's used to make the Victoria Cross taken?

25. What name is given to the ceremonial placing of a sword on the recipient's shoulder during a knighthood?

The answers to these questions are in Appendix G. Here's how to rate your performance:

➤ 20 or more—You're in line for an honor.

➤ 13-19—A regal effort.

➤ 6-12—Do some revision in the Tower.

➤ 5 or fewer—Respond "yes" to the name of this quiz!

The Least You Need to Know

➤ The Order of Chivalry originated in medieval times.

➤ The Peerage took off during the reign of William the Conqueror.

➤ Today, honors are based on merit either for service or achievement.

➤ It is only recently that huge numbers of celebrities have been honored.

Chapter 5

The Di Revolution—Sprucing Up Those Royals

In This Chapter

➤ Princess Diana's family background

➤ The fashion sense of the House of Windsor

➤ How Diana sharpened the Royal Family's image

➤ The Princess' charitable nature and public adoration

There can be little doubt: For much of this century, the members of Britain's Royal Family haven't exactly set the fashion world alight or captured the public imagination by way of their dress sense. Indeed, what they choose to wear tends to amuse rather than inspire, yet there have been some welcome exceptions and, among them, Princess Diana was by far the most notable.

This chapter focuses on the way in which Di revitalized the House of Windsor's image, not only because of the *haute couture* designs she wore, but also the warmth that she exuded and the care that she showed for others. Her impact on the royals and the rest of society was highly significant, for it radically altered perceptions on both sides.

To start, let's take a look at Diana's background and the fashion track record of the family that she married into. That way you can make up your own mind as to the hows and whys of 20th-century royal garb.

Lady Diana Spencer: English Roots, American Ancestry

Entering the world during the early evening of July 1, 1961, the Honorable Diana Frances Spencer was born into a solidly aristocratic English family, yet one with strong connections to the other side of the Atlantic.

Her parents were the Viscount and Viscountess Althorp, otherwise known as Johnnie and Frances, who resided in Park House. Located on the queen's Royal Sandringham estate in Norfolk, this 10-bedroom residence boasted guest cottages, a swimming pool, a tennis court, and a cricket pitch (kind of like an English *Field of Dreams*). It was, however, the least of the Spencers' links to royalty.

The Queen Mother, was, in fact, godmother to the couple's eldest child, Sarah, while their next daughter, Jane, had the Duke of Kent as her godfather. For her part, young Diana didn't have such prestigious godparents, yet, like her sisters, she was a cousin to Queen Elizabeth II's children several times over, and they all shared a common ancestor in King Charles I.

Hear Ye, Hear Ye
"Let not poor Nelly starve."
—*Charles II on his death bed, requesting that his favorite mistress, Nell Gwynne, should be well taken care of*

That's right: At birth Diana was related to her future husband, Prince Charles. Yet, given that his family was descended from a long German lineage, it was actually she who had more British ties. Diana, you see, was a descendant of that "Merry Monarch" Charles II, thanks to the illegitimate offspring that he produced with a string of mistresses, not to mention those that resulted from the extramarital philandering of George IV and James II.

Ah yes, Diana's was a colorful heritage and as if all of the royal connections weren't enough, she was also related to many other famous people from all walks of life. These included political, military, and national leaders such as Sir Winston Churchill, Oliver Cromwell, Lawrence of Arabia, King Juan Carlos, Prince Otto von Bismarck, the Aga Khan, and presidents George Washington, Calvin Coolidge, and Franklin D. Roosevelt. Then, there were the philosopher Bertrand Russell; painter John Singer Sargent; and celebrated writers Jane Austen, George Orwell, Graham Greene, Samuel Pepys, Barbara Cartland, Ralph Waldo Emerson, Louisa May Alcott, and Virginia Woolf.

Heiress Gloria Vanderbilt was another noted relative, as was tycoon Nelson Bunker Hunt and celebrities Rudolph Valentino, Humphrey Bogart, Lillian Gish, Lee Remick, Olivia de Havilland, and Orson Welles.

Diana's American ancestry was on her mother's side of the family. Frances' great-grandfather, Frank Work, was a Manhattan stockbroker and self-made millionaire. His daughter was also named Frances but better known as Fanny, and the first of her two husbands was the Englishman James Roche, the future 3rd Baron Fermoy. They had three children—Frank, Maurice, and Cynthia, all of who moved to America with their mother after her divorce—and, when James died in 1920, Maurice inherited the title of the 4th Baron Fermoy and settled permanently in Britain. He became a Tory Member of Parliament and mayor of King's Lynn. In 1931, the Baron wed Ruth Gill (making her Lady Fermoy) and King George V provided them with the Park House home. Diana's mother was born there five years later.

Meanwhile, in the case of the Spencers, there had been a line of earls, dukes, and duchesses stretching back to the 15th century. During the late 1700s, King George III conferred the title of Earl Spencer on one of Diana's ancestors and this has been passed down the generations all the way to Di's young brother, Charles, who is the current Earl Spencer.

Di's father, Johnnie, was born in 1924, a godson to Queen Mary. In his youth, he was an affable and attractive man, and he occasionally even escorted Princess Margaret in a foursome with newlyweds Prince Philip and Princess Elizabeth. In 1950 he was appointed *equerry* to King George VI, and when Elizabeth acceded to the throne, he became Master of the Queen's House.

On June 1, 1954, Johnnie married 18-year-old Frances Roche, making her the youngest bride to walk down the aisle of Westminster Abbey this century. The wedding was the biggest society event of 1954, with a guest list that included the queen, Prince Philip, the Queen Mother, and Princess Margaret. The other guests probably didn't know which way to look. The following year Baron Fermoy died, prompting Lady Ruth Fermoy to hand over Park House to Johnnie and Frances.

Unfortunately, as would be the case with Diana and Charles, this was a fairy tale marriage that didn't work out. Thirteen years and five children later (a son named John died shortly after birth in 1960), the Spencers separated.

Palace Parlance
An **equerry** is an officer of the royal household who attends to members of the Royal Family. An equerry may also be charged with supervision of the horses belonging to a royal or noble household.

Royal Rebuttal
Following the Spencers' marital split, some people asserted that Frances had deserted her husband and children. This, however, wasn't true. The day after their mother left Park House, Charles and Diana joined her at her rented apartment in London's exclusive Belgravia district. Initially, they visited their father on weekends and during school breaks, and Christmas 1967 found the whole family gathered at Park House.

Frances fell for wealthy businessman Peter Shand-Kydd and Johnnie won custody of the children. This court ruling was largely due to the respectability of his title, as well as some timely assistance from an unexpected source: Frances' mother, Lady Ruth Fermoy, gave evidence against her daughter during the court proceedings!

During the mid 1970s, Johnnie would become the eighth Earl Spencer, Charles would replace him as Viscount Althorp, the three girls would become Ladies, and all of them would move from Park House to the traditional Spencer family home at Althorp. The house was built in 1508 by Sir John Spencer, a sheep farmer who became one of the wealthiest men in England, and revised in the late-18th century. The home is surrounded by a 600-acre park set within a 13,000-acre estate. Inside there are marble floors, crystal chandeliers, and one of the country's finest collections of antique furniture and classic paintings.

Oh yes, if life at Park House had been one of closeted privilege, with a nanny, six servants, and private tuition, then that at Althorp was like stepping into another world and a bygone age. In fact, it would be in the middle of a plowed field on the Althorp estate, during a weekend pheasant shoot in November 1977, that Lady Diana Spencer would first meet Prince Charles. Clearly, they were both members of Britain's social elite, yet they still came from considerably different backgrounds.

Windsor Style, Mark I: A Whiff of Pomp and Circumstance

If you want some idea as to how the Royal Family has attired itself throughout this century, you need look no further than the occasion when short-sighted writer E.M. Forster bowed to the cake at a wedding reception thinking it was Queen Mary, the wife of George V.

Aside from Edward VII and Edward VIII, both of who loved fancy clothes, the Windsors have never been noted for their fashionable line of casual wear. Nor, for that matter, has their taste ever been considered particularly subtle. From yellow, pink, and turquoise outfits of the queen to the fruit-filled hats of the Queen Mother, the designs have often been ridiculed, yet even these items are refreshing compared to the staid and stuffy look of many of their peers and predecessors.

Of course, there is the glamorous side to the royal role; those formal events when, in the case of the women, an elaborate evening gown, dazzling jewelry, and glittering tiara will more than match the occasion. Given the kind of jewelry that we're dealing with here, together with a style of dress that is increasingly outmoded yet extremely dignified, the queen, for instance, has no problem standing out in a crowd.

No, where the problem lies is in the area of less formal public occasions, when the royals' conservative tastes usually emerge. The suits the men wear are pretty standard. (Although when Charles and Prince Philip appear outside Scotland's Balmoral Castle sporting their kilts, this is a less familiar sight for foreign eyes.) The women, on the other hand, have to be more design-conscious and it's in this respect that they sometimes…er, let themselves down. At least as far as the public and press critics are concerned.

A Right Royal Tale

Edward VIII recalling events surrounding his investiture as the Prince of Wales: "When a tailor appeared to measure me for a fantastic costume designed for the occasion, consisting of white satin breeches and a mantle of surcoat of purple velvet edged with ermine, I decided things had gone too far. What would my Navy friends think if they saw me in this preposterous rig? There was a family blow-up that night, but in the end my mother, as always, smoothed things over. 'You mustn't take a mere ceremony so seriously,' she said. 'Your friends will understand that as a prince you are obliged to do certain things that may seem a little silly.'"

While fashions come and go, those royal outfits stay pretty much the same. Admittedly, during the late 1960s and early 1970s, the queen's hem lines did creep dangerously close to her knees (while still remaining below them, of course), but overall I suppose the fairest thing you could say about Her Majesty's wardrobe is that it's colorful and timeless. Most women wouldn't even consider wearing those clothes, yet what they perhaps fail to appreciate is that London couturiers such as Norman Hartnell and Hardy Amies have ensured that the outfits are functional in a royal way.

You see, when you're the queen, a princess, or a duchess, and you're stepping out of cars, getting onto boats, or jumping off a horse, those skirts mustn't ride up and expose a royal thigh. At the same time, the outfits have got to be comfortable, considering all of the sitting, handshaking, and waving that has to take place. Finally, they have to be easy to climb in and out of; on a strenuous foreign tour in a hot climate there may need to be half a dozen costume changes in the space of a day.

Off-duty, the countryside look appears to be the thing: tweed jackets and plain pants (or kilts) for the men, sweaters and tweed skirts for the women…unless you're Princess Anne, in which case an anorak, baggy pants, and boots are often the norm. Unfortunately, the sight of the queen in her "casuals," complete with headscarf and, in recent years, glasses, only adds fuel to the flames of public perception that the royals have just stepped out of a time-warp.

Windsor Style, Mark II: Jet-Set Di

When she first entered onto the royal scene as Prince Charles' fiancée, Lady Diana Spencer appeared to fit in with the Windsors in terms of her attire. Still only 19 and not as slim as she would be in future years, "Shy Di" often sported long skirts, high necklines, and casual knitwear. Then her sister Jane introduced her to the fashion team at *Vogue* magazine and things began to change.

Jane had been an editorial assistant at the mag, so she set up a meeting in which Diana was able to explain to the fashion editors how she wanted to create a high-impact, glamorous image that oozed sophistication. Further meetings followed, before the *Vogue* team decided that, for her first official public engagement, up-and-coming British designers Elizabeth and David Emanuel should cater to Lady Di. What they in turn came up with was a sexy, off-the-shoulder black taffeta dress that Diana wore to a fund-raising reception for the Royal Opera House at Goldsmith's Hall in London on March 9, 1981. Eyebrows were raised inside Buckingham Palace, but the result was instant press hysteria and public fascination. The Palace insiders lowered their eyebrows and bowed to popular opinion.

The Emanuels subsequently designed the incredible wedding dress that Diana wore in July of that year, and within a year of that memorable event, the new exponent of British fashion slimmed down from a size 12 (U.S. size 10) to a size 10 (U.S. size 8). Designer wear was now the norm for the much-adored Princess (if not for her royal relatives), and, when she undertook her first foreign tour to Australia in 1983, she traveled with 90 trunks full of costumes that had been created for her by no fewer than 21 different fashion houses!

On Her Majesty's Service

Ladies (and in certain cases gents), if you want to give your eyes better definition, follow a tip that Princess Diana picked up from Elizabeth Taylor when the two of them first met in 1982. According to Liz, she enhances her legendary violet-colored eyes by applying strong liner to the upper lids and brilliant blue to the inner rims of the lower ones.

Fortunately, being a royal, she didn't have to tip the bellboy for carrying them. Everyone from private citizens to heads of state was dazzled by the combination of the stunning clothes and the elegant young woman who wore them. Furthermore, they admired her originality; at a 1985 gala in Melbourne, Australia, Di adapted a necklace that had belonged to Queen Mary (she who had been mistaken for a wedding cake) and wore it as a headband. The following year she turned up at the America's Cup ball in a sensational Murray Arbeid gown comprising a black top and flame-red skirt together with arm-length gloves, one red, the other black.

At the same time, complementing the fabulous clothes was Di's refined use of cosmetics—which she had learned from her favorite beautician, Barbara Daley—as well as the ever-evolving hairstyles which, by the late 1980s, were running up a tab of around $18,000 a year. Add to that a total expenditure of about $2 million on more than 750 outfits and 100 evening gowns, and it's no wonder that the princess was increasingly being referred to as "Dynasty Di."

In her final years, following her split from Charles, Diana truly confirmed her status as the first and, so far, only jet-set princess of the British monarchy, hobnobbing with the rich, the famous, and the celebrated in exotic locales around the world. Equally comfortable in jeans and a T-shirt as in expensive designer clothes, she gradually refined her style, wearing an incredible array of outfits that were both trendy and classically sophisticated.

Diana looks back at photographers on her arrival to a dinner at the National Gallery of Art in Washington. (Photo courtesy of UPI/Corbis-Bettmann)

Meanwhile there were all of those gowns that she no longer needed. What to do? Well, on June 25, 1997, acting on the advice of her eldest son, Prince William, Diana had 79 of her dresses auctioned off at Christie's in New York.

Collectively these raised $3.26 million which, together with the $2.5 million that was accrued from catalog sales and tickets to the previews, was donated by Diana to AIDS and cancer charities.

Which bring us to another, major way in which Diana differed from her counterparts in the House of Windsor…

From a Handshake to a Hug: The People's Princess

Outdone only by Princess Anne, the queen, and Prince Philip in terms of the number of public functions that she undertook during her years as a member of the Royal Family, Diana also left an indelible imprint on the global consciousness by way of her unforgettable humanitarian behavior.

The patron or president of more than 70 organizations, Di was heavily involved with charitable causes just like the rest of the royals, yet where she broke new ground was in territory that other public figures had previously feared to tread. The most notable example of this occurred during the mid- to late 1980s, at a time when some people were afraid to breathe the same air—let alone touch—an AIDS victim. In full view of the news cameras and press photographers, and possibly against the advice of the Palace (opinions differ on this), Diana made a point of embracing and shaking the hands of AIDS patients when she visited them in the hospital. The same applied to people suffering from other socially undesirable ailments such as leprosy, mental illness, alcoholism, and drug addiction. This was a sample of the care, compassion, and desire to confront ignorance that touched hearts everywhere.

Meanwhile, the public was also amazed to see the way in which Di related to her children. I mean, for goodness sake, she not only held their hands while walking along, but, when reuniting after having spent some time apart, she actually *hugged* them! This was virtually unprecedented public (and possibly private) behavior for a member of the royal household. You should note that when the queen returned from a six-month overseas tour of duty during the mid-1950s, eight-year-old Charles had to make do with a brusque handshake from his monarchical mom. What else did he expect? A peck on the cheek?

A Right Royal Tale

Today, aggressive news hounds constantly pursue the royals, but things haven't always been this way. Up until the late 1960s, TV and radio were actually banned from covering certain royal events, as it was assumed that some members of the public would be wearing unsuitable clothes or be situated in undesirable locations while watching or listening! It was the queen who eventually ushered in a new era of openness when, in 1969, she allowed the BBC to film *Royal Family*, a landmark documentary about life at home with the Windsors. In terms of press and public relations, this was a winner, but it also helped open the floodgates to intrusive media coverage.

The cold and damp of the British winter—and on occasion, the autumn, spring, and summer too—necessitates first-rate heating systems in the royal palaces, yet apparently nothing can endow the residents with the kind of warmth that the Princess of Wales exuded.

When Prince William was hit over the head with a golf club at school in June 1991, Diana was by his side as doctors at the Royal Berkshire Hospital performed a CAT scan to check for brain damage. She then accompanied her son in the ambulance that took him to London's Great Ormond Street Hospital for Sick Children, where he underwent surgery for a depressed fracture of the skull. In the meantime, Charles, satisfied that everything possible was being done, left to entertain European Community officials at a Covent Garden opera production of Puccini's *Tosca*…which is just what his father would have done. When Prince Philip's young wife, Princess Elizabeth, went into labor with their first-born on November 14, 1948, the expectant father didn't have the patience to hang around. Rather than wait for the birth, he went off to swim and have a game of squash (similar to racquetball) in another part of the Palace. His game was interrupted by the news that Charles had been born.

Diana didn't fit into this royal mold. She often cared for William and Harry herself instead of leaving them under the supervision of a nanny, and when she was away from them she kept in constant contact via the telephone. By royal standards, the princes were experiencing a fairly balanced childhood, as well as unconventional exposure to the harsh realities of everyday life. When Diana's friend, Adrian Ward-Jackson, was dying of AIDS, she ensured that her sons got to meet him.

Although media attention guaranteed that the public was informed of many of Diana's ground-breaking humanitarian acts, most people weren't so aware of countless acts of kindness that Diana performed when no cameras or microphones were around. From privately helping homeless individuals who she encountered on the street to repeatedly visiting patients who were confined to hospital beds, Diana, "Queen of Hearts," fully earned her posthumous title as "the People's Princess."

The Least You Need to Know

➤ Princess Diana was steeped in the aristocracy on both sides of her family.

➤ Di had American ancestry and stronger English roots than Prince Charles.

➤ Diana grew into her twin roles as a fashion icon and jet-set princess.

➤ "The People's Princess" broke new ground by way of her humanitarian deeds and public displays of affection.

Part 2
Divide and Conquer (802-1216)

For almost a thousand years now the Brits have successfully fended off the greedy aspirations of aggressive foreigners trying to invade their shores. In the beginning, however, they had to learn a few tough lessons before perfecting the methods of defense and counter-attack.

Over the course of more than two centuries, vicious Vikings raided the English coast in order to seize power from the Anglo-Saxon kings. Then, having seen off the Scandinavians once and for all, the Anglo-Saxons got themselves into more trouble at the hands of the covetous Duke of Normandy. Thereafter things settled down into some sort of routine, with royal relatives constantly battling one another in their on-going struggle for the throne. Murder, treachery, and abuses of power were a part of everyday life until the nobles and the clergy finally decided enough was enough. Getting their collective act together, they contrived to limit the strength of the monarchy.

As you'll see, it wasn't easy being a king.

Chapter 6

Prize Fights: Anglo-Saxons Versus the Great Danes

First, let me start by saying that we have a lot of kings to work our way through in this chapter: 21 in all. Second, there are various spellings for many of their names, since the English spoken during the period we're covering (802-1066) differed considerably from the language today—and even that differs quite a bit depending on where you live. Furthermore, thanks to the Viking invasions of England, some of those royal names were foreign, and they've also changed over the years. Basically, I've gone with the modern, anglicized version of all the names, so if you see them spelled differently elsewhere, don't give me a hard time! Okay, having gotten that issue out of the way, I can now tell you that this chapter is bursting at the seams with bloody treachery and juicy gossip.

Believe me, today's royals are saints when compared to their predecessors. Along the way, while the Vikings keep entering the picture and disrupting the status quo, you'll get to see how the English monarchy really started to develop a line of succession. Or at least how it tried. There were just too many power struggles going on to keep the peace. Are you ready? Let's go...

This Land is My Land: Alfred Overcomes the Vikings

In Chapter 2, I explained how, by the start of the eighth century, England was divided into seven kingdoms. One of these, Mercia, rose to power under the rule of King Offa (757-796), but then, after Egbert acceded to the throne of Wessex in 802, the balance of power shifted decisively toward that kingdom.

In 825, Egbert and his army defeated the Mercians at the Battle of Ellandun, and two years later the kingdom of Northumbria also succumbed to him. As a result, in 827 Egbert effectively became the first king of England.

A Right Royal Tale

According to legend, while once traveling alone without food in a remote part of western England, King Alfred took refuge in a farmhouse. One day, while the farmer was out in the fields, his wife was baking some cakes and doing a spot of housecleaning. Suddenly noticing that the cakes were burning, she flew into a rage against the lazy king. "Look here, man," she apparently shouted. "You hesitate to turn the loaves which you see to be burning, yet you're quite happy to eat them when they come warm from the oven!" Some mortals could have had their heads chopped off for talking to a king in such a manner, but Alfred was humbled and attended to the cakes.

Ever since 787, the Vikings had been making raids along the English coastlines. In 836 King Egbert defeated a Danish invasion force at Hingston Down, and following his death in 839 it fell to his successors—Ethelwulf (839-855), Ethelbald (855-860), Ethelbert (860-866), and Ethelred I (866-871)—to keep them at bay. As you can see, the House of Wessex was full of Ethels. Shortly after Ethelred's accession to the throne, the Danes tasted victory in East Anglia, and five years later he was killed battling these same invaders at Merton. His successor was Ethelwulf's youngest son, Alfred.

At the age of 22, Alfred immediately had to contend with the Danes' advances on Wessex and a situation whereby the various kingdoms were in total disarray. What he managed to do was assemble a united force representing the whole of England, and, after fighting nine separate battles against the Danes within the space of a year, he succeeded in holding them off until 878. At that point, the Danes finally invaded Wessex, but they didn't stay for long.

Alfred had retreated to a temporary base in the marshes of Somerset, where, having cultivated an underground movement, he formed an army that dealt the Danes a heavy defeat at the Battle of Eddington.

Now came a deal. In return for the Danish leader Guthorm withdrawing his forces from Wessex and becoming a Christian, Alfred agreed to recognize the Danish control over

East Anglia and parts of Mercia. In this way, England was divided and the partition, formalized by another treaty in 886, was known as the "Danelaw."

Alfred had numerous *burhs* built around his kingdom in order to prevent similar invasions from taking place again, and he also formed a fleet of ships, which earned him the title "father of the English Navy." At the same time, having traveled to Rome as a young man and observed how things were done there, Alfred introduced decent laws, promoted education, and supported the arts. He himself was illiterate, but later in life he taught himself Latin, learned to read and write, and translated a work of Pope Gregory that he sent to each of his bishops.

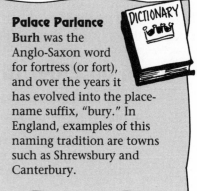

Palace Parlance
Burh was the Anglo-Saxon word for fortress (or fort), and over the years it has evolved into the place-name suffix, "bury." In England, examples of this naming tradition are towns such as Shrewsbury and Canterbury.

Alfred the Great (849-899) forced the Angles and Saxons into submission and ruled all of England that wasn't occupied by the Danes. (Picture courtesy of Corbis-Bettmann)

Known as the King of the Saxons, he was never officially pronounced king of England. A long time after his death, however, the title "Alfred the Great" was conferred upon him—the only time that an English monarch has been honored this way.

From an Elder to a Martyr: Spread a Little Power

For 75 years after the death of Alfred the Great, England consolidated its power by way of a continuous family line holding onto the throne.

The first to succeed Alfred was his son, Edward I, the Elder, whose eldest sister married Ethelred of Mercia. Her newfound power helped Edward to re-conquer the midlands and southeast of England and drive out the Danes.

Subsequently, the princes of West Wales also acknowledged Edward as their overlord. On his death in 925, he was succeeded by his son, Athelstan, who was the first English sovereign to be crowned on the King's Stone at Kingston-upon-Thames. He was also the first monarch to have his likeness officially reproduced on coins, fitting in with his self-styled image as "Emperor of the British and Ruler of all England." Some say that Athelstan was, in fact, the first King of all England, but, as I've already pointed out to you, Egbert (802-839) was deserving of that title. Still, Athelstan was more than entitled to his reputation as a great warrior. In 927, he was recognized as overlord by the rulers of northern England—some of which now includes the southern parts of Scotland—when he conquered Northumbria. Then, 10 years later, he defeated a combined force of Scots, Welsh, and Vikings at the Battle of Brunanburh. This placed him firmly in Scotland, although two of his nephews died during the conquest.

Athelstan's father, Edward the Elder, had recognized that being married three times and siring a load of children helped establish a dynasty. Athelstan, on the other hand, never married and had no offspring. Still, his sisters followed in their father's footsteps and even outdid him, marrying no fewer than five European monarchs and so adding to England's wealth and prestige.

For his part, Athelstan liked to spend his social time collecting jewelry, art, and relics, and he was also a loyal patron of monastic communities. His tomb is in the monastery at Malmesbury.

Athelstan was 44 when he died, and in 939 he was succeeded by his young half-brother Edmund I, who had been second-in-command at the Battle of Brunanburh. During his time on the throne he kept up the family's good work of subduing the Norse Vikings, but murder prematurely ended his reign.

A Right Royal Tale

On May 26, 946, a robber named Leofa was sitting among the congregation at Puckle church in Gloucestershire, when he was set upon by Edmund I. Six years earlier the king had banished Leofa for his crimes, and now, seeing him make a suprise return, the monarch grabbed the thief by the hair and dragged him to the ground. Unfortunately, even back in those days criminals were armed. Leofa overpowered Edmund, pulled out a dagger, and stabbed him in the chest. Conflicting stories would surface about the king's death, but Leofa wouldn't be around to confirm or deny them. Shortly after the murder, attendants rushed in and tore him limb from limb.

As a result, yet another brother, Edred, became king. Only 16 years old when he took over in 946, Edred soon found himself having to face off with a man going by the delightful name of Eric Bloodaxe. With that appellation few people wondered about Eric's line of business. He'd been the king of Norway back in the 930s, but, after bloodying his axe on the heads of his seven brothers, he was expelled.

Nevertheless, that piece of good news for the Norwegians turned into a bad roll of the dice for the residents of Northumbria, where the Vikings had been ruling from within the old Roman walls of York since the 870s. Eric decided York would be the perfect place to further indulge his fun-loving nature, but King Edred didn't agree. After Eric had installed himself as king of Northumbria, Edred immediately reasserted his own authority by marching north with his forces, wreaking havoc in the Norse-held territories, and then returning south. On his way back, however, old Bloodaxe's forces took a swipe at Edred, prompting the English king to do an about-face and threaten Northumbria with complete annihilation.

Those poor Northumbrians! What would you have done in their position? There they were, forced to choose between the rule of Eric, who had already proved himself too violent for his bloodthirsty fellow countrymen, and Edred, who was threatening to turn their buildings into rubble. Well, they made their decision, and personally I think it was a good one. In 949, Eric was expelled. Back he came in 952, but then two years later Edred's army did unto Eric what Eric had done unto others; Mr. Bloodaxe fell in battle at Stainmore and Northumbria's independence was at an end.

So, for that matter, was the period of Edred's rule. In 955, at the age of 25, he died without a wife or children. His successor was Eadwig (now there's a name to savor), the 16-year-old son of Edmund I who himself only lived to the age of 20. It appears that illness plagued the Wessex family, and there weren't any antibiotics on the shelves to help cure their maladies. Still, during his short reign Eadwig managed to make quite an impact in his homeland, even if this wasn't for all the right reasons.

This is how the story goes. On the day of his consecration, Eadwig went missing. Bishop Dunstan, an influential friend and advisor to Edred, was dispatched along with another clergyman to track down the unruly 16-year-old, but when they accomplished their mission the sight that greeted them virtually took their breath away. Eadwig, you see, was…er, performing his royal duty with a young lady named Elfgifu (another name to savor). She was the daughter of a noblewoman, and when Dunstan saw this he immediately dragged Eadwig away, making him an enemy for life—which only amounted to four years, so it wasn't such a bad deal. Dunstan would go on to become Archbishop of Canterbury and, after that, a saint. In the meantime, by marrying Elfgifu, Eadwig underlined the fact that Dunstan had walked in on a moment of tender love rather than a royal roll in the hay.

Hear Ye, Hear Ye
"No fleet however proud / No host however strong, / Was able to win booty for itself / In England, while that noble king / Occupied the royal throne."
—*Tribute to Edgar the Peaceable in The Anglo-Saxon Chronicle, 975*

What he didn't manage to do, however, was convince everybody that he was fit to be king. These doubters included his own brother, Edgar, who had taken over the rule of Mercia and Northumbria at the age of 14. Clearly, yuppie ambition isn't anything new. Two years later, he was king of Wessex and, with the three most powerful kingdoms now under his control, he was effectively the first ruler of a united England. This differed from his predecessors who had been kings "of all England," in that they were basically kings of Wessex with a military hold over the other kingdoms.

The years of 959 to 975 would later be referred to as the reign of Edgar the Peaceable, due to the fact that there were very few raids by Vikings or anyone else during his time on the throne.

The second of his three wives reputedly came from a nunnery before serving as his mistress for many years, yet Edgar ensured that the Church turned a blind eye. After recalling Dunstan from exile and making him Archbishop of Canterbury, the King founded 40 religious houses in England and helped instigate a monastic revival there. He also introduced a legal code based on the laws of his great-grandfather, Alfred the Great, and was responsible for the Hundred Ordinance, which divided shires into hundreds. With three saints alive and canonized during this era, this peaceable monarch benefited from good advice, and he in turn invested the Church with considerable power.

Edgar wasn't formally crowned until 14 years after his accession, at which point all of the Scottish and Welsh kings recognized his supreme authority, as did the general public. When he died two years later in 975, the eldest of his four sons, 12-year-old Edward II, stepped onto the throne, but this would be anything but a peaceable reign. Immediately the in-fighting started, with Edgar's third wife claiming that her son Ethelred was the rightful heir.

For three years the bad blood continued, until a fateful day in 978 when Edward decided to visit his 10-year-old stepbrother at Corfe Castle in Dorset. On the king's arrival, Ethelred's agents pretended to welcome him, but the greeting was just a ruse to get close enough to use their knives.

Edward died of his stab wounds and he would later be canonized by his unwitting brother, leading to the name by which he is now best known: King Edward the Martyr. Meanwhile, said brother acceded to the throne as planned, kicking off what proved to be a long and largely undignified reign.

Tug of War: Dispossession and the Rule of the Canutes

If the era of Edgar the Peaceable had been distinguished by a relative lack of trouble from the Vikings, the same could hardly be said for that of Ethelred II. He had acceded to the throne as a pawn in the power game of those around him, and that's pretty much how things would remain for the rest of his life.

Unable to trust his political and military generals during a period when the Danes were stepping up their acts of aggression, Ethelred II often took advice from a court of favorites who were ill-equipped to make suggestions in such matters. One of his most disastrous policies was the payment of Danegeld, whereby he attempted to buy off the greedy Vikings with money. As other leaders have discovered, trying to appease an aggressor is often a fatal mistake. As soon as something is offered the other side wants more, and this was the case with the Danes.

In 1009, Sweyn, the king of Denmark, decided that the English throne was his for the taking, and no amount of Danegeld could persuade him otherwise. The clock was now ticking for Ethelred, and four years later his time ran out. Fleeing to Normandy, he left England entirely in the hands of the Viking invaders. Robert the Good, the brother of Ethelred's second wife, Emma of Normandy, provided the deposed king with protection, yet he didn't need it for long.

Back in England, after only five weeks on the throne, Sweyn died as a result of falling off his horse in Gainsborough, Lincolnshire. It was February 1014, and no sooner was he six feet under than Ethelred II re-entered the scene. Ethelred reigned again for two more years before passing away at the age of 48.

"Ethelred the Unready" would be the nickname forever associated with this lackluster king; while "unready"

> **On Her Majesty's Service**
> This advice is for all prospective heads of state: If you want a relatively peaceful term of office don't upset your country's religious leaders. Take the example of Ethelred II, who, according to St. Dunstan, made an unforgivable slip-up as a baby that foretold the slaughter of the English. What was his crime? At his baptism, the future king peed in the font!

could be applied to him in the modern sense, the Saxon meaning for the word was "with no policy" because he refused to take good advice. Still, he did manage to sire 14 children with his two wives (11 of them with the first, Elfgifu). Meanwhile, a couple people who entered the picture late in his reign pointed toward what lay ahead for his successors.

One of these people was Robert the Good, who had given Ethelred II refuge when he fled to Normandy, and who was the grandfather of William the Conqueror. (You'll learn about William the Conqueror in the next chapter.) The other, meanwhile, was Canute, son of King Sweyn, who had accompanied his father on the victorious expedition to England that drove Ethelred II out in the first place. When Ethelred died in April 1016, Canute decided to follow Pa Sweyn's example and aim for the English throne.

Palace Parlance
The **Witan** was the council of the Anglo-Saxon kings, once considered to be the first English parliament. In Old English, *witan* means "meeting of wise men."

His initial attempt to take the city of London was thwarted by Ethelred's son, Edmund II, who was promptly proclaimed king by the Londoners. When the *Witan* met in Southampton, however, Canute was chosen to be monarch. Do I have to tell you what happened next? You've got it: A series of squabbles took place on various battlefields, during which Edmund II's bravery earned him the name "Ironside." After Edmund's forces defeated the Danes at Oxford and Canute's men scored a decisive victory in Essex, a truce was called and an agreement drawn up: Edmund would control Wessex in the south while Canute would rule over Mercia and those beleaguered Northumbrians in the north. The second part of the deal, however, was somewhat worrisome.

It was agreed that whoever survived the other would inherit the throne of all England. Now, given the track record of those shifty Danes, would you have signed your name to such an agreement? Ironside did, and within no time at all he was dead, the cause unknown! No one's ever cleared up this mystery, but rest assured that the words "murdered" and "Danes" have often come into play.

Not that Canute I, king of England, was prepared to stop there in his consolidation of power. He had Edmund's younger brother Eadwig murdered, and Edward's sons Edward and Edmund exiled in Hungary. That left the way for Canute's own offspring to come to the throne. He'd had two sons with his first English mistress, Elfgifu of Northampton, who was acknowledged as queen of Denmark, and another two children with his wife who was none other than—now hear this—Emma of Normandy, the widow of Ethelred II! Talk about a golddigger! In England, Emma's son Hardicanute was regarded as the rightful heir to the throne. Another contender was Harold Harefoot, son of Canute and Elfgifu, and then there was Alfred, who was the fruit of the union between Emma and Ethelred II. As the saying goes, two's company but three's a crowd, so one of them had to go and Alfred pulled the short straw. He was murdered, courtesy of some assistance from Earl Godwin of Wessex (more on him in a minute).

In the meantime, Canute himself was doing fine. He turned out to be a good and just leader, and he was very generous to the Church. Hey look, all he'd ever wanted was English citizenship! Consequently, when he died in 1035, he was buried in Winchester Cathedral. This opened the way for Harold Harefoot to become Regent, while the rightful heir, his half-brother Hardicanute, was preoccupied with his duties as king of Denmark. For a couple years, therefore, they were almost joint monarchs, but then in 1037 Harold was elected king, and he ruled England until he died three years later. Actually, this was good timing on his part, as Hardicanute had just been getting ready to invade England in order to reclaim his throne.

A Right Royal Tale

On arriving in England to claim the throne in 1040, one of Hardicanute's first acts was to desecrate the dead body of his half-brother, Harold Harefoot. On his orders, Harold's body was dug up, and the head was cut off and thrown into the River Thames. It didn't drift there for long, however. Those were the days when people regularly went fishing along the Thames, and one such person just happened to drag up a heavy load in his net: the disfigured remains of Harold Harefoot. Subsequently buried in the cemetery of St. Clement Danes in London, the decapitated body would at long last be accorded the dignity of resting in peace.

Now, you'd think that Hardicanute would have been happy with his lot, but no. Preparing for an invasion had cost a lot of money—all for nothing.

This was the fault of the English, who should never have elected that half-breed Harold Harefoot as king in the first place. His solution, therefore, was to impose a "fleet tax" on the two-timing citizens. Needless to say, that didn't exactly enhance his popularity, and not too many tears were shed when the mean-spirited Viking died of convulsions at a drinking party in June 1042. He left no wife and no children.

A Confessor and His Abbey: The First Edward III

The eldest son of Ethelred II and Emma, Edward was the penultimate Anglo-Saxon king. Having fled to Normandy with his parents when Sweyn invaded England in 1013, he'd remained there through the reign of Canute. When the latter died in 1035, Edward failed in an attempt to seize the throne; fortunately, a couple of people in high places were unexpectedly pulling for him.

One of these people was Hardicanute, who'd been waging an ongoing battle with Magnus of Norway and saw his half-brother as a means of blocking the greedy aspirations of the Nordic upstart. The other was Earl Godwin of Wessex, who was thinking in terms of the future social status of his own family. Between Hardicanute's bequest for Edward to succeed him as King and Godwin's ability to realize ambition by way of his powerful political influence, Edward's 1042 accession to the throne was pretty straightforward.

Three years later the Essex Earl could see his dreams materializing when Edward married Earl's only daughter, Edith. Now there was a chance of a Godwin grandson one day becoming king of England! The honeymoon didn't last long, however. Godwin was one of several Saxon nobles who weren't happy about Edward's close affiliation with several Norman advisors he'd met during his years in Normandy. Then, when Edward had a Norman named Robert Champart appointed as Archbishop of Canterbury, Godwin was infuriated.

In response, and with no grandson in sight, Godwin started hatching a plan for his own son, Harold Godwinson, to become the next king. A rebellion against Edward was unsuccessful, however, and the reigning monarch, aware of the role that the Earl had played in the murder of his step-brother, Alfred, retaliated by banishing Edith to a monastery and exiling Godwin from the kingdom. That happened in 1051. A year later Godwin was back with an invasionary force, and he and his family attracted such strong support among the people that the king was obliged to restore them to favor.

The upshot of all this was that Edward now had to expel many of his Norman friends while using Harold Godwinson as his chief advisor for the rest of his reign. At the same time, he still managed to display his Norman bias by announcing that, upon his death, his cousin William, Duke of Normandy, would succeed him on the throne.

In 1052, the same year as Godwin returned with his invasionary force, Edward III instigated the construction of Westminster Abbey. With the exception of Edward V and Edward VIII, this has been the site of every monarch's coronation since that of William the Conqueror in 1066. Today, not a stone of the original building remains above ground. It was demolished and largely rebuilt during the reign of Henry III (1216-1272), and then consistently revamped until it was completed in the late-18th century.

When Westminster Abbey was consecrated on December 28, 1065, Edward was too ill to attend. He died the following January. Because of his fairness and piety, he was given the title of Edward the Confessor, placing him between a

Royal Rebuttal
Another powerful earl during Edward III's reign was Leofric of Mercia, husband of Lady Godiva. According to legend, Godiva was so upset with the taxes that poor people had to pay that she rode naked on a horse through Coventry as a protest to have her husband lower the taxes. Not true. The couple did exist but there's no record of her naked ride.

Hear Ye, Hear Ye
"Sir king, I have been often accused of harboring traitorous designs against you, but, as God in heaven is just and true, may this morsel of bread choke me if even in thought I have ever been false to you."
—*Earl Godwin of Wessex, 1053, just moments before a lump of bread stuck in his throat and choked him at the royal dinner table*

common man and a saint; a century later he would indeed be canonized. During the Plantaganet era (1216-1399) there was a whole new cycle of Edwards, and these repeated the numeric titles I, II, and III.

Meanwhile, on his deathbed, the Confessor had named his successor. This wasn't William, Duke of Normandy, but Harold Godwinson. The legitimate heir, however, was Edward's own grandson, Edgar. The whole issue of the heir to the throne—appointed or rightful—remained unsolved...for now.

The Least You Need to Know

➤ Egbert of Wessex was the first King of all England.

➤ Danelaw was the partition of England that saw one part of the country ruled by Alfred the Great and the other part ruled by Guthorm of Denmark.

➤ The first ruler of a united England was King Edgar.

➤ Ethelred II vainly tried to buy off the Viking aggressors by paying them Danegeld.

➤ Edward the Confessor was responsible for the construction of Westminster Abbey.

The French Are Coming— The Norman Reign

During the 150 years or so since its foundation, Normandy had become so powerful that, by the middle of the 11th century, it was virtually a separate state from the rest of France. Indeed, although the Normans spoke French, they shared certain traits with their Viking ancestors—not the least of these was their territorial ambition. Unfortunately, England, in its usual state of disarray following the death of Edward the Confessor, was a prime target.

In this chapter, we'll glance at the events leading up to the Norman invasion and those surrounding the conquest. It was the start of a whole new era in England in which a predominantly Anglo-Saxon population suddenly found itself under the thumb of the Norman and French minority. Continental language and culture had a major impact on English society, while the Norman/French style of rule and administration represented an important step forward. Still, some things never changed; Royal Family squabbles and power struggles continued to make the pages of ye olde tabloide papers. Let's now see what those occupied Brits were reading about.

Death in Sussex: William Conquers Harold

Having become the Earl of Wessex in 1053 upon the death-by-choking-on-a-lump-of-bread of his father Godwin, Harold Godwinson forged a solid reputation for himself as an astute general and reliable aid to Edward the Confessor. Then an apparent lack of foresight let him down. According to William of Normandy's later assertions, while Harold was serving as an emissary to William's court in 1064, Harold swore an oath of allegiance to William and relinquished his own claims to the English throne. At the same time, William would also claim that back in 1051 his cousin King Edward III had promised him the right of succession. When, in 1066, the dying Confessor named Harold the next king, Harold immediately acted upon the Confessor's words, despite his alleged pledge to William, and had himself crowned. Consequently, William felt that he'd been double-crossed.

Of course, all this is based on William's words. Who knows whether either Edward or Harold had made the promises William claimed. Regardless, he stuck with his story, and the word "invasion" now entered his thoughts. This same word was also on the minds of a pair of other likely lads: Harold's brother Tostig, who had been exiled since the autumn of 1065, and a Nordic king going by the name of Harald Hardrada. In September 1066, these two landed in Yorkshire with more than enough men to distract Harold away from the south of England, where he'd been waiting for the inevitable Norman attack. What he didn't want was to be waging war on two fronts with different enemies, so he quickly marched north with his forces and clobbered Tostig and Mr. Hardrada at the Battle of Stamford Bridge.

Hear Ye, Hear Ye
"Six feet of ground or as much more as he needs, as he is taller than most men."
—*Harold II's response when asked by his brother, Tostig, how much he was prepared to yield to the King of Norway*

Hear Ye, Hear Ye
"See, I have taken England with both my hands."
—*William the Conqueror after landing on the English coast, stepping off his boat, and falling flat on his face, September 28, 1066*

That was on September 25. Three days later the Normans landed at Pevensey in the south of England, prompting Harold and his men to break into a trot as they headed back toward London. They arrived there on October 5, pausing just long enough to collect what fresh troops were available before setting off again to intercept the advancing Normans. At about 9:00 a.m. on Saturday, October 14, 1066, the two sides met six miles north of Hastings.

The 7,000-strong Saxon army—many of whom were foot soldiers with long and heavy battleaxes—lined 10 to 12 deep along the top of a ridge, while 7,000 Normans—sword and axe-wielding foot soldiers, archers, and fast-moving mounted knights in armor—gathered at the bottom of the ridge about 400 yards away. The Normans made the first move, attacking the Saxon lines before being forced to retreat. Harold's troops pursued the aggressors down the hill and were met with a strong counterattack. The Normans launched another assault on the ridge and, when the plan didn't work, William had his troops pretend to run away.

The Saxons were drawn toward William's troops, who then turned around and hit the Saxons with a surprise attack. The tactic worked.

The Battle of Hastings lasted about 10 hours; when it was over, the green fields were covered with dead bodies, including those of King Harold II and his brothers Gyrth and Leofwine. According to the Bayeux Tapestry—a famous depiction of William's heroics before, during, and after the battle—Harold had received an arrow in his right eye. He was probably finished off, however, by the sword of a knight. The last of the Anglo-Saxon kings, Harold was also the last monarch of England to be defeated by a foreign invader.

On Christmas Day 1066, William the Conqueror was crowned king of England at Westminster Abbey.

Castles, Taxes, and the Feudal System

William had gotten what he wanted, but the same could hardly be said for his English subjects. This was occupation by an invasion force, just like any we've witnessed or seen presented by 20th-century media. People were scared, angry, and rebellious. As a result, the new king decided to built castles, lots of them, in which the nobility he had brought with him from Normandy could take refuge, and from where they could preside over the surrounding land and their subservient English peasants. The Tower of London was among the first such castle to be constructed, and it would set a trend: Over the next 600 years approximately 2,000 castles sprang up all over Britain.

English land had been confiscated from the Anglo-Saxon nobility. William kept a vast amount of it for himself, and then awarded the rest to the Norman barons who had helped him in his conquest. These barons subsequently divided their land into *fiefs* and handed them out to *vassals* in return for a specified amount of military service. Not that the vassals would do that service themselves. That job would fall to the knights, who, in accepting some land from the vassals, became subvassals of the king. This was the *feudal* system, Norman-style, and it was meticulously operated.

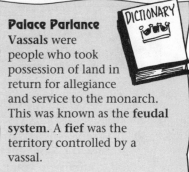

Palace Parlance
Vassals were people who took possession of land in return for allegiance and service to the monarch. This was known as the **feudal system**. A **fief** was the territory controlled by a vassal.

The barons had to pay feudal dues to the king, and even though the fiefs were scattered all over the kingdom, William ensured that the fees were regularly collected. Together with a system of national taxation and the revenue earned from the massive royal estates, this income guaranteed the stability and independence of the Royal Court. Furthermore, without the sort of tax-loopholes available today, few if any people got away with not paying what was demanded of them. Taxpayer non-compliance was especially rare after 1086, when William initiated a public census that set standards still being aspired to.

An aerial view of the Tower of London, adjacent to Tower Bridge and the River Thames. (Photo courtesy of UPI/Corbis-Bettmann)

Basically, the king sent out commissioners to collect information on who owned what—land, equipment, you name it—and how much it was worth. Evidence was given under oath (meaning that it was best not to lie), and the results were collated in the Norman capital of Winchester, where they were recorded in the legendary Domesday Book. William the Conqueror, as you can tell, was no fool.

Furthermore, it was made very clear that the vassals' first loyalty was to the king, not the barons, and few were about to argue. When crossed, William displayed a tremendous capacity for cruelty. For example, when northern earls rebelled in 1069, William responded by destroying their villages, burning their crops, and killing all of their cattle. While most citizens, especially those peasants who had to work on the feudal territories for virtually nothing, resented their Norman ruler, many also admired him.

Because crimes were severely punished, England was a safer place than before the Conquest. Convicted rapists, for example, were castrated—a punishment in accordance with William's own stand on sexual morality. Unlike many of his fellow monarchs, he was faithful to his wife, Matilda of Flanders, with whom he sired four sons and five daughters. He was also a leading reformer of the English Church, replacing nearly all the Saxon bishops and abbots with stricter and more highly trained ones from the Continent. Celibacy was imposed on the clergy, and if any men of the cloth strayed from their duties they could be tried by their superior officers in the specially set-up ecclesiastical courts.

On Her Majesty's Service

If you want to see the Domesday Book, it's kept at the Public Record Office in London. A glance at its pages will give you a fair idea as to the extent of William the Conqueror's survey. Unless you're a true scholar, however, you'll probably be bored to tears by what you're reading.

Then there were the changes William introduced to the English legal system, not the least of which was the introduction of trial by jury (derived from the French word *jure*, meaning truth). Indeed, as a result of William I's reign, England became a more civilized and united nation.

An avid deer hunter who cleared the New Forest of all its buildings and inhabitants in order to create game reserves, the Conqueror nevertheless died in 1087 as a result of his adventures pursuing humans. Having just captured the French town of Nantes, William was thrown from his horse after it trod on hot embers. When he passed away the following day, some people who had been attending to the king decided to partake in a spot of royal looting.

His weapons, armor, and clothes were all stolen, as were his bedsheets; the corpse was left practically naked. Then at the burial, the body was broken in half as it was forced into a stone coffin. The grave was reinterred in 1522, only for the new site to be looted several years later. All that was left of the first Norman king on the English throne was a thigh bone (I kid you not), and although that bone was accorded the dignity of a reburial, it too was destroyed during the French Revolution! There is, however, a relatively happy ending to this story. During the 1980s, that much-missed thigh bone was rediscovered—French authorities confirmed that it was authentic, and so, on September 9, 1987, it was finally laid to rest under a new tombstone. Personally, I'm surprised it wasn't given a full State funeral.

Would you mess with this man? William I, the Conqueror and king of England in full battle dress. (Picture courtesy of Corbis-Bettmann)

Malice Among Brothers: Rufus, Henry, and Robert

While William I lay dying, he bequeathed the English throne to his second surviving son, also named William but nicknamed Rufus because of his extremely red complexion. The eldest son, Robert, was deemed too generous and easygoing, and so he was made Duke of Normandy. This decision would prove to be highly unpopular.

Short and stout, with fair hair and a stutter, William II could be witty and generous to his own supporters, yet these were not the character traits that most people would identify him with. Instead, this man named Rufus was known for being cruel, ruthless, greedy, violent, and crude. He fell out with the church after imposing heavy taxes, and when Archbishop of Canterbury Lanfranc died in 1089, Rufus didn't appoint another for four years, during which time he kept the revenues normally allotted to the post. Then, a few years after the Benedictine monk Anselm filled the position, William had a row with him, exiled him to Rome, and seized all of his assets.

Meanwhile, aside from the church, the King also had problems with England's French-speaking barons, many of whom owned land both in England and in Normandy. This meant that they owed some of their allegiance to William's brother, Duke Robert, who was staking his claim to the English throne. In 1088, the duke's supporters led a baronial revolt in Normandy, but the uprising was crushed by William, and in 1090 he led an invasion of Normandy as a show of strength to subdue Robert. The following year, and again in 1093, Rufus repelled a couple of attempted invasions by Malcolm III of Scotland, and then in 1095 he suppressed yet another baronial uprising, this time in Northumbria.

A Right Royal Tale

During the reign of William II, as the gap between rich and poor, noble and peasant continued to widen, those with the money dressed themselves ever more extravagantly. Women decked themselves in increasingly flashy jewelry, while the men wore flamboyant, puffed-up tunics that stretched below their knees. It also became fashionable for men to wear shoes with curved, pointy toes. Apparently, however, none of this finery could rival the trends that were taking place within the king's court. According to contemporary accounts, red-faced Rufus surrounded himself with longhaired, "half-naked," effeminate young men. Of course, all of this prompted widespread speculation that the monarch, who never married, was gay.

As you can see, it wasn't an easy reign for the king, who was, to his credit, responsible for the construction of Westminster Hall. Like his father, William II had a great passion for deer hunting, and on August 2, 1100, while on a chase in the New Forest with, among others, his younger brother Henry, he took an arrow to the head. The arrow had been fired by a close friend named Walter Tyrell, and while the incident was passed off as an accident, speculation to the contrary has raged ever since. The fact that Henry, the heir to the throne, was around at the time has fueled the flames of a conspiracy theory, as has Henry's behavior immediately following his brother's death. While peasants wheeled a cart carrying the body of the unloved king to Winchester, Henry rushed there and seized the royal treasury, having first confronted courtiers who thought that this should be the possession of his eldest brother, the Duke of Normandy. Robert, however, was off on a crusade, so Henry quickly had himself crowned as the new king of England at Westminster Abbey on August 5.

Henry I was the only one of William the Conqueror's sons to be born in England. Although he was more placid and more studious than his father or brother Rufus (earning him the nickname "Beauclerc," which means "fine scholar" in French), he could display their ruthlessness and cruelty. Reportedly, he once pushed a man to his death from the top of Rouen Castle for betraying the Royal Family. On the other hand, he also knew how to win over his Saxon subjects far more successfully than his Norman predecessors had.

In the year of his accession, Henry issued a Charter of Liberties that promised fair rule, while the *Curia Regis* (Latin for "King's Council") was set up to settle disputes between the monarchy and the people. There again, in line with Norman tradition, Henry was a strict enforcer of the law, meting out harsh punishments to those who stepped out of line, and thus earning for himself yet another nickname; "The Lion of Justice." In 1100, Henry married Edith, the daughter of the late Malcolm III of Scotland and a great-granddaughter of Edward the Confessor, a union that went some way toward placating both the Scots and the Saxons. Still, to keep the Normans happy, she adopted the name of Mathilde, or Matilda, and the couple had two children, a daughter also called Matilda and a son named William.

Meanwhile, brother Robert still hadn't given up on his claim to the throne. In 1101, he launched an abortive invasion of England and ended up signing the Treaty of Alton, which confirmed that Henry I was the rightful king of England and that Robert should remain Duke of Normandy. Henry also agreed to pay his elder brother a pension, but by 1106 he'd had second thoughts about that, as well as the whole question of Norman rule. He therefore went to war with Robert, and, after defeating him at the Battle of Tinchebrai, imprisoned him in Cardiff Castle for the rest of his life. He would spend more than half of his reign there in Normandy.

A Right Royal Tale

On landing in Normandy to tame his brother, Robert Curthose (so-called because he was reportedly quite short), Henry I made a pact with the Church, promising Bishop Erlo of Sees that he was simply fighting for peaceful co-existence. Believe that if you will! The bishop, happy with what he heard, now took advantage of the conciliatory atmosphere by telling the King and his colleagues that they should all crop off their fashionable but "unseemly" long hair and beards. No sooner had the king agreed than the bishop whipped out a pair of scissors and went to work. Afterward, clean-shaven and having received the sacrament, Henry and his men were ready for business.

William was now the new Duke of Normandy and heir to the throne. However, the king's only son would never accede. In 1120, while returning from Normandy to England, 17-year-old William drowned when the White Ship that he was traveling on hit a rock and filled with water. Henry's wife, Matilda, had died two years earlier, and so, unwilling to take the chance of naming their daughter as his heir, the King married Adela of Louvain in 1121 and tried again. The fact that Adela subsequently failed to produce an heir or even a daughter was probably due to her (although I wasn't in the bedroom with them, so I can't be sure). After all, Henry still holds the record of having sired more acknowledged illegitimate children than any other English monarch. The irony is that he just didn't leave a male heir.

The king's daughter Matilda subsequently married twice—her second husband was Geoffrey Plantaganet, Count of Anjou—and Henry persuaded the barons to accept her as his successor. After Henry died of food poisoning at the start of December 1135, however, those same barons transferred their support to Matilda's cousin, Stephen...and what a mistake *that* turned out to be.

Stephen's Folly: Civil War and Stalemate

"Nineteen long winters."

That's how the 1135-1154 reign of King Stephen has been described—for very good reason. Stephen had been one of those who had sworn to accept Henry I's daughter Matilda as heir to the throne; then, as soon as Uncle Henry died, what did Stephen do? That's right, on December 22, while Matilda was still in France, where she lived with Count Geoffrey of Anjou, Stephen had himself crowned. Matilda should have rushed back to England earlier so that the ensuing disaster may have been averted.

Easygoing but horribly naive, Stephen had only been on the throne a short time before trouble reared its ugly head. In 1136, the Earl of Norfolk led a rebellion against Stephen, and, although the king initially managed to suppress this and other revolts, he made the fatal mistake of being lenient with the rebels. This meant they were soon free to attack him again. Stephen's predecessors never would have made such a simple mistake, and by 1138, able to see the direction in which the winds of fortune were blowing, the rats started to desert the sinking ship.

One of these deserters was Robert, Earl of Gloucester (pronounced "Gloster"), one of Henry I's many illegitimate sons. Robert withdrew his support for Stephen and aligned himself with Matilda. Her uncle, David I of Scotland, shortly followed suit by invading England. The Scots didn't need much excuse to invade. As it happens, Stephen defeated David at the Battle of the Standard in Yorkshire, but Matilda had already seen enough. The king's support was hemorrhaging badly, the writing was on the wall, and it was time to pack her luggage.

Hear Ye, Hear Ye
"He was adept at the martial arts but in other respects little more than a simpleton."
—*Contemporary writer Walter Map's assessment of King Stephen*

Matilda's first husband had been an emperor of the Holy Roman Empire (actually a loose collection of countries—he was German) and she'd held onto her title, so we'll now refer to the usurped monarch as *Empress* Matilda. King Stephen himself was married to another Matilda who, to avoid confusion, we'll *simply* call Matilda.

Anyway, in 1139 Empress Matilda landed in England and joined Robert of Gloucester in the west country. Stephen didn't think it right to make war on a woman. So early in the year 1141, that woman was making war on him: civil war. Anarchy now swept across England as some barons took the opportunity to build illegal castles and plunder other people's property. The country was in a state of uproar and nobody felt safe.

Empress Matilda's forces defeated Stephen at the Battle of Lincoln and imprisoned him in Bristol Castle. With the help of Stephen's brother, Henry, Bishop of Winchester, she then declared herself queen. When she arrived in London for her expected coronation, however, this "Lady of the English"—as supporters had already proclaimed her—was chased out by angry citizens who weren't prepared to accept a woman on the throne or the taxes that she had already imposed on them.

In the meantime, the other Matilda was rallying the King's forces. Empress Matilda's half-brother and loyal friend, Robert of Gloucester, was captured and the would-be queen's army was on the run. Her other loyal friend, Bishop Henry of Winchester, had already realigned himself with his brother Stephen. The two Matildas now exchanged allies—the king for Robert of Gloucester—and the civil war resumed. Empress Matilda and her men were soon surrounded at Oxford Castle, but while their situation looked desperate the Empress wasn't about to give up. She broke out of the castle and, camouflaged in a white nightgown and accompanied by three knights, ran across the snow all the way to London.

Reunited with Earl Robert (and, soon afterwards, her nine-year-old son Henry, who had come from Normandy to support his mother), she vowed to keep on fighting. And so she did, for another five years. During these years she suffered further losses but no one side could finish off the other. Then, in 1147, Robert died, and at that point Empress Matilda decided enough was enough. The following year she retired to Normandy, and it was left to Henry to fight for his own right of accession.

Having succeeded his father, Geoffrey, as Count of Anjou in 1151, Henry landed in England and made a full-tilt assault on Stephen two years later. The king, weary from battle and disheartened by the deaths of his wife and his son Eustace, no longer had his heart in the struggle. He therefore agreed to a deal: According to the Treaty of Westminster, Stephen would see out his reign, but on his death the crown would be passed to Henry of Anjou instead of the King's son William.

Empress Matilda, meanwhile, lived until 1167, more than long enough to see her son take the throne that she had been denied. She wasn't at Westminster Abbey for his 1154 coronation, however, nor did she ever return to England. After all, England didn't really hold many happy holiday memories for her.

The Least You Need to Know

➤ On October 14, 1066, William the Conqueror defeated King Harold II at the Battle of Hastings. This defeat ended the Anglo-Saxon reign and commenced that of the Normans.

➤ William I was a ruthless leader, but his enforcement of Norman-style laws and the feudal system made England a safer and better-organized country.

➤ A landmark public census was carried out in 1086 and the results were entered in the Domesday Book. This census helped William assess taxes owed to him.

➤ One of England's most unpopular kings was the tyrannical William II (known as Rufus), while one of its most disastrous was the overly lenient King Stephen.

Lust For Power—The Day of the Angevins

In This Chapter

➤ Henry II's legal reforms and his religious and family conflicts

➤ The overseas adventures of Richard the Lionheart

➤ King John's unpopular policies and disputes with the Church

➤ The turbulent but fruitful reign of Edward the Confessor

After the anarchy and pandemonium of Stephen's reign, it was vital for the English monarchy to reassert its authority and establish a centralized system of law and order that could withstand periodic mismanagement. As you'll see in this chapter, Henry II, one of the greatest of medieval rulers, was just the man for that job.

Richard the Lionheart, on the other hand, spent more time dealing with issues abroad than at home, while his brother John, although as keen as his father Henry to extend royal justice, ran into trouble when he punished lawbreakers but broke laws himself. The result was a charter of rights and privileges that also forced the monarchy to fall into line. After all, let's face it: Those rulers could get pretty unruly at times, couldn't they?

Henry II: Justice of the Peace?

Before we get started with Henry's reign, let me first clear up something with regard to his family name. Some books group together the royal houses of Angevin and Plantagenet under the Plantagenet title, but I'm adhering to convention and keeping them separate.

Angevin, the name usually applied to the English monarchs from 1154 to 1216, derives from the lordship of the medieval county (and later duchy) of Anjou in western France. Henry, you should remember from Chapter 7, became the Count of Anjou on the death of his father Geoffrey. He then went on to create a wider Angevin empire, also comprising Normandy, Maine, and Aquitaine, and this royal family line therefore continued up to and including the reign of Henry's brother John, when Anjou was lost to the French.

After John's death, the Plantagenet dynasty came into force, ruling from 1216 to 1399, and then splitting into a pair of rival houses, Lancaster and York, until 1485. So why, you may well ask, are the Angevins and Plantagenets sometimes lumped into one group? Well, even though Henry II was the first of the Angevins (for the reason that I've just explained), his surname was actually Plantagenet. He acquired this name from the nickname given to his father, Geoffrey, who used to wear a badge consisting of a sprig of flowering broom.

In French, *plante genet* (the botanical name is *Planta Genista*) means "flower broom." So there you have it. For a few hundred years the English had a bunch of flower brooms on the throne, and the first of them, ruling from the House of Angevin, was Henry II. He started his reign by destroying the castles that had been illegally built by rebellious barons during the civil war era of King Stephen. Later he invaded Ireland and commenced 700 years of English rule there before suffering the betrayal of his wife, Queen Eleanor, and sons Henry, Richard, and Geoffrey, who all plotted to overthrow him. They united with rebel nobles in East Anglia and encouraged invasions by the kings of Scotland and France. All were unsuccessful. When, toward the end of his life, Henry learned that yet another plot by Richard also involved his beloved youngest son John, the king's heart was broken. He died of a fever at the age of 56.

The death occurred at Chinon Castle in France, for Henry had spent a lot of his time there. A tough and athletic man, he traveled incessantly through his empire—the most powerful in Europe—which stretched from the Scottish borders to the Pyrenees. In fact, before marrying Eleanor of Aquitaine, the recently divorced wife of King Louis VII of France, he'd already ruled most of that country from the Channel to the Loire. It was Eleanor who had the land between the Loire and the Pyrenees.

Hear Ye, Hear Ye

"Now in Ireland, now in England, now in Normandy, he must fly rather than go by horse or ship."
—*King Louis VII of France talking about Henry II*

Henry was no fool. In fact, he was a great intellectual, and it's therefore appropriate that, during his reign, some English scholars who were expelled from Paris founded a university in a town named Oxford. The king's interests were many and so were his spheres of influence. Let's now take a closer look at two of his main interests.

Creating Common Law

Henry II extended the area of authority of the royal courts by radically increasing the number of officially recognized offences and pleas. Now anyone could use these courts for civil actions involving land disputes, including those citizens located in remote parts of the country that were visited by traveling justices. Consequently, a lot of cases that previously would have been heard in local courts were relocating to the royal courts, which were widely regarded as being more professional and fair.

As a system of common law increasingly replaced local laws across the nation, the royal courts helped boost the king's image as well as his income. Don't forget, by widening the legal net, he was able to accrue even more money than before from fines and so on. Of course, William the Conqueror had been responsible for initiating many of the laws that Henry II was now simply embellishing. One of those ideas was a jury system.

Under Henry, the jury became par for the course within the royal courts, although the jury wasn't used in the same way then that it is in modern times. Instead, it would be a case of the king's justices summoning ordinary citizens and forcing them to disclose, under oath, the names or descriptions of any criminals who they were aware of in their neighborhood. Anyone named would then be summoned to trial at a royal court. In this use, the jury was simply a means of accusing or indicting a criminal. Where the system more closely resembled a trial jury, on the other hand, was in a royal court case dealing with a land dispute, where the jurors not only gave evidence but also came up with a decision. In 1166, the Assize of Clarendon established trial by jury for the first time.

Having a centralized system of common law and *assize courts* that negated the need for local courts and rules was clearly desirable for the king and popular with most people. Where this policy got Henry into trouble, however, was when the Church took exception to the Crown meddling in ecclesiastical affairs.

> **Palace Parlance**
> Assize courts, dating back to the reign of Henry II, were presided over by judges who traveled on circuit to hear criminal and civil cases. The Courts Act of 1971 abolished this system in Britain.

Murder in the Cathedral: The Death of Thomas à Becket

Henry didn't think that clergy should enjoy special dispensations when they committed crimes, yet that's what he was seeing: the ecclesiastical courts punishing serious misdemeanors by administering figurative slaps on the wrist of the guilty clergy. The king felt that there was no justification for this leniency, or for cases to be appealed to the papal court in Rome. Criminal clergymen were no different than other criminals, Henry argued; as such, they should be tried in civil courts without the right of papal intervention, unless sanctioned by the English monarch. In 1164 the Constitutions of Clarendon made Henry's notion law, and, from Henry's point of view, that should have been that. But it wasn't.

Royal Rebuttal
Nobody knows the precise statement that provoked the murder of Thomas a Becket. According to the account of Edward Grimm, Becket's biographer who was wounded during the slaying, Henry had moaned, "What miserable drones and traitors have I nourished and promoted in my household, who let their lord be treated with such shameful contempt by a low-born clerk!" Impressive words, but impossible to prove.

On Her Majesty's Service
Following the murder of Thomas a Becket, Canterbury Cathedral became a popular destination for pilgrims from all over Europe through the Middle Ages. Today many people still visit, but in order to keep the Cathedral in good repair, the Chapter has recently imposed an admission charge on tourists. Real worshippers can get in for free, however, so it may pay to look humble.

Two years earlier he'd appointed his Chancellor, Thomas a Becket, as Archbishop of Canterbury in the hope that Becket would weed out abuses within the church. After all, Becket had always been on the King's side in his disputes with the clergy, so what better man to have as the head of the church than his closest ally? Well, no sooner had Becket become Archbishop than he resigned as Chancellor and sided with the church against the king. Objecting vociferously to the Constitutions of Clarendon, he went into exile in Normandy after learning that Henry intended to try him for contempt.

Six years later Becket was back, and the row between the church and the Crown continued. The struggle would end in tragedy. According to the most widely recounted version of the story, on December 29, 1160, after having had another confrontation with Becket, Henry flew into a rage and screamed, "Will not someone rid me of this turbulent priest?" The king would later claim that his words were simply a rash expression of anger. Regardless, four of his eager-to-please knights evidently took him at his word.

Becket was standing at the high altar during divine service at Canterbury Cathedral when the knights came up from behind and hacked him to death.

Henry II would pay for this crime in many ways. First, with Becket instantly viewed as a martyr by the masses (he would later be canonized), the King was forced to do public penance as ordained by the Pope.

The penance included walking barefoot through the streets of Canterbury until he reached Becket's tomb in the Cathedral, where he confessed and asked for pardon before being lashed across his bare back by a number of monks. Henry must have worried about being unpopular to have agreed to this treatment. In addition to Henry's humiliating penance at the grave, the Constitutions of Clarendon largely had to be withdrawn. Finally, Henry's family viewed—or at least used—Becket's murder as reason enough to try to overthrow the king.

The church had won this battle with the English monarchy. The war, however, would go on.

The Lionhearted Crusade of Richard I

If Henry II spent a lot of his time traveling, his son Richard I was hardly ever around. Indeed, after acceding to the throne in 1189 he spent only seven months of his 10-year reign in England. In his absence, Chancellor William Longchamp and then Richard's brother John presided over the royal government.

So, what was the king doing? Well, soon after his accession, he sold state and Church property, as well as charters giving English towns greater freedom of self-government, in order to raise the money he needed for the Third Crusade. During medieval times, the crusades were basically military expeditions undertaken by Europeans to recover the Holy Land from the Muslims. Christianity was on the rise and anti-Semitism was already rife: When Jewish leaders had turned up uninvited at Richard's coronation banquet, they'd been beaten and, in some cases, murdered, leading to copycat treatment of Jews all over London. Still, the Christians didn't always get their way. There were nine crusades in all and ultimately the Muslims kept control.

"By God's feet," Richard had half-joked when struggling to raise enough money for the Third Crusade, "find me a purchaser and I will sell London itself!" For in truth, even though he was a dashing hero overseas, Richard the Lionheart (translated from the French *Coeur de Lion*) just used England as a source of revenue. This was not a subtle man; having married Princess Berengaria, he did little to disguise the fact that he was gay.

Three great rulers of Western Christendom set off for Jerusalem to confront the Muslim leader, Saladin, who had captured the Holy City a couple of years earlier: Richard I; King Philip II of France; and the Frederick I ("Barbarossa") of Germany, ruler of the Holy Roman Empire. Unfortunately, the venture got off to a bad start when Barbarossa drowned in Anatolia before even arriving in the Holy Land, while the obvious animosity between the English and French led to Philip's early return home.

Richard demolished the Muslims at Acre in Palestine, and then defeated Saladin at Arsouf near Jaffa, yet the main objective of taking Jerusalem was never realized. Instead, an agreement was reached with Saladin, who promised to protect the Christian pilgrims traveling there.

Meanwhile, as he made his way home, Richard was taken prisoner by another of his crusading allies, Duke Leopold of Austria, who he'd somehow contrived to insult when they were in Acre. Leopold handed Richard over to Barbarossa's replacement as the Holy Roman Emperor, King Henry VI of Germany, who demanded a massive ransom of 150,000 silver marks for Richard's release. And who did he demand the ransom money from? Why, those free spenders the English, of course! It took two years for the money to be raised, during which time the king's young brother, John, conspired with Philip II of France to keep Richard in prison. I tell you, whenever that English Crown looked like it might be up for grabs, all bets were off in terms of loyalty. In the end, Henry got his money and, to show his gratitude, Richard paid England the rare honor of a visit. Richard then left for France and never returned.

Man with a mission: The lion-hearted Richard I. (Picture courtesy of Corbis-Bettmann)

In France, Richard waged war on King Philip, and after he'd routed the French army at Gisors in 1198, he asserted, "God and my right did this, not I." Actually, he said the words in French, and thereafter "Dieu at mon droit" became a motto on the Royal Coat of Arms.

The following year, while besieging the Castle of Chalus, Richard was hit in the shoulder by an arrow. He tried to pull out the arrow, but only succeeded in removing the shaft, leaving the arrowhead embedded. Gangrene soon set in, and within 12 days the Lionheart was dead.

King John: A Troubled Man

The youngest son of Henry II, Richard's successor was often called "John Lackland" because of the way his father had divided his possessions among the elder sons. In other words, he "lacked land." Get it? Well, even if you don't, he certainly did, because within five years of acceding to the throne, all of the provinces in France that he'd inherited had been lost to the French. He didn't lose his throne, though; he dealt with the claim of his nephew, Arthur, by murdering him with his own hands.

Meanwhile, of course, the loss of Normandy meant that those Normans living in England no longer had a divided allegiance; they were now solidly English! John would subsequently take an unsuccessful stab at winning back the territories, and in the last year of his life suffer a double catastrophe. First, with English nobles rising up against him, the French would invade England, and Prince Louis would capture the Tower of London in the process. Second, the chest John carted around with him—a chest containing cash and his own Crown Jewels—would fall into a river at the neck of the Wash (an inlet of the North Sea between Norfolk and Lincolnshire) and never be seen again.

Hear Ye, Hear Ye
"I forgive you my death. Live on...and by my bounty behold the light of day."
—*Richard the Lionheart on his deathbed, talking to the man who had fatally wounded him*

Royal Rebuttal
Robin Hood supposedly lived during the reign of King John. Although historians point to a man who stole from the rich and gave to the poor, he didn't woo a girl named Maid Marion or have a friend named Friar Tuck. These details were 16th-century add-ons, as was the idea of him hanging around Sherwood Forest. In the original story it was Barnesdale Forest.

Nevertheless, in between the loss of the French territories in 1204 and his death from dysentery in 1216, John had numerous other problems to occupy his mind...

Excommunicated in His Prime

Pope Innocent III had supported John in his conflicts with Philip Augustus of France, but then John got into an ultimately disastrous squabble with the Pope over the election of a new Archbishop of Canterbury. After Hubert Walter died in 1205, the Cathedral's canons elected his replacement by secret ballot, while the clergy elected another man based on a directive from the king. Innocent, meanwhile, opted for a third man, Stephen Langdon, but John refused to accept him. The ball was now in the pope's court. He served an ace.

In 1208, Pope Innocent III issued an Interdict against England banning all church services except baptisms and funerals. After all, people had to have *some* fun. Then, the following year, he and John really went at it; John confiscated the land and buildings of the Church, and Innocent excommunicated the English king. In 1212, the Pope even went so far as to declare that John was no longer the rightful monarch. Where he got the authority to come up with that I'm not too sure, but Philip Augustus of France was more than prepared to agree, and more than prepared to invade England on the Pope's behalf. It had nothing to do with self-interest, of course. John, recognizing that he was firmly up against the ropes, finally gave in, declaring England a papal fief (under the Pope's sphere of influence) and also accepting Stephen Langdon as the Archbishop of Canterbury. If only he'd agreed to these terms in the first place, there would have been a lot less fuss. Now, however, he was conceding defeat to an enemy who was still poised for action.

Accepting the Magna Carta

No sooner was Stephen Langdon installed as Archbishop of Canterbury than he began stirring up trouble against his longtime oppressor the king. Since the beginning of his reign, John had been very unpopular with England's barons—and almost everyone else. His heavy taxes and the long-running dispute with the pope were both seen as abuses of royal power, while the disastrous loss of territory to the French reflected how he was dragging the country through the mire.

On Her Majesty's Service
Following John's June 15, 1215, endorsement of the Magna Carta, numerous copies were made and distributed around the kingdom. Today, the British Library's Manuscript Saloon contains two of the four surviving copies, while the other two are in the archives of Lincoln and Salisbury Cathedrals. All differ slightly in size, shape, and contents, with last-minute revisions included in the Lincoln and Salisbury copies.

Following yet another terrible defeat against the French, at the Battle of Bouvines in 1214, the Archbishop decided that it was time to make his mark. He and the barons all got together at Bury St. Edmunds, and between them they came up with a list of demands and an ultimatum for King John: Either accept what we're asking or be prepared for civil war. John being John wasn't going to agree to anything immediately (just ask Pope Innocent III), but at least he didn't reject the demands. He just said he would need time to consider them. Actually, he wanted to haggle.

By the next year, the barons were getting restless, so after plenty of negotiating, John agreed to meet them at a field in Runnymede, which was situated about halfway between his residence at Windsor and theirs in Staines. The date was June 15, 1215, and after the two sides turned up, there was a short ceremony, confirming that this was an important occasion—and royal to boot. Next, the barons presented their demands in the form of a Great Charter, as it was called, and John reluctantly affixed the royal seal to it. Contrary to Hollywood's version of events, he didn't sign his name.

So, what did it say? There were actually four different versions of the Magna Carta. The original from 1215 was revised in 1216 with certain clauses removed, and there were more changes for the third version in 1217. Henry III endorsed the fourth and final one in 1225, but let's stick with the original for now. The first version had no fewer than 63 clauses that attempted to lay down the rights and responsibilities of the monarch and the people, but particularly the barons and the Church. After all, they'd devised it. Chief among these were curbs on the king's ability to tax the barons, guarantees regarding the rights of the Church and city corporations, and a stipulation that people couldn't be arrested or imprisoned just because the king said so; arrests and prison sentences should be left to the established legal mechanism.

John may have put his wax seal to this document, but abiding by all the rules and regulations was another matter. Having renewed their allegiance to the king, the barons were very aware of the shaky nature of his word, so in their eyes Pope Innocent looked more like Pope Guilty when, in August 1215, he contrived to "annul" the Charter. After all, considering that John had agreed to England being a papal fief, what were the Archbishop and barons doing, making all the rules without his say so? That Stephen Langdon was clearly ungrateful for all that the Pope had done to get him installed at Canterbury. Boy oh boy, give him a little power and it goes straight to his head! As punishment, Innocent suspended the Archbishop for two years, and furthermore he decreed that John didn't need to adhere to the Magna Carta.

The result was civil war. Of course, the barons immediately turned to the French for assistance in their fight against the English kzing, and the rest I've already told you about. Suffice it to say that when John died, the civil war was still raging, and the situation was less than pleasant for his nine-year-old son Henry to inherit.

The Least You Need to Know

➤ The Angevins and Plantagenets all shared the Plantaganet surname.

➤ Henry II, a reformer of the law and the Church, ran into trouble when his dispute with Thomas a Becket led to the Archbishop's murder.

➤ Richard the Lionheart only spent seven months of his 10-year reign in England, but he used the country to finance his overseas exploits.

➤ During King John's reign, England lost all of its French territory, and his rows with the Pope led to excommunication from the Church of Rome.

➤ The Magna Carta (or Great Charter) was endorsed by John on June 15, 1215, and served to curb the power of the monarchy.

Part 3
Medieval Mischief
(1216-1485)

If the Dark Ages ended around the time that William the Conqueror came on the scene, then this part of the book spells the last part of the Middle Ages. This period saw the same old struggles continue: between England and France, kings and nobles, kings and religious leaders, and kings and kings.

Medieval monarchs were always full of mischief but short on money to pursue some of their mischievous activities. Teams of advisors had to be called upon to discuss how funds could be raised, and these teams came to be known as parliaments. *Eventually, Parliament was the only arm of government that was able to impose taxes, and it also worked with the king in devising new laws.*

Still, if the early Middle Ages had witnessed the rapid growth of England's population as well as the country's wealth, then the late Middle Ages saw more than a quarter of that population wiped out by a series of terrible plagues. No, life wasn't always so merry in olde England, but I'll do my best to lighten things a little.

Chapter 9

Trouble in the Isles—The Plantagenets

In This Chapter

➤ The foreign favoritism of Henry III

➤ The legal reforms and battling adventures of the "Hammer of the Scots"

➤ Edward II's court of favorites and diabolical death

➤ Deadly disease and incessant hostilities between the English and French during the reign of Edward III

➤ Richard II's dishonest deal with the rebel peasants

As I progress from one chapter to the next, I keep thinking "I'll never top the last one," yet those mischievous monarchs and their dastardly deeds ensure that I do. This chapter is a case in point. If you think you've already read all there is to know about treachery and murder, wait until you see what I've got lined up for you this time. No, it's not that I'm trying to indulge you in a carnival of carnage, but the methods devised for some of those medieval murders and executions really do take some believing.

Nevertheless, instead of reveling in gruesome details, the majority of this chapter focuses on other aspects of the Plantagenet years: the successes, disasters, advances, achievements, and disappointments. It also highlights how an incompetent ruler could sire a wonderful successor and vice versa. This was an extremely important time in the history of both England and its monarchy, for a fair amount of what took place at that time laid the foundation for what we're familiar with today.

Boy King: Henry III

Because Henry III was only nine years old when he acceded to the throne in 1216, he initially had two Regents ruling England: William the Marshall and Hubert de Burgh. After William died in 1219, de Burgh ran things on his own until Henry reached the age of 20, at which point the King took full control of the government.

In the meantime, England, of course, was still in a state of civil war following the death of Henry's father, John. Consequently, the French supported by the barons were, as ever, trying to stake their claim to the throne. Because the barons didn't really have any problems with the boy king, however, many of them began to switch sides. After the Regents managed to repel the French attacks at Lincoln and at Sandwich, the *Dauphin*, Louis, finally gave up. In 1217, the Treaty of Lambeth established peace.

Palace Parlance

Dauphin was the title given to the eldest son of the King of France. The Dauphin's wife was the **Dauphine**.

When Henry started to execute his duties as king, he retained Hubert de Burgh as his chief adviser, but it soon became clear that the monarch wasn't cut out for rule. The nobility resented the increasing amount of French influence within the Royal Court, most notably in the form of Peter des Roches, who was the Bishop of Winchester, and Peter des Riveaux, who was appointed Treasurer of England in 1232. This same year Hubert de Burgh, after years of tremendous service to the Crown, was dismissed on blatantly trumped-up charges of treason.

Richard Marshall, the Earl of Pembroke and son of the late regent, William, provoked a new rebellion among the barons. As a result, the king dismissed Peter des Riveaux and his bunch of hangers-on, but by 1236 Henry was at it again. He married Eleanor of Provence, and, buoyed by this union, he immediately installed three of her uncles in leading government positions. Other French relatives followed, and the annoying effect on both the nobility and the people was compounded by the manner in which their king allowed the pope to impose heavy taxes, while recruiting lots of French and Italian priests to the English Church.

At the same time, Henry was spending the taxpayers' money like water. His unsuccessful forays into Wales and France, as well as his ludicrous attempts to make his second son, Edmund, King of Sicily, and his younger brother, Richard, the Holy Roman Emperor, pushed him into bankruptcy. The barons had seen enough. Led by Simon de Montfort, Earl of Leicester and husband of the king's sister, the barons met at Oxford in 1258 to decide on how to deal with Henry's mismanagement. The resultant Provisions of Oxford—another attempt to place power in their hands, not the king's—were presented to Henry, who reluctantly agreed to abide by the rules, although he totally resented taking orders from a council (or parliament).

Within three years, surprisingly supported by King Louis of France and the nosey pope, Henry had repudiated the Provisions of Oxford, and within another three he once more found himself at the center of a civil war (known as the Barons' War). At Lewes in 1264, his forces, led by eldest son Edward, were roundly defeated by those of Simon de Montfort, who could now see the way to the throne opening for himself. Henry was captured and Edward gave himself up, and in 1265 de Montfort summoned what is widely recognized as the first English Parliament.

A Right Royal Tale

The first Parliament of 1265 convened in London, probably in the Palace of Westminster. Then, during the next century, Parliament divided into the House of Lords and House of Commons. The lords met in Westminster Palace's White Chamber and the Commons—which held its inaugural meeting in the White Chamber—met in Westminster Abbey. Thereafter, from 1548 the Commons met in Westminster Palace's Chapel of St. Stephen, until the Palace was largely destroyed by fire in 1834. Plans were then drawn up for the construction of the present Houses of Parliament—both Commons and Lords—by Sir Charles Barry and Augustus Pugin. These houses now stand in the Westminster district of Central London.

In truth, this was really a gathering of de Montfort's supporters, comprised of knights, the clergy, town representatives, and just a few nobles. Feeling excluded, the majority of barons were none too happy with "the good Earl," as de Montfort had come to be known. Therefore, after Prince Edward escaped from captivity in 1265, they joined up with him, raised a large army, and confronted de Montfort in the Battle of Evesham. Henry III was pushed into the front line of de Montfort's forces in the hope that he would be killed by his son's army—or, better still, the son himself! He was quickly recognized, however, and hauled to safety. Instead, de Montfort was killed, and thereafter Henry returned to the seat of power while relying ever more heavily on Edward to restore law and order.

Edward I: Laying Down the Law

At around six feet tall, Edward "Longshanks," as he was nicknamed, enjoyed a distinct height advantage over many of his fellow Englishmen. Fortunately for those Englishmen, he also displayed a far greater flair for ruling than his hapless father.

It was while returning from the Eighth Crusade to the Holy Land in 1272 that Edward learned of Henry III's death. Being that he didn't arrive back in England until 1274, it was fortunate that the usual lineup of aggressors wasn't waiting for him, casting their beady eyes on the throne. Instead, he could return as king and concentrate on the task of pulling the Welsh and the Scots into line.

The Welsh chieftain, Prince Llywelyn, was proving himself to be a royal pain in the you-know-where. Raids were taking place along the English border, so in 1277 Edward ordered Llywelyn to pay homage to him.

The prince refused, so the king invaded North Wales and exacted the land from Llywelyn. Soon, however, Llywelyn was up to his old tricks again, and by 1282 Edward had had enough. He returned to Wales, and by the end of the year, Llywelyn was in London. At least his head was: stuck on top of a high pole.

Sound uncommonly brutal? It was brutal, but it wasn't uncommon. Troublemakers during Edward's reign were often dealt with in this manner—Llywelyn's brother David, for example, was hung, drawn, and quartered before also having his head severed and displayed on top of a pole at the Tower of London. Then there was that trusty old Saxon custom of stripping off the skin of church robbers and nailing it to the church door. These were gruesome times!

Getting back to Wales, the Principality was incorporated into England in 1284, and in 1301 the king would make his son—the future Edward II—Prince of Wales. In the meantime, Edward I delved into an area that had interested many of his recent predecessors: reforming English law.

Responsible for establishing many new regulations, clarifying old ones, weeding out corrupt officials, and reorganizing the law courts, Edward also laid the foundations for representative democracy in 1295 when he summoned the "Model Parliament." While this Parliament comprised earls, barons, knights, and the clergy, it also included numerous men who had been elected to represent the common people, and as such it was a fore-runner of today's House of Commons.

Royal Rebuttal
Edward I sired 19 children with two wives, yet the story that he presented the Welsh with a son who'd been born there at the time of his victory and couldn't speak a word of English was a 16th-century myth. Edward II was born in Wales in 1284 but he could speak English, and he didn't become Prince of Wales until 1301.

Not that the king, his court, or many of his subjects believed in equal rights for everyone; the Jews were now being treated in a manner—although not on the same scale—that would be revived several hundred years later by the Nazis. Forbidden by law in 1275 to lend money at interest, a number of Jews were then accused of having debased the currency three years later and hanged for their "crime." For others, the persecution took the form of beatings or murder, and Jews weren't allowed to leave the country without first obtaining royal permission. Permission wasn't easy to come by, but then in 1290 England's entire Jewish population was expelled—and no doubt happy for it.

The Jews wouldn't return in any great numbers until Oliver Cromwell deposed the monarchy during the mid-17th century. Still, the Jews weren't of any great consequence to Edward I, because they were small fry when compared to greater adversaries such as the Scots. In 1290, Margaret, Maid of Norway and heir to the Scottish throne, died en route to claim her inheritance. Three nobles immediately vied to take her place, so in 1292 Edward was asked to act as the adjudicator. And the winner was…

John Balliol, an Anglo-Norman who subsequently showed his immense gratitude to Edward by refusing to join him on a campaign in France. Instead, he chose to form the Auld Alliance with the French.

Edward was hurt. More than that, he was angry, and when medieval kings were angry with rival rulers, there was only one thing to do: invade. So Edward invaded, and in 1296 he defeated Balliol at Dunbar. Then, as a sign that Scotland was now under his rule, he carried the *Stone of Scone* all the way to Westminster; the Scots weren't having any of that.

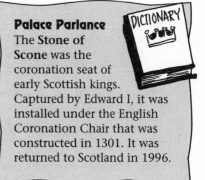

Palace Parlance
The **Stone of Scone** was the coronation seat of early Scottish kings. Captured by Edward I, it was installed under the English Coronation Chair that was constructed in 1301. It was returned to Scotland in 1996.

The next year, while Edward was trying to regain some territory that Grandpa John had lost in France, the Scots under William Wallace reoccupied their own land and scored a great victory at the Battle of Stirling Bridge.

Edward immediately returned from France and earned his nickname "Hammer of the Scots" by thrashing Wallace at the Battle of Falkirk. Wallace escaped, but six years later he was betrayed into the hands of the English king. Guess what was Wallace's fate? That's right, he was hung, drawn, and quartered, and his head was stuck on a pole and displayed on London Bridge. I guess he could have been flayed. Meanwhile, a new Scottish resistance movement led by John Comyn and Robert the Bruce had risen out of the ashes of Falkirk. Bruce eventually murdered Comyn, and in 1306 had himself crowned king of Scotland. Edward, of course, was furious, and at the then-ripe old age of 68 he girded himself for battle one more time. He never made it to the field. As his forces were advancing north, Edward I keeled over and died.

The Undoing of Edward II

Edward II was anything but his father's son. Naiveté, poor judgement, and an overdependence on friends plagued his 20-year reign and resulted in his horrific downfall, one of the worst suffered by any English monarch.

Before Edward II came to the throne at the age of 23, his father had tried to break up his very close friendship with an undesirable named of Piers Gaveston. Yet, as soon as the old man was dead, the new king sent for his favorite and made him Earl of Cornwall. Not a good move. Gaveston was, among other things, obnoxious, and he immediately set about winding up many of his fellow nobles. He referred to the Earl of Gloucester as "whoreson," which didn't go down too well with said Earl, while the Earl of Warwick was given the charming epithet "the Black Hound of Arden." In 1308, a year after Edward II's accession, Gaveston was unceremoniously exiled for being a harmful influence on the king. The king missed him terribly, and a year later Gaveston was back. Parliament could see that the situation was getting out of control, so in 1310 a committee of Lord Ordainers was set up to improve the way the country was being run. Their solution: Take away some of Edward's governmental power and place it in the hands of his cousin Thomas, Earl of Lancaster.

The move didn't solve what should have been done with that pest, Gaveston. Warwick, "the Black Hound of Arden," came up with a more permanent solution; in 1312, Edward's pal was kidnapped and beheaded. Simple as that. Despite the long tradition of Plantagenet anger, however, Edward never avenged his friend's death. His passivity was one factor in his downfall.

Another was his wife, Isabella, the "She-Wolf of France," whom he'd married about six months after his accession. Together they produced four children, yet it wouldn't be unfair to question whether they were all truly his. Isabella, you see, grew tired of competing with the men in her husband's life, and so she sought affection elsewhere. Her wandering eye would ultimately prove to be Edward's undoing.

Hear Ye, Hear Ye
"I feel that marriage is a joining together of man and woman, maintaining the undivided habit of life, and that someone has come between my husband and myself, trying to break this bond."
—*Queen Isabella, 1325*

Meanwhile, helping him on his way was a devastating defeat dealt to the English army by Robert the Bruce at the Battle of Bannockburn in 1314. Other defeats followed, resulting in Scotland assuring itself of independence from England. Still, nothing seemed to perturb the king all that much. He just continued with his other interests, and chief among these by 1320 were a couple of new bosom buddies, a father and son going by the names of Sir Hugh Despenser and Hugh Despenser. These two businessmen were soon helping out with the country's financial administration, and while Edward may have been happy with this state of affairs, the barons certainly weren't.

In 1322, led by the Earl of Lancaster, the barons rose up against the monarch but were beaten down at the Battle of Boroughbridge in Yorkshire. Then, in 1325, Queen Isabella went to visit her brother, the King of France, supposedly to protest about his seizing most of Gascony. Her main motivation for going there, however, was to reunite with her lover, Roger Mortimer, who she'd helped escape from the Tower of London after Edward had imprisoned him for his rebellious activities against the Crown.

Isabella's young son, Edward, Prince of Wales, joined the lovers in France, and there they all stayed for quite a time without Edward II even raising an eyebrow. The pope, on the other hand, raised both and threatened the French king with excommunication for being a party to this illicit love nest.

Mortimer and Isabella (with young Edward in tow) therefore moved on to the Low Countries, where they raised the nucleus of an army to invade England and overthrow the witless king. Once there, they knew they'd also be able to count on the support of the barons, as well as numerous others who were fed up with him.

In 1326, the invasion force landed in Suffolk, and almost immediately the king beat a retreat westwards from London. Isabella and Mortimer's army grew in size and strength as it made its way across England, and, when it reached Bristol, Sir Hugh Despenser was captured and hung. His son was with Edward II, both of whom would soon be trapped in Wales. The king was imprisoned in a number of different castles, deposed, and then sent to Berkeley Castle in Gloucestershire. Hugh Despenser, on the other hand, was tried, hung, drawn, quartered, and...no, not decapitated, but disemboweled! What's more, Isabella was there to enjoy the show.

Edward II was deposed and murdered on his wife's orders. (Picture courtesy of Corbis-Bettmann)

Still, she wasn't quite so entertained when, following her husband's formal renouncement of the throne in favor of 14-year-old Prince Edward, Parliament didn't appoint her as her son's regent. Instead, they set up a Council of Regency headed by young Edward's cousin, Henry of Lancaster. Isabella and Mortimer weren't about to put up with that, so they quickly usurped the regency and proceeded to rule in the name of Edward III.

As for Edward II, his wife and her lover didn't waste much time deciding what to do with him. The only question was how to do it. They didn't want tell-tale marks on his body to make it obvious that he'd met a violent end, so they finally opted for the method of execution normally meted out to homosexuals during medieval times: a red-hot iron inserted up the rectum to burn out the bowels. Ugh! It's difficult for me to even write that!

The Good Soldier: Edward III

Although Mortimer and Isabella had engineered Edward III's early accession to the throne, Edward could see right through their dirty little deeds. After having been king for just three years, he set about avenging his father's murder. Roger Mortimer, the bogus regent, was arrested, tried before Parliament, and hanged at Tyburn. Isabella, the king's mother, was more gently treated by way of an enforced retirement.

A Right Royal Tale

In 1328, the year after his accession, Edward III married his only wife, Philippa of Hainault. The union would produce 13 children, and after Philippa's death in 1369, the King turned to his last mistress for comfort and advice. Her name was Alice Perrers, and she became such a dominant force in the increasingly senile monarch's life that people actually suspected her of witchcraft. The liaison helped to hurt his image, yet it only served to enrich her. When Edward was on his deathbed, she knew that the good times were nearly over, so, aware of her lousy reputation, she stripped the rings off his fingers and ran away.

Edward III was the antithesis of his father. He was astute in his choice of advisors and he never had to deal with a rebellion. He reigned for an incredible 50 years, a time of some very notable events. In 1332, Parliament divided into two houses, the Lords and the Commons, and 10 years later English—rather than French—became the official language used there and in the law courts. In 1348, Edward also founded the Order of the Garter. This was also the time of the Black Plague and the 100 Years' War, two episodes that had a profound impact on late-medieval society.

The Most Noble Order of the Garter

Founded by Edward III in 1348, this chivalric brotherhood was designed to embody the ideals of King Arthur's Round Table. The order was limited to a membership of 24 people in addition to the king and his son, the Black Prince. (The Black Prince picked up his title based on the color of his armor; his birth name was Edward.)

Normally, only members of the British or other royal families can belong, but recent times have seen some notable exceptions to this rule, such as Sir Winston Churchill.

Apparently, it was while at a dance that Edward picked up a garter belonging to the Countess of Salisbury, tied it around his leg, and shouted, *"Honi soit qui mal y pense!"* ("Shame on him who thinks evil of it.")

Bubonic Plague and Black Death

In 1347 the bubonic plague arrived in west and central Europe, courtesy of the pilgrim ships traveling from the east and carrying black rats infested with fleas. The effect was devastating. Victims would develop swellings in the groin and armpits, suffer a terrible fever, and very often die.

The disease was also highly contagious, and by 1349 "The Black Death" had already claimed the lives of about 1.4 million people in England, out of a total population of just 4 million; in Europe, about 25 million people, or a third of the population, would perish. The tragedy would continue until 1351, followed by lesser outbreaks at irregular intervals culminating in the Plague of London in 1665. The following year the Great Fire of London would end the tragic cycle. (You'll learn about the Great Fire of London in Chapter 18.)

In terms of the sociological impact, England's prosperous south wasn't permanently affected, yet elsewhere the changes instigated by the Black Death were far-reaching. There was now a shortage of labor to cultivate the land, so landowners were forced to give up the old feudal traditions in favor of paying proper wages. At the same time, with demand outstripping supply, traders and craftsmen were able to charge higher prices for their products and services. In a strictly ordered society, such changes wouldn't have been possible so soon without the advent of the plague.

The 100 Years' War

Stretching from 1337 to 1453, the 100 Years' War would actually last 116 years, but hey, when things went on that long who was counting?

The whole thing started almost immediately after Edward III's accession, when he decided to stake his claim to the French throne because his mother was French. Even if she didn't have a royal French connection, he probably would have found another excuse to try taking the land. The French didn't say, "Oh sure! Here, it's all yours!," so Edward declared war on them. Sounds fair enough.

During the first phase of the war, England had the upper hand. One of the greatest victories in the country's history was scored by Edward II and the Black Prince at the Battle of Crecy in 1346, where there were 200 English deaths compared to 10,000 French.

Hear Ye, Hear Ye
"Is my son dead, unhorsed, or so badly wounded that he cannot support himself?"
—*King Edward III, when asked by knights to come to the assistance of his son, the Black Prince, at the Battle of Crecy, 1346*

Numerous other victories followed, leading to the Treaty of Bretigny in 1360, whereby Edward traded his claim to the French throne in return for holding onto Calais, Guienne, Gascony, and Poitou. Clearly, there was nothing like a little land (or a lot of it) to calm down the king.

Within a few years, however, the French went onto the attack, declaring war on England and regaining much of the territory that they'd been forced to sign away. After Edward III's death, Richard II and Henry IV presided over a relatively peaceful period that included only short bursts of fighting, but then on the accession of Henry V, the whole conflict exploded all over again. I tell you about this period in the next chapter; for now all you need to know is that by 1453 only the town of Calais remained in English hands.

Richard II and the Peasants' Revolt

Edward III's eldest son, also named Edward, actually died a year before the king. One of Europe's most feared military commanders, he caught an ultimately fatal infection while fighting in Spain and passed away at the age of 46. The new heir to the throne was therefore his son Richard.

Only 10 when he acceded in 1377, Richard II sat back for the first four years while his uncle, John of Gaunt, ran the country. Then it looked as if John might be running it into the ground. The Black Death had seen a rise in wages for many of England's peasants (or had seen the novel idea of being paid some wages), and this in turn had led to price increases.

Parliament responded by passing legislation to control wages, but no similar restraints were imposed to curb the rate of inflation. Obviously, this move affected the living standard of the working classes, and when Parliament then decided to raise funds for the government by imposing a series of poll taxes, the patience of ordinary citizens was tested to the limit.

The poll tax was levied on each person irrespective of wealth or income, meaning that a millionaire paid no more than a pauper. At first, many cash-strapped peasants simply evaded paying, but then in 1380 an even higher poll tax was introduced, and when government officials were dispatched to collect outstanding payments, the peasants saw red. Blood red. Under the leadership of John Ball and Jack Straw, a rebel mob from Essex joined forces with one from Kent led by Wat Tyler, and together all 100,000 men marched on the City of London in June 1381. The poll tax registry was burned, houses were looted, and both the king's treasurer and the Archbishop of Canterbury were murdered. Now King Richard II came into his own. The rebels had carried his flag en route in the belief that he would stand up for their cause, and initially he didn't disappoint them. (During the 1980s, British Prime Minister Margaret Thatcher imposed a poll tax of her own and meet with similar results: riots in the streets.)

On June 14 and 15, the 14-year-old monarch met with the Essex and then the Kent rebels and agreed to their demands for the abolition of *serfdom*, low-fixed land rents, and an unconditional pardon. Wat Tyler got so carried away with this success that he immediately made more demands, angering the mayor of London, who took out his sword and killed him. In the midst of this situation, the king showed a cool head by quickly telling the aggrieved peasants that he himself would be their leader. He then displayed a calculating mind by reneging on his agreement as soon as the rebellion began to die down.

Uprisings around the country were crushed, and 200 people are estimated to have died, including the 15 rebels who were hanged at St. Albans, John Ball among them. Still, the Peasants' Revolt wasn't without its eventual successes. For one thing, landowners were now scared to stir up their workers too much, so serfdom soon died out. As for the poll tax, as Margaret Thatcher would one day learn for herself, it was just best to abolish it.

> **Palace Parlance**
> **Serfdom** is a form of slavery whereby workers aren't allowed to leave the land on which they work. In England, the Statute of Labourers of 1351 prevented workers from changing jobs in search of higher pay.

The Least You Need to Know

➤ The first English Parliament was summoned by Henry III's adversary, Simon de Montfort, in 1265. Thirty years later, the "Model Parliament" for modern forms of government was convened.

➤ Decapitation and disemboweling were among the favorite methods of execution in medieval England.

➤ Edward II was condemned to death by his wife and her lover.

➤ A European outbreak of the bubonic plague from 1347 to 1351 resulted in the "Black Death" of more than a third of England's population.

➤ The 100 Years' War between England and France actually lasted from 1337 to 1453.

➤ The imposition of a poll tax led to the Peasant's Revolt of 1381.

Rule of the Lancastrian Hens

In This Chapter

➤ Revenge leads to ruin for Richard II

➤ The tiring reign of Henry IV

➤ Henry V and his victories against the French

➤ The triumph and tragedy of "The Maid of Orleans"

The less bloodthirsty among you will be glad to know that this is a more sedate chapter…relatively speaking. It focuses largely on the House of Lancaster and its three kings, all named Henry. It also serves to illustrate that almost the entire period was consumed by battles of one type or another—between countries, dynasties, and even the common people. England's fortunes swung one way and then the other, yet in spite of all the triumphs and disasters, the nation was now one of the dominant forces on the face of the map.

We'll start off by taking a look at how Richard II's long-harbored grudges turned him from a responsible monarch into an out-of-control tyrant—a change of personality that spelled personal disaster. Then we'll move on to the first of the Lancastrian kings, Henry IV, whose reign was dominated by rebellions on all fronts. By contrast, the all-too-short tenure of his son, Henry V, marked one of the most successful periods of warmongering in English history, while that of his successor (yes, Henry VI) quickly reversed the good fortune.

Yes, there's nothing like consistency, and during the reign of the Lancastrians, there was nothing like consistency.

The Overthrow of Richard II

Following Richard II's surprising show of strength during the Peasants' Revolt, his advisers continued to govern England, yet the atmosphere of rebellion was never very far away.

The barons, of course, could always be counted on for a quick uprising, and in 1387 a number of them got together and overthrew the government of the king's advisers. Calling themselves the Lords Appellant, these rebels included Richard's uncle, Thomas, Duke of Gloucester, who'd helped run the country, and Henry Bolingbroke, son of John of Gaunt, the other uncle who had ruled. John of Gaunt, the fourth son of Edward III, had recently faded more into the background, but he was keeping an eye on the throne for his son.

In seizing power, the Lords Appellant banished or killed many of the king's close friends and advisers, yet, although Richard appeared to let their behavior pass, in truth he was just biding his time. In 1389 he decided to take control of the government himself, and for the next eight years he did pretty well, reaffirming English rule in Ireland and signing a peace treaty with the king of France, whose *eight-year-old* daughter, Isabella, he married in 1396! Ever since the death of his first wife, Anne of Bohemia, a couple of years earlier, Richard had been consumed with grief, yet following his union with Isabella that grief turned into a very unpleasant form of anger.

In 1397, without warning, Richard took revenge on the Lords Appelant who had impeached his favorites a decade earlier. Some, including his Uncle Thomas, Duke of Gloucester, were murdered, while the others were exiled. Among the latter was Henry Bolingbroke, who in 1399 not only had to deal with the death of his father, John of Gaunt, but also suffer the injustice of having the family's estates seized by the king. This humiliation was too much for Henry to bear, and it spelled the beginning of the end for Richard II.

A Right Royal Tale

During the reign of King Richard II, the legendary Geoffrey Chaucer wrote his most famous work, *The Canterbury Tales*. Born in or around 1340, Chaucer had previously worked in the court of King Edward III, initially serving as a page to the king's son Lionel, and working for Edward in a number of different roles, including London's Controller of Customs. This took place in 1374, but back in the early 1360s, Chaucer had already started to compose poetry. Between 1387 and 1398 he wrote his *Canterbury Tales* and thanks to the wonderful rhyme and astute observations about the vices and virtues of English life, his work would inspire countless future generations of poets.

While the king was away on an expedition in Ireland, Bolingbroke returned from exile on the pretext of claiming back his father's assets. Almost immediately, however, he realized that he had the backing of almost everyone in England if he also wanted to claim the throne. He did. Richard returned from Ireland to find himself with neither an army nor a clue as to what he should do next. He ran away to Wales, but was caught and brought back to London, where he was forced by Parliament to declare himself unfit to rule and hand over the Crown to his cousin, Bolingbroke, the new Henry IV.

Still, Richard wasn't totally without friends, and those who wanted to hold onto power knew it. He was therefore hustled from the Tower of London to Pontefract Castle in Yorkshire, and when the deposed king's supporters began rising in his favor they inadvertently sealed his fate. In 1400, amid mysterious circumstances, he was pronounced dead. Some say he starved himself to death, others that he was murdered. His 12-year-old wife of four years wanted to believe he was still alive. What's your guess?

Henry IV: Exhausted From Battle

In one fell swoop he'd successfully seized the English throne, yet in future years Henry IV probably wondered why he'd ever bothered. Almost from the start he had to contend with insurrections by the Welsh as well as those closer to home, and in the end, the physical effort and mental strain just wore him out.

The trouble began in 1401. Owain Glyndwr (pronounced "Owen Glendower"), a descendant of Llywelyn, the last independent Prince of Wales, asked the king to deal with an English neighbor named Lord Grey of Ruthin, who apparently had swiped some of the Welshman's land. Henry knew all about the perils of upsetting the nobles, so he ignored Glyndwr's plea, which was a *big* mistake. The Welsh weren't exactly happy about being annexed to England in the first place, and evidently this latest example of shoddy treatment was the straw that broke the camel's back.

Glyndwr quickly assembled some forces (which is what you normally do when you've been snubbed by the king) and waged a guerilla war against the English that soon resulted in him controlling most of Wales. Ruling his country like a monarch, Glyndwr next made pacts with certain English nobles who had fallen out with their king. Among them were the Earl of Northumberland and his son, Henry Percy, better known as Harry Hotspur, yet before these two could join forces with Glyndwr's they were intercepted by Henry IV and soundly beaten at the Battle of Shrewsbury in 1403. Harry Hotspur was dead, yet his father would be back to fight another day. He too, however, would eventually die in the heat of rebellion.

> **On Her Majesty's Service**
>
> The first king to speak English as his native language—his immediate predecessors spoke French—Henry IV had several different titles. While "Bolingbroke" came from the castle where he was born, he was also the Earl of Derby, the Duke of Hereford, and the Duke of Lancaster. His mother had been Blanche of Lancaster, hence the origin of the Lancastrian branch of the Royal Family.

In 1404, Owain Glyndwr set up an independent Welsh parliament and had himself crowned Prince of Wales. He also made a treaty with the French, whose King was still smarting over the fact that Henry had murdered his son-in-law, Richard II. Glyndwr would continue to defy the English for several more years, but eventually Prince Harry of Monmouth, son of Henry IV, managed to erode his power, and when Glyndwr died in 1416 he was little more than a fugitive.

In the meantime, the king had all forms of other problems to deal with: an itchy skin problem that some people unkindly described as leprosy, as well as a potential usurper of his throne in the form of... prince Harry of Monmouth! That's right, it was a case of "the son also rises" as the prince set up his own court and posed a silent threat to his father. There was no need for him to rush things, however. Henry IV was an ill and exhausted man. He died in 1413 at the age of 55.

Henry V: Bane of the French

During the reign of Henry IV, the 100 Years' War with the French had pretty much fizzled, but when his son Henry V came to the throne all bets were off.

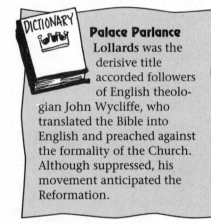

Palace Parlance
Lollards was the derisive title accorded followers of English theologian John Wycliffe, who translated the Bible into English and preached against the formality of the Church. Although suppressed, his movement anticipated the Reformation.

Of course there were the usual domestic issues; putting down a *Lollard* uprising and swatting a plot by a group of nobles to place his cousin, Edmund Mortimer, Earl of March, on the throne. However, the main item of business had to do with the French and taking back all of that territory that Henry viewed as rightfully his, but that his stupid ancestors had gone and lost. Naturally, the king of France, Charles VI, didn't share Henry's opinion about ownership, so 1415 saw a renewal of hostilities.

After a five-week siege, Henry and his troops captured the port of Harfleur in northwest France, which is where, according to William Shakespeare, the English monarch drove his men on by urging, "Once more into the breach, dear friends, once more"...." Shakespeare, however, wasn't even born yet, so his words shouldn't be taken too seriously. Besides, as you'll see a little later on, he quite enjoyed fiddling with the facts. Then it was on to Agincourt where, on October 25, 1415, one of the all-time great battles was fought.

Henry's forces were exhausted, which is why he'd implored them with, "Once more into the breach"...." About 2,000 men had lost their lives in Harfleur, and now there were only around 8,000 left to contend with, oh, say, 50,000 French! (Estimates vary, but everyone agrees that it was a case of a little against a lot.) However, it seems the French still hadn't learned the lessons of the Battle of Crecy just under 70 years earlier: Pitched cavalry don't do very well against knights on foot armed with longbows. In fact, they do very badly.

The longbow, you see, was quicker to load and fire than the crossbow, and it provided the user with a far greater striking distance than the sword or the arrow. The men on horses were sitting targets, which was something at least 6,000 Frenchmen quickly discovered to their detriment. By comparison, fewer than 400 English lost their lives. You've heard of *Mission: Impossible*? This was the real thing. Henry returned to England as an all-conquering hero. Flags and tapestries were draped over buildings, and people lined the streets of London as their king took a five-hour victory ride.

An engraving of Henry V in the days when he was Prince of Wales. (Picture courtesy of Corbis-Bettmann)

Still, Henry hadn't yet finished. He returned to France to recapture Normandy in 1420, and in May of that year dictated the provisions of the Treaty of Troyes. This made him Regent of France and heir to the French throne, and he duly celebrated by taking Charles VI's daughter, Catherine, as his bride. The following year a son was born, another little Henry, who would one day accede to the thrones of both England and France. Unfortunately, that day wasn't long in arriving.

In 1422 Henry V returned to France to do a little more battling. After all, Charles VI may have signed a treaty, but that didn't mean his nobles were adhering to it—a bad habit that they shared with their English counterparts. So, back Henry went and again he scored some handsome victories. Then, at the height of his power, he was struck down by dysentery.

Only in his mid 30s when he died in Vincennes, Henry V didn't live long enough to become king of France, yet by going out on top he was guaranteed instant immortality: an undefeated champion and one of the greatest of all English monarchs. Had his life been longer he could have suffered some setbacks and tarnished his record. Of course, while we can't know what could have happened with Henry, we do know what happened with his son and heir: He made a quick job of undoing his father's fine work.

Henry VI: Born to Lose

At nine months, he was the king of England. At a year old, he was king of France. After that, it was all downhill for Henry VI. Humphrey, Duke of Gloucester served as Regent of England while John, Duke of Bedford, acted as Regent of France when Henry VI was a child.

Both regents were brothers of Henry V, but there were also numerous relatives playing the power game, and once again the courtiers would all have their beady little eyes on the King, not to mention his throne. In the next chapter, I'll tell you how the murderous habits of these family rivals led not only to Henry's downfall, but also to out-and-out war. For now, however, let's concentrate on simpler stuff, like the doomed monarch's love of all things cultural, and the manner in which his overseas rule was undermined by a French peasant girl.

King of Culture

A deeply religious man, Henry VI had a great enthusiasm for building and education, even though, by all accounts, he was pretty simple-minded.

A Right Royal Tale

During an era when barbarism was in vogue and good taste didn't enter the thoughts of executioners, Henry VI was a far more compassionate and forgiving king than many of his regal counterparts. Take the occasion when he was traveling to London from St. Albans. Passing through a place going by the delightful name of Cripplegate, Henry saw the quarter of a man stuck on top of a tall stake. Asking what it was, he was told that it was the remains of someone who had betrayed him. "Take it away," the king responded. "I will not have any Christian man so cruelly handled for my sake." The quarter was duly removed.

Among his greatest personal achievements during a disastrous reign was the founding of Eton College, where there's a statue of him outside at the front, and King's College, Cambridge, which he reportedly conceived in 1441. He laid the foundation stone there that same year, and the original intention was for a grand total of 12 scholars to attend.

In 1446 that plan was revised and the number of scholars rose to 70, along with 10 priests and 16 choirboys.

Construction work on King's College began in 1445 and it went through various stages before it was completed in 1515, quite a few years after Henry's death. Meanwhile his wife, Margaret of Anjou, was one of the founders of Queen's College, Cambridge.

Tussling with Joan of Arc

As Regent of France, the Duke of Bedford had a pretty thankless task. There he was, presiding over foreign subjects who weren't the least bit receptive to English rule, and who could blame them? The thought that they might see tasty French meals increasingly replaced by England's culinary offerings would have upset anyone. There again, they really weren't feeling too confident about their chances of overthrowing their oppressors.

The late King Charles VI had basically been as mad as a hatter toward the end, and now his son, the Dauphin Charles, appeared to be weak and uninspired. He certainly didn't inspire his people, and they were badly in need of some royal motivation right now. The English, under the Duke of Bedford, continued to tighten their stranglehold on the country by way of further military victories, until only Orleans stood between the Duke and total domination. Then, just when all appeared to be lost, came the divine intervention of a 16-year-old farm girl named Jeanne d'Arc, or Joan of Arc.

Hear Ye, Hear Ye
"The King of Heaven bids me tell you that you shall be anointed and crowned in the Church of Rheims."
—*Joan of Arc, upon seeing King Charles VII*

Joan turned up at the court of the Dauphin insisting that she had to tell him how, while she'd been tending to her father's sheep in Domremy, the voices of Saints Michael, Catherine, and Margaret had come to her and said that she alone was capable of driving the English out of France. If you turned up at the White House or Buckingham Palace during a time of crisis and proclaimed a similar line, do you think you would gain a personal audience with the President or the Queen? Well, in 1428 it somehow worked for Joan of Arc, which just goes to show you how desperate the Dauphin and his colleagues must have been!

The Dauphin liked what he was hearing, but initially he didn't take Joan too seriously. She was serious however, and when she asked for the chance to realize this great ambition, the Dauphin gave his consent. What did he have to lose? (The little credibility he had left, *that's* what he had to lose.) The next thing anyone knew, Joan of Arc was decked out in silver armor and riding a white horse at the head of an army making its way toward Orleans.

Her faith in herself and the word of the Lord started to rub off on those around her, and before long the incredible had happened: The English turned on their heels and left Orleans to the French. Other successes followed, and within a year Joan had come through on the King of Heaven's promise; Charles VII was crowned in Rheims Cathedral amid widespread euphoria.

Having achieved her own version of *Mission: Impossible*, Joan should have stopped there. The French soldiers, however, were convinced that she was the key to getting rid of the English once and for all, so she stayed on to lead the good fight. Now Joan had faith and she was extremely brave, but for all her success she wasn't a military genius. Her leadership was bound to come unstuck somewhere down the line, and it did during an attack on Paris. The assault failed and Joan was captured by fellow French, the Burgundians, who ruled the city and were at war with the French king. They in turn sold her to the English.

Hear Ye, Hear Ye
"We are lost, for this maid was indeed a saint."
—*An English soldier witnessing the burning of Joan of Arc*

Being that they were dealing with a woman who dared say she was fighting according to the Lord's wishes, a clerical court presided over by the Bishop of Beauvais contrived to try her for heresy and witchcraft. It was a shameful trial, resulting in an inevitable "guilty" verdict and a diabolical sentence.

For her crimes—or, in reality, the crimes of her captors, both English and French—Joan of Arc was burned at the stake in the marketplace of Rouen. Five years later there would be a posthumous retrial and she would be proclaimed innocent. In 1920, "the Maid of Orleans" would be canonized.

Following Joan's death in 1431, the French and English kept on fighting. After all, this was the 100 Years' War and so far they'd only been going at it for 94 years. Now, however, the initiative was with the occupied rather than the occupiers. The Duke of Bedford did his best with limited resources, but after the Burgundians had wisely switched their allegiance back to the fellow countrymen, he made the mistake of turning down a peace offer that would have left the English in control of Normandy and Aquitaine. They wouldn't get a chance like that again.

Bedford died in 1435, Henry VI assumed personal rule of England two years later, and bit by bit the French started to claw back their land. In 1449 they recaptured Normandy, and by 1453 Calais was the only town still left in English hands. The 100 Years' War was at an end, but Henry's biggest problems were just about to begin.

The Least You Need to Know

➤ At the time of their marriage, Richard II's second wife, Isabella of France, was just eight years old.

➤ Owain Glyndwr (Owen Glendower) set up an independent Welsh parliament during the reign of Henry IV.

➤ On October 25, 1415, Henry V and his 8,000-strong army defeated a French force of about 50,000 men at the Battle of Agincourt.

➤ Henry VI founded King's College, Cambridge, but he was king during the era when a peasant girl named Joan of Arc helped drive the English out of France.

Chapter 11

A Large Dose of Treachery—The Yorkist Dynasty

In This Chapter

➤ Double-dealing and deadly deeds end the reign of the Lancasters

➤ The history according to historians as opposed to William Shakespeare

➤ The unsolved mystery surrounding the disappearance of the two princes

➤ The overthrow of the Yorkists by Henry Tudor

➤ Time for another painless test of your knowledge

Okay, it's back to the action in this chapter; plenty of fighting, murder, treachery...and even a tasty new form of execution for you to revel in! ("Tasty," as you'll see, being the operative word.) What's more, for all of you conspiracy theorists out there, I've also got a right royal whodunnit, which almost plays out like a game of Clue—"It was Colonel Mustard with the piece of rope in the kitchen"—except that in this case the cast of villainous suspects are none other than the members of the English monarchy.

As things tend to get a little complicated here, I'll try to simplify them. After all, there's a lot to learn about the centuries of history in the English monarchy. Just to let you prove what you have learned, however, I'll give you a chance to get top marks in the quiz that appears at the end of this chapter!

Domestic Strife—The Wars of the Roses

As I told you in the last chapter, during Henry VI's early years on the throne he had two uncles working on his behalf: Humphrey, Duke of Gloucester, was the Regent of England, and John, Duke of Bedford, was the Regent of France.

Bedford died in 1435, and it appears that he was a relatively decent man who did his best with the bad lot of trying to hold down the French. Gloucester, on the other hand, was forever conducting battles of his own back in England, vying with his cousin Edmond Beaufort, Duke of Somerset, and with William de la Pole, Duke of Suffolk, to see who could gain the upper hand with the king.

In 1437, that king assumed the personal rule of England, and in 1445 he married the 15-year-old French princess, Margaret of Anjou. By all accounts she was a tough and confrontational woman, but she was also fiercely loyal to her weak, affable, and childlike husband. That meant when the going got tough there was at least one person who would stand up for him.

Hear Ye, Hear Ye
"Henry VI's head was too small for his crown."
—K.B. McFarlane

In 1447, the Duke of Gloucester was arrested out of the blue and charged with plotting to do away with the king. Whether or not the accusation were true is open to conjecture, as is the validity of the official announcement soon afterwards that he had died of a stroke. That left Somerset and Suffolk to, well, duke it out. Before long, Suffolk was also accused of treason and exiled for his sins. Then he was arrested and executed at sea. Two down, one to go…but maybe not.

The sole survivor out of the three influential dukes was, of course, Edmund Beaufort of Somerset, who was a descendant of Edward III by way of illegitimate Plantagenet family lines. Beaufort and Margaret of Anjou weren't exactly bosom buddies, but they soon found themselves in the same camp when another and vastly more powerful player entered the scene. This player was Richard, Duke of York, a cousin of Henry VI who was descended from the Plantagenets on both his father's and his mother's sides. What's more, these lines were legitimate (now there's a shock), and one of them went back even further than the single line of descendency of the king himself. In Richard's and many other people's eyes, Richard had more right to be on the throne than did Henry VI.

Of course, Henry didn't share Richard's view, nor did his wife Margaret or the sly Edmund Beaufort. Nevertheless, being that the monarch's marriage hadn't produced a child, Margaret assured Richard that he would be her husband's heir. In light of the country's miserable losses to the French, popular support virtually dictated this succession. In 1454, however, the king's wife did have a child, Edward, and all of "Dicky" Plantagenet's best-laid plans were thrown into turmoil. So, for that matter, were those of Margaret shortly thereafter, for when her husband succumbed to a bout of mental illness that same year, the Duke of York was asked to fill in for him as protector. In essence, therefore, the ambitious, would-be king was, among other things, "protecting" the new heir to the throne. Talk about a mess!

To make matters worse for Margaret, she soon lost her strongest ally, the Duke of Somerset, who was locked away in the Tower of London, while her loyal courtiers were dismissed and replaced by people faithful to Richard. (These people were called *Yorkists*.) You can imagine Margaret's relief when Henry made sufficient recovery and was again declared sane. Richard was ousted at Christmas 1454, Henry resumed the throne, and the Duke of Somerset was sprung from the Tower so that he and Margaret could serve as regents in the event of the king suffering a relapse.

Up to this point Richard had tried to be subtle in terms of his intentions. Now he didn't care. He gathered together his forces, Margaret and the Duke of Somerset gathered together theirs, and in 1455 they met head-on at the Battle of St. Albans. This was the first of the Wars of the Roses. Richard won, Somerset was killed, and the recently deposed protector once again took over the government.

At this crucial moment, poor Henry once again lapsed into madness; consequently, as the Yorkists replaced Lancastrians in all the key positions of power, there didn't seem to be a need for the king to have a quick "stroke" or meet with an accident. No, they reasoned, surely it would only be a short time before his heart would give out of its own accord, and then the House of York could take over without any unnecessary bloodshed.

Royal Rebuttal
The Wars of the Roses were so called because the emblem associated with the Lancastrians was a red rose and the emblem associated with the Yorkists was a white one. Henry VI never actually used a red-rose badge, however, and the phrase itself wasn't employed in print until the mid-18th century. William Shakespeare did, nevertheless, allude to the symbols in his play, *Richard III*.

Henry's demise wasn't as quick as planned. Henry's mind may have been failing him, but his body wasn't about to let him down. In fact, it held out quite nicely until, by 1459, his mind made another recovery. Margaret had been waiting for this mental restoration. Her army at the ready, she once again launched herself into battle on the king's behalf. After the Yorkists were defeated at Ludford, Parliament declared Richard a traitor and he fled to France. Henry VI was back on the throne, but not for long. The next year, 1460, the Duke of York's second-in-command, Richard Neville, Earl of Warwick ("The Kingmaker"), defeated the Lancastrians at the Battle of Northampton. Henry was captured, Margaret escaped to Scotland, and the Duke of York this time didn't mess around. He claimed the throne for himself, *but not for long!*

Within weeks, Richard was killed when Margaret returned from "north of the border" to defeat his forces at Wakefield. So the Wars of the Roses continued, with the sides trading victories in a very violent game of musical thrones. Richard's son Edward (not to be confused with Henry's son, the Prince of Wales) took over as Duke of York and in 1461 he also took over as England's monarch, being crowned Edward IV as a result of the efforts of "Warwick the Kingmaker." He would later also be deposed by "Warwick the Kingmaker." The two men fell out with each other during the late 1460s and Warwick switched over to the side of Margaret. Henry had once again been imprisoned in the Tower, but after Warwick's forces defeated Edward IV's in 1470, he was released and restored to the throne, *but not for long!*

A Right Royal Tale

Edward IV was a man of voluminous appetites and questionable manners. In other words, he was a typical English king. Married to Elizabeth Woodville, with whom he had 10 children, Edward was a notorious womanizer known for passing his mistresses onto his courtiers after he himself had grown tired of them. All of the exercise must have kept him pretty fit, yet in later years he managed to grow fat thanks to his penchant for food and drink.

In 1471, Edward returned from exile in Flanders and scored two resounding victories, defeating and killing Warwick at the Battle of Barnet, and then defeating Margaret at the Battle of Tewkesbury in which her son, Edward, Prince of Wales, was also killed. Henry VI was captured and, days later, on May 27, he was killed in the Tower. Margaret was subsequently imprisoned and then released in 1476 in return for a ransom paid by the French King. She would die in her native Anjou six years later.

In the meantime, England would enjoy a period of well-earned peace during the remaining years of Edward IV. The Wars of the Roses, so to speak, would come to an end when the House of Tudor would replace the House of York in 1485 (more of this toward the end of this chapter). In the 30 years from when they first commenced, however, the battles amounted to a grand total of about 13 weeks, an average of three days per year.

Law and Order: Edward IV

Despite the on-going squabbles with the Lancastrians during the first half of his reign, Edward IV set out from the beginning to revive royal finances and refine England's legal system, and in both respects he succeeded. At the same time, he also wasn't above bending the rules to suit his own ends.

Edward's successful ventures in the wool industry not only reduced Crown debts, but also helped boost England's cloth exports to record heights during an era when the country's overall volume of trade doubled. At the same time, the Lancastrian estates he seized weren't turned over to his supporters among the landed gentry. Instead, he held onto them so that they made money directly for that Crown.

This was the age when wealthy wool merchant William Caxton set up England's first printing press in a house close to Westminster Abbey. It was also the age when Edward IV became the first monarch to address the House of Commons.

To Edward's credit, the Court of Requests was introduced so that peasants had a means of legal recourse against landlords who charged exorbitant rents. At the same time, however, Edward would meddle with the established court system as he pleased, replacing judges who didn't conform to his wishes and even bribing juries in order to ensure that the end results were "just." In addition, the first documented uses of torture took place during his reign. Whoever said that medieval monarchs sometimes employed Mafia-style tactics?

Edward, meanwhile, also suffered from that well-known royal habit of falling out with family members. His 1464 marriage to Elizabeth Woodville, the widow of a commoner and daughter of a knight, caused a deep rift with his cousin, Earl "Kingmaker" Warwick, who could see his dominant position being threatened. Then, in 1477, the king accused his own brother, George, duke of Clarence, of treason. There's nothing like a spot of animosity between royal siblings. On February 18, 1478, the duke was murdered in the Tower of London and the story goes that the mode of his execution was a new means specially invented for the occasion; supposedly—are you ready for this?—he was drowned in a large cask of malmsey wine.

A Right Royal Tale

In William Shakespeare's play, *Richard III*, Richard III has the Duke of Clarence drowned in a butt of malmsey wine. Of course, Edward IV was really responsible, but actor Vincent Price was probably grateful to Shakespeare for his version of events. Price, you see, performed the playwright's scene in three different films:

➤ He portrayed the unfortunate duke in the 1939 version of *Tower of London*.

➤ He played the role of Richard III in the 1962 remake.

➤ In 1973's *Theatre of Blood*, he played a crazed actor who murders drama critics using methods found in Shakespearian plays, including dumping his victim into a cask of wine while reciting Shakespeare's lines.

As it happens, in a figurative sense Edward IV would inflict the same fate on himself: drinking like a fish, stuffing his face, and chasing women until, by the age of just 40, he was utterly worn out. He died on April 9, 1483, and the throne was passed to his 12-year-old son, Edward V. Meanwhile, Edward IV's brother, Richard, Duke of Gloucester, was appointed protector, and what a sorry state of affairs *that* assignment would turn out to be.

Princes in the Tower—The Very Short Reign of Edward V

Edward, Prince of Wales, and his 10-year-old brother Richard, Duke of York, were living in Ludlow Castle near the Welsh border when their father died. On May 4 they traveled to London and moved into the royal apartments at the Tower. At that time, the Tower was a palace as well as a prison, so there was nothing unusual about their move. In fact, it was a far more conventional arrangement than, say, the marriage of the Duke of York, who wed the Duke of Norfolk's little daughter, Anne Mowbray, when he was less than five years old. By the ripe old age of eight he was a widower!

Edward's coronation was scheduled for Sunday, June 22, and Parliament was summoned to meet three days later. For the heir to the throne, however, things never got that far. On June 10, his uncle and Protector was apparently informed by the Bishop of Bath and Wells that when Edward IV had married Elizabeth Woodville, he was already betrothed (or engaged) to Lady Eleanor Butler. In those days, a betrothal was considered as much of a commitment as marriage, so this meant that Edward and Elizabeth's union was invalid and that their children were illegitimate. It also meant that Richard the Protector was actually the rightful heir to the throne, a tidbit of information that he, of course, felt duty-bound to pass on to Parliament.

The coronation was immediately canceled, and on June 25, Parliament felt it had no choice but to approve the protector's accession as Richard III. On July 6, he was crowned and anointed at Westminster Abbey. Meanwhile, what was to become of the little princes? Well, Richard was still supposed to protect them, of course, and throughout the summer of 1483 they were reportedly sighted on numerous occasions at the Tower of London. Then, sometime in September, they disappeared and were never seen again.

Given the history of the English monarchy up to that point, the words "foul play" come to mind, yet to this day the mystery surrounding the fate of the princes has never been fully resolved. In 1674, during the reign of Charles II, the skeletons of what appeared to be two boys were discovered in a chest buried 10 feet under a flight of stone stairs in the White Tower. Everyone believed them to be the bodies of the two princes and so they were reburied in an urn inscribed with their names at Westminster Abbey. Then, in 1933, an eminent physician as well as a dentist carried out a detailed forensic examination of the bones. The results confirmed that they belonged to a 12- and 10-year-old boy; however, without dental records, there was no way of corroborating their identity.

The fact that little Edward V and his younger brother were murdered in 1483 therefore appears fairly certain. However, who was responsible? There have been numerous theories. The most popular and obvious one, of course, is that Richard III ordered the killings in order to strengthen his own hold on the throne. The theory goes on to claim that Sir James Tyrell was duly dispatched to the Tower with a group of hired assassins and while the princes were asleep, they smothered them with their pillows. Tyrell is said to have admitted to the crime 20 years later.

Fact or fiction? The death scene of the two princes in the "Bloody Tower." (Picture courtesy of Corbis-Bettmann)

This version of events was advanced after Henry VII and the House of Tudor had over-thrown Richard III. Of course, it was in Henry's best interests to confirm Richard's wickedness in order to justify overthrowing Richard. By having historians/propagandists such as Sir Thomas More and Polydore Vergil point their fingers directly at Richard, however, Henry has also prompted certain theorists to question whether he himself was the guilty party. After all, Richard was only on the throne for a couple of years before dying in battle, so what about the possibility that he had indeed protected the princes and that they had then been murdered by the Tudors as a means of sullying his name?

This conspiracy scenario is possible but unlikely, especially as the forensic tests on the bones confirmed that they belonged to a 12- and 10-year-old, not a 14- and 12-year-old. What's more, being that the bodies were buried 10 feet under a flight of stone stairs; it doesn't look as if the perpetrators intended that they would be found.

Finally, the crime has numerous other suspects: those many relatives who also coveted the Crown for themselves. Chief among them was Henry Stafford, the Duke of Buckingham, who reportedly was plotting to usurp Richard III. By murdering the princes and making it look as if Richard was responsible, he'd possibly clear the way for his own

Today, if you visit the Tower of London, you can see where the two young princes, Edward and Richard, were allegedly murdered. The theory is that they were killed in the Bloody Tower, so-called for its long history of slayings—the princes were supposedly suffocated. They were then buried in the adjacent Wakefield Tower and are now laid to rest near the White Tower.

Richard III, the most vilified of English kings. Accusations of him murdering the two princes may have been as unfounded as Shakespeare's por-trayal of him as a hunchback. (Picture courtesy of Corbis-Bettmann)

accession. Once again, however, the fact that the bodies weren't intended to be found kind of spoils the theory.

That still leaves us with Richard III as the guilty party. At the very least he'd been responsible for looking after the princes and there's no doubt that they disappeared while in his care. The only problem is that William Shakespeare also had Richard pegged for the murders, and we all know what a reliable historian Shakespeare was, don't we?

The Much-Maligned Richard III

Poor Richard or evil Richard? Who knows? All things considered he doesn't appear to have been a very savory character, but then, who was? One thing's for sure; contrary to Shakespeare's portrayal, he wasn't a hunchback with a withered arm. Perhaps one shoulder was slightly higher than the other, but so what? The royal tailor just had to cut some extra cloth.

The year of Richard III's accession was a troubled one for the new king. Not only did his two young nephews disappear, but he also had to contend with an attempted coup by his cousin and former friend, the Duke of Buckingham. Retribution was swift. Buckingham was arrested, tried, and executed. In 1484, the year in which court defendants were first entitled to seek bail, Edward, Prince of Wales, the only child of the king and his wife Anne Neville, died. The following year Queen Anne also died, and it was at that moment, just when Richard could have done with some free time to mourn, that Henry Tudor, Earl of Richmond, made his move on the throne.

Exiled in France, Henry felt that his Lancastrian ancestry entitled him to be the monarch every bit as much as Richard III. In fact, *more* than Richard III! Henry landed in Milford Haven, West Wales, where he hoped his Welsh background might help stir up a little extra support for his cause; as added support, he also brought along several thousand French mercenaries for the inevitable battle. This would turn out to be the final War of the Roses, fought on Bosworth Field in Leicestershire (pronounced "Lester-sheer") on August 22, 1485.

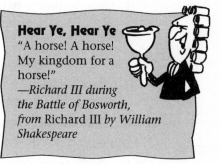

Hear Ye, Hear Ye
"A horse! A horse! My kingdom for a horse!"
—*Richard III during the Battle of Bosworth,* from Richard III *by William Shakespeare*

Henry's army of about 8,000 men came face-to-face with Richard's force of around 12,000. Still, not everyone had made a final decision yet as to which side they should throw their support behind. Lord Stanley, for one, had raised about 5,000 of the men who were due to fight for the king, but then he had a change of heart. Who knows, perhaps he had an uncanny eye for picking a winner. Whatever the reason, his defection meant that, in the thick of battle, Richard's forces were outnumbered. Still, the king didn't give up, cutting men down until he was within striking distance of Henry himself. Then Richard was downed, and the crown he had been wearing that day was placed on the head of Henry VII by—who else?—Lord Stanley.

The story is that Stanley had plucked the crown from a hawthorn bush, yet there were no contemporary reports to substantiate that claim. What is known, on the other hand, is that Richard III was buried in an unmarked grave, and that Henry VII spent just over 10 pounds on a coffin that was subsequently used as a horse-trough before being broken down to make steps to the cellar of the White Horse Inn.

Are You a Complete Royal Idiot? Quiz #2

All right, it's the moment you've been looking forward to—when you can prove to your friends what an expert of British Royalty you're becoming! Get out that quill and start scribbling your answers…

1. What were the first names of Lady Diana Spencer's parents?
2. What title did King George III confer upon one of Diana's ancestors?

3. Who designed Princess Diana's wedding dress?

4. What did the Anglo-Saxon word "burh" mean?

5. Who was the first English king to have his likeness officially reproduced on coins?

6. Which viciously named Norwegian ruler installed himself as King of Northumbria during the 10th century?

7. What was the Witan?

8. Who, according to legend, rode naked through the streets of Coventry as a protest against taxes on the poor?

9. What was the name of the system whereby people were granted land in return for their allegiance and service to the monarch?

10. When William the Conqueror carried out a landmark public census in 1086, where were the findings recorded?

11. What was the scholarly nickname of Henry I?

12. Henry II was the first of the Angevin kings, but what was his surname?

13. Which Archbishop of Canterbury did Henry II's knights murder?

14. Which Angevin king spent only seven months of his 10-year reign in England?

15. During whose reign did Robin Hood supposedly steal from the rich and give to the poor?

16. What or who was the "Dauphin"?

17. Who was known as "The Hammer of the Scots"?

18. What is the Stone of Scone?

19. Who was "The She-Wolf of France"?

20. What all-encompassing name was given to the battles waged between England and France during the 14th and 15th centuries?

21. What was the name of the popular uprising provoked by the imposition of a poll tax during the reign of Richard II?

22. Which king scored a famous victory at the Battle of Agincourt?

23. Which royal dynasty had the white rose as its emblem?

24. What was the method by which Edward IV reportedly had his brother George, Duke of Clarence, murdered?

25. In which specific building were Edward V and his brother Richard supposedly murdered?

The answers to these questions are in Appendix G. Here's how to rate your performance:

➤ 20 or more—The royals would be proud of you.

➤ 13–19—The royals *could* be proud of you.

➤ 6–12—Go into exile and do your homework.

➤ 5 or fewer—You ought to be hanged, drawn, and quartered!

The Least You Need to Know

➤ The Wars of the Roses were waged between the Houses of Lancaster and York over the course of 30 years.

➤ When Henry VI suffered bouts of madness, his wife, Margaret of Anjou, fought his battles for him.

➤ The young princes were almost certainly murdered, but no conclusive proof has ever been found that Richard III was responsible.

➤ In 1485 the Battle of Bosworth ended the life of Richard III, the reign of the Yorkists, and the Wars of the Roses. Henry VII became the first Tudor monarch.

Part 4
Soft Beds, Hard Battles (1485-1625)

We're now entering a classic period in English history, comprised of landmark events; a renaissance in the arts; and colorful, legendary characters such as Henry VIII and his six wives, "Bloody Mary," Elizabeth I, Sir Walter Raleigh, Guy Fawkes—a custom-made cast for authors and scriptwriters.

The start of the Tudor era coincided with the end of the Middle Ages and a time when the power of the monarchy was at an all-time high. You may be shocked to learn that none of the Tudor rulers were overthrown or executed, and that one of the first female monarchs also committed some of the most gruesome crimes. Indeed, even though the Tudor years consisted of tremendous economic growth and unprecedented stability for a royal dynasty, they were also plagued by an incredible amount of tyranny.

Part 4 ends with the uniting of the English and Scottish thrones through the peaceful accession of the House of Stuart, and the Pilgrim Fathers setting sail on the Mayflower in search of a fresh start in the New World.

Yes, these were, as the saying goes, the best and the worst of times.

Chapter 12

Takeover of the House of Tudor

In This Chapter

➤ Young impostors fall foul of Henry VII

➤ The king asserts his power and increases his profits

➤ Oceanic adventures in search of foreign riches

➤ Henry's astute marital maneuvers

Aware that his claim to the English throne wasn't exactly built on a rock-solid foundation, Henry VII, the first of the Tudor monarchs, had to appease the people if he wanted his dynasty to survive. At the same time, he also knew that dissidents and potential usurpers had to be left in no doubt as to whom was boss. This king therefore had to tread a very fine line, and by and large he really did succeed in this respect.

This chapter tells the story of a canny monarch who made up in intelligence, endeavor, strength of character, and sophistication what he lacked in charisma and personal appeal. I'll tell you how he quashed the attempts of pretenders to his throne, revamped the legal system so that rebellious nobles were brought into line, used his businessman's acumen to increase vastly both his and the country's wealth, and engineered a series of shrewd marriages to ensure peace and stability.

The start of the Modern Age required vision, determination, a cool head, and a steady hand on the part of those in positions of power, and in Henry VII, England had a man who was more than up to the task.

Henry VII and those Revolting Pretenders

Henry VII came to the throne in 1485, and in 1486 he married Elizabeth, the eldest daughter of Edward IV and sister of the little princes in the Tower. The warring houses of Lancaster and York had at last been united. Hereafter there were some Yorkist plots, but they now only really took place near the Welsh and Scottish borders. Still, being that Henry's royal line of descendency was an illegitimate one on his mother's side (making him the great-great-great-grandson of Edward III), numerous other people had much better claims to the throne.

After defeating the last Yorkist king, Richard III, Henry Tudor is offered the crown that fell off of Richard's Head. (Picture courtesy of Corbis-Bettmann)

His wife Elizabeth was one of them, but evidently she was happy with the way things had worked out. (Besides, even though there were no rules against women acceding to the throne, said women had, as you may have noticed, so far been bypassed.) Similarly, most individuals with stronger claims wisely kept a tactful silence, and so it was really left to a number of impostors to stir up trouble.

Take one Lambert Simnel, a 10-year-old baker's son who asserted that he was Edward Plantagenet, the Earl of Warwick. Edward Plantagenet had a stronger claim to the throne than did the reigning monarch, and under this false pretext Simnel had himself crowned in Ireland. Such nonsense could have very easily resulted in a quick spot of hanging, drawing, and quartering, but Henry decided to go easy on the boy. After overcoming his supporters, he did young Simnel the indignity of putting him to work in the royal kitchen. At least he must have been good at making the bread.

Not so fortunate, on the other hand, was another youngster named Perkin Warbeck. Warbeck pretended to be Prince Richard of York, who had supposedly escaped from the Tower of London when his elder brother Edward V was murdered. Again, he found acclaim in Ireland and on his arrival in Flanders, Margaret of Burgundy "recognized" him as her nephew. Which was all very nice, except that Henry hit back by threatening to put the kibosh on the Flemish wool industry. Warbeck next moved on to the friendly confines of Scotland, and in 1495 he should have taken heed of the way the King dealt with Lord Stanley.

As you'll no doubt recall from the last chapter, Stanley was the man who did the old switcheroo on Richard III and fought for Henry Tudor at the Battle of Bosworth. Now that Henry was installed on the throne, Stanley was up to his old tricks, except that this time around he'd aligned himself with Perkin Warbeck—a foolish move. I mean, did he really expect Warbeck to succeed? Henry VII swiftly had Stanley arrested and executed. Yet again, Perkin Warbeck didn't take heed—another foolish move.

When, in 1497, a revolt appeared to be brewing in Cornwall, southwest England, Warbeck took himself there. The king's army subsequently crushed the rebels and some of the leaders were tried and hanged. Warbeck, however, was treated fairly leniently and he was confined to a form of house arrest. Then he tried to escape and was locked in the Tower, where he next started plotting a coup with the real Edward Plantagenet, Earl of Warwick. This conspiracy proved to be Warbeck's final foolish move, as it did for Warwick. Henry saw to it that both men were hanged.

Thereafter things quieted down as far as any other would-be pretenders were concerned. The king had been forced to flex his muscles and the dissidents had paid the price. No longer would the monarchy allow itself to be undermined by those who avoided playing by the rules.

Hear Ye, Hear Ye

"I am a better astrologer than you. I can tell where you will be— in the Tower of London!"
—*Henry VII, prior to imprisoning an astrologer whom, having forecast the king's death, wasn't able to foretell his own future*

Breaking the Barons by Way of the Star Chamber

As we've seen over the course of the past few chapters, during the Middle Ages, England's nobility had quite a lot of say as to how the country was being run. Whenever things weren't going the way the nobility wished—which was quite often—there would be a baronial uprising that often involved enlisting the services of nosey foreigners to help in the escapades. "The barons are revolting" must have been a common saying during medieval times.

In 1215, the Magna Carta had been the means by which the nobility and the clergy attempted to curtail abuses of royal power, while also, of course, improving their own lot in life. Just under three centuries later, it was the turn of the monarchy to curb abuses of power on the part of the barons, thus strengthening its own position.

Take the occasion when, early in his reign, Henry VII dropped in on the Earl of Oxford at Hedingham Castle for a cup of tea and a chat. The guard of honor that greeted him wore military uniforms and sported the Oxford badge. Talk about threatening! "These are your servants?" the King asked the Earl. "They are my retainers, assembled here to do you honor," Oxford replied, to which Henry immediately retorted, "I thank you for your hospitality, but I like not to have my laws broken in my own sight."

Shortly afterward, the genial host was hauled up before a special court and fined the then-enormous sum of 15,000 pounds. The punishment shocked and infuriated Oxford, but it also taught him and his fellow nobles that it might be worthwhile abiding by the law instead of upsetting the monarch. The special court where Oxford appeared was the Court of the Star Chamber, which Henry revived in 1487. Comprised of Privy Counsellors (handpicked advisors to the sovereign) and two chief justices, this court handled civil and criminal cases and ensured that there was no disparity between the treatment of rich and poor.

A Right Royal Tale

Henry VII's reign saw an increase in the number and variety of tortures that were meted out. These included the use of such charming devices as the rack, the wheel of a cart or wagon, the vice, and the ever-popular length of wire.

In light of this event, it was ironic that the king himself viewed personal wealth as the key to his own power. Handing out fines was a favorite way of punishing offenders, as was Henry's penchant for accepting extremely valuable "gifts" in return for a royal pardon. In 1491, after he and his large army had successfully invaded France, he agreed to withdraw the English forces on receipt of a huge wad of money from the French sovereign. This kind of behavior disgusted many of Henry's subjects, but having inherited a country in debt, he soon managed to turn things around.

Taxes were strictly collected and the revenue earned from royal land was doubled during Henry's reign. In addition, Henry's personal wealth tripled, and over the years he invested more than 100,000 pounds into jewelry. In modern terms, his jewelry purchases would be worth billions. So even though Henry VII earned himself a reputation as a penny-pinching monarch, he was also wise, and he wasn't afraid to invest in what he considered to be good prospects, whether they were at home or overseas.

Look Yonder: It's Cabot's New-Found Land

As I hope you all know, it was in 1492 that Christopher Columbus discovered America. Columbus had been born in Genoa, Italy; another adventurer to hail from this region was Giovanni Caboto. Living in England's West Country city of Bristol, Caboto—otherwise known as John Cabot—shared Columbus' notion of traveling west across the Atlantic in order to more easily attain the riches that lay waiting in far east places such as Cathay (China). The only problem was, how to raise the funds that he would need to undertake that kind of voyage. The solution: Appeal to the entrepreneurial instincts of King Henry VII.

Aware that his royal counterparts in Spain and Portugal were involved with voyages of discovery that could net them untold riches, Henry met with Cabot in Bristol and, on hearing the plan, agreed to provide a fleet of five ships that would enable Cabot to make his trip. As for the deal (and with Henry there was always a deal), in return for permission to annex any lands that he might discover, Cabot had agreed not to interfere with the exploits of the Spanish and Portugese and to give the king 20 percent of the profits.

Cabot set sail in 1496, only to turn back after encountering a factor that not even the monarch could do anything about: the English weather. The journey was rescheduled for the following May when Cabot hoped conditions would be better. The weather was milder in May, and Cabot set sail once again, although this time only one tiny ship, the Mathew, was made available to him. That ship boasted a crew of just 18 men. The vessel made its way across the Atlantic for about seven and a half weeks before, on June 24, the lookout sighted what amounted to a "new-found land." That's right, Newfoundland, except that Cabot and his men actually thought they were sailing around the tip of Asia rather than off the coast of North America. Don't forget, at that time they didn't even know North America existed.

On Her Majesty's Service
During the reign of Henry VII, Bristol was England's second city, having grown wealthy thanks to the shipping of Cotswold wool, Iceland fish, and Bordeaux wine. This success was remarkable considering that the men who sailed from there had to contend with choppy waters that were often difficult to navigate. This led to the saying that vessels had to be "all shipshape and Bristol fashion."

After roaming around and finding little aside from the fish in the sea, Cabot returned to England and was greeted like a hero by the king. Rewarded with the then-generous sum of 10 pounds, as well as an annual pension of 20 pounds, he never did locate a quick route that would transport him to where the treasures of the east lay waiting. Nevertheless, the conquest of the Atlantic was underway.

Royal Marriages, English Dynasty

I told you that Henry VII was shrewd, didn't I? This shrewdness went beyond his legal crackdowns and moneymaking schemes to the way in which he used marriages to firmly establish his Tudor dynasty and maintain peace. If the Tudors didn't have much royal blood in them to start with, they certainly had a lot more flowing through their veins by the time that Henry departed this world.

On Her Majesty's Service

If you want an impression of what Henry's wife, Elizabeth of York, looked like, you can see her effigy carved alongside that of her husband on their tomb in Henry VII's chapel in Westminster Abbey. Less lifelike but altogether more accessible, however, is the portrait of the Queen that appears on every deck of playing cards. These cards were first invented in 1486.

As previously explained, the king's marriage to Elizabeth of York had obvious dynastic advantages, but these were small fry compared to their children's romantic matches. Their eldest son and heir, Arthur, was paired with the Spanish princess, Catherine of Aragon. Then, following Arthur's death shortly afterward at the age of 15, Henry secured a special dispensation from the pope for Catherine to marry her late husband's younger brother, the future Henry VIII. (In the next chapter I'll delve into the can of worms that union opened up.) Clearly, Henry VII was determined that, by hook or by crook, the Aragon girl would stay part of the family and eventually become Queen.

That left the king's two daughters, Margaret and Mary, and they both played their part in making conciliatory marital gestures to a couple of age-old adversaries. By marrying James IV of Scotland, Margaret linked the English and Scottish royal families—a union that had repercussions I'll tell you about soon. Mary, on the other hand, married King Louis XII of France. He would die in 1515 and she would then wed someone closer to home: Charles, Duke of Suffolk.

Following the death of Elizabeth of York in 1503, Henry VII threw his own hat (or crown) into the ring, and the woman he firmly set his eyes on was one of Europe's most wealthy heiresses, Joanna of Castile, the widow of Philip of Austria. Unfortunately, however, Queen Joanna was quite mad, and although Henry tried his best to ignore this little drawback while thinking about all of the money he could lay his hands on, even he had to admit defeat in the end. You see, Joanna refused to be separated from the embalmed body of her late husband and it therefore accompanied her wherever she traveled. For money Henry was willing to make many concessions, but this one was too much.

Henry VII died in 1509. Never the most popular of kings due to the manner in which he distanced himself from the people, he nevertheless left England both prosperous and at peace. No one could have predicted what was to follow...

The Least You Need to Know

➤ The accession of Henry VII in 1485 heralded the start of the House of Tudor and the dawn of the Modern Age.

➤ The Court of the Star Chamber, revived by Henry VII in 1487, helped curb the power of the barons and ensured equal treatment for rich and poor alike.

➤ In 1497 John Cabot discovered what is now probably known as Newfoundland.

➤ Henry VII's marital maneuvering united the Houses of Lancaster and York, and helped link the English and Scottish thrones.

Chapter 13

Don't Lose Your Head—The Turbulent Reign of Henry VIII

WELL, DEAR, I WOULDN'T WANT YOU TO LOSE YOUR HEAD ABOUT ANYTHING...

In This Chapter

➤ Henry pursues leisure activities and foreign policy while leaving England in the hands of his Lord Chancellor

➤ A troubled divorce leads to retribution and excommunication

➤ The despotic monarch runs rampant as he severs all ties with the Church of Rome

➤ Love, despair, infidelity, and a record number of royal marriages

Henry VIII was one of those legendary characters whose life makes for fascinating reading, but who in reality was probably well worth avoiding. An incurable pleasure-seeker, he was also a tyrannical monster who solved arguments and undesirable situations by simply executing whomever he deemed responsible for the predicaments that entangled him.

The fact that Henry often caused these predicaments didn't seem to matter, for he was a man of violent contradictions and wild excesses: an avaricious eater, keen womanizer, profligate spender, hardy adventurer, and out-and-out autocrat. His word was the law, and anyone who crossed him was crossed out. No British monarch has ever been more powerful than Henry VIII or more famous… and *that* line leads me straight into telling you to close your eyes and imagine you're in Merrie Olde England. On the other hand, keep your eyes open so you can read about his royal escapades.

Fun at Home, Meddling Abroad

The fun-loving Henry VIII who acceded to the throne in 1509 was very different from the tyrannical, grossly overweight, and diseased physical specimen of later years. A couple months short of his 18th birthday, he was tall, handsome, and relatively thin. He was also a man of many talents: a sports enthusiast, a linguist, a poet, a composer, and a musician. (It has, in fact, been suggested that he wrote "Greensleeves," the song that has come to be closely associated with his era.)

A man of many talents and hearty appetites: The legendary King Henry VIII. (Picture courtesy of Corbis-Bettmann)

Henry loved pursuing leisure activities such as hunting, jousting, riding, tennis, archery, and dancing, and he also saw to it that the money his father had accumulated wasn't left to gather dust. Oh no, this king was determined to enjoy himself. He spent freely on banquets, tournaments, and, when the spirit of adventure really got the better of him, a quick invasion of France! After all, having a punch-up with the French was always good for a few laughs.

As it turned out, this wasn't a victory on the scale of, say, the Battles of Crecy or Agincourt, but at least a few towns were captured, so Henry felt he'd made his mark. Closer to home, the English got into a tussle with those other enemies of choice, the Scots. Actually, the Scots started the skirmish by invading England while Henry was abroad, and in charge of this slimy operation was none other than King James IV. You might remember from the previous chapter that James was married to Henry's sister Margaret, but, as the saying goes, an in-law isn't the same as a blood relative. (Not that blood relations would have made much difference with regard to the Royals; they were all at each other's throats anyway.)

James IV paid for his bad manners at the Battle of Flodden Field in 1513. There, he and most of his nobles were killed as their large Scottish army was completely routed. Meanwhile, the king himself really didn't want to get bogged down in the affairs of State, so in 1515 he appointed Thomas Wolsey as Lord Chancellor of England and let him run the government. Wolsey warmed to the task, in the process becoming one of the most powerful ministers in the country's history and enriching himself immeasurably.

Wolsey assumed the titles Bishop of Tournai, Bishop of Lincoln, and Archbishop of York as he rose within the Church and reaped the associated incomes and acres of land. The Pope made him a cardinal, and he lived in fabulous style—York Palace and Hampton Court were his star residences. Even the sovereign had trouble matching the opulence that Wolsey was fast growing accustomed to. In 1525, the cardinal tried to curry favor by passing over ownership of Hampton Court to the king, although he continued to live at this residence.

Though well aware of the power with which he was granting the cardinal and the amount of influence being enjoyed by both the Church and the pope, Henry always knew that the ultimate say rested with him. Besides, while his chancellor was running England in a grand manner, he was able to dabble in foreign policy, something that Wolsey was only too happy to encourage. The perfect encapsulation of how these two vain, egotistical, calculating, and power-hungry men operated was a summit meeting Wolsey organized near Calais in 1520 between Henry and the new French King, Francis I.

> **On Her Majesty's Service**
> Take a trip along the River Thames just west of Central London and you'll see a number of royal palaces and estates. Chief among them is Hampton Court, the 1,000-room residence built for Cardinal Wolsey in 1514. Enlarged during its occupation by Henry VIII and William III, it now supposedly accommodates the ghosts of two of Henry's wives, Jane Seymour and Catherine Howard.

Taking place over the course of three weeks, this meeting featured such outrageous extravagance—Wolsey had laid on 300 servants and fountains full of wine—that it was known as the Field of the Cloth of Gold. Naturally, it was one of those back-slap-and-suck-up occasions when everyone was on his best behavior, with the two kings enjoying each other's company and feigning mutual admiration. Despite the show, however, the meeting accomplished nothing.

The French were agog at the splendor of Henry's (or was it Wolsey's) court, yet no peace treaty was signed and the two countries were soon at war again. Henry had probably planned for this outcome. During his reign, he enthusiastically continued with his father's work of establishing a strong navy, separating it from the army for the first time and building it to the point where it could challenge Spanish maritime supremacy. A total of about 80 ships were added to the fleet, including the appropriately named and proportioned *Great Harry*, a 1,000-ton vessel that was then the largest ever known. And so things continued.

The foreign exploits and domestic indulgence of England's king and lord chancellor only really succeeded in frittering away much of the late Henry VII's hard-earned savings. The taxpayers had to pick up the tab for this waste of money, and the growing sense of dissatisfaction eventually caused division in the ranks. By 1527 even Henry VIII was losing confidence in Thomas Wolsey. Soon, however, he'd have even greater reason to be displeased with the chancellor.

No Divorce? Goodbye, Church of Rome!

For Henry, the situation was getting desperate. He'd now been married to Catherine of Aragon for nearly 20 years, yet, in spite of her giving birth eight times, they only had one surviving girl, Mary, to show for all the effort. The king needed a son to be his rightful heir—after all, the men who had ruled so far had done a perfectly good job, hadn't they? His eyes therefore started wandering, and they soon settled on a young lovely by the name of Anne Boleyn. Obviously, Catherine had made some effort to provide the monarch with a boy, but the results just weren't up to expectations. No, he'd have to divorce her and marry Anne. Wolsey would take care of the arrangements. Unfortunately, Wolsey couldn't.

Charles V, the Holy Roman Emperor, was Catherine's nephew, and so while the pope would have normally consented to Henry's wishes, in this case he just couldn't afford to upset Rome's ruler. Caught, so to speak, between the devil and the deep blue sea, the pope's initial reaction was not to react at all.

Hear Ye, Hear Ye
"Had I but served God as diligently as I have served the King, He would not have given me over in my grey hairs."
—*Thomas Wolsey on his deathbed, 1529*

Wolsey tried to get a favorable answer out of the pope and then pitched to a visiting Roman cardinal, but all to no avail. Months passed by without the response the king desired. Henry was furious. He'd always been used to getting what he wanted; now he was sonless and unable to improve his situation by divorcing Catherine and marrying his new love. Someone had to be responsible for this mess; Henry decided to blame Thomas Wolsey.

The chancellor's fall from grace wasn't pleasant. Banished from the Royal Court and divested of his wealth and most of his titles, Wolsey withdrew to York only to then be charged with high treason. Just before he came to trial, however, he died en route to London.

No sooner was Wolsey out of the way than Henry replaced him with a lawyer and intellectual named Sir Thomas More. Three years later, however, having watched England's volatile king sever virtually all connections with the Church of Rome, this former Treasurer of the Exchequer resigned his post. In 1533, Henry subsequently had Archbishop Thomas Cranmer annul his marriage to Catherine of Aragon, opening the way for Anne Boleyn to become the new queen that January. Another daughter, Princess Elizabeth, was born later in the year. That birth didn't make Henry VIII a happy man. To add to Henry's woes, the pope then excommunicated him.

The English Reformation

Henry had called a handpicked Parliament that he knew would back him up in his dispute with the Pope. That Parliament approved his marriage to Anne Boleyn, and now, in 1534, it passed the Act of Supremacy, declaring the king to be "Supreme Head on earth, under God, of the Church of England." Most of the country's power brokers swore an oath recognizing him as such, but there were a few dissenters —among them was former Chancellor, Sir Thomas More. This righteous man wasn't prepared to do the bidding of a puppet Parliament that he felt had no right to say who the head of the church should be. Henry found this protest intolerable. He promptly had More imprisoned and, in 1535, hanged.

Now assuming the role of a virtually unopposed, totally out-of-control despot, the king appointed Privy Counsellor Thomas Cromwell as Vicar-General of England. This was a fancy title for the job of assisting Henry in enforcing the Act of Supremacy; closing down the country's monasteries, stripping them of their assets, and selling off the land for a fat profit. Meanwhile, John Fisher, the Bishop of Rochester and opposer of Henry's divorce from Catherine of Aragon, was subsequently made a cardinal by Paul III. The monarch took this appointment as a personal affront, and by now you know what happened when Henry felt affronted. Fisher was arrested and, in 1535, beheaded. Beheading, as you'll soon see, was Henry's favorite form of execution.

> **Hear Ye, Hear Ye**
> "I die the King's faithful servant, but God's first"."
> —*Thomas More's last words*

William Tyndale, on the other hand, was strangled and burned at the stake after he was caught in Brussels in 1536. Tyndale had been on the run for many years while he defied the king by translating the Bible into English. His work forms the vast majority of the Authorized (King James) Version of 1611. Henry, however, opposed Tyndale's work and had ordered a translation by Thomas Matthew. Matthew's translation formed the basis of the Great Bible that was first published in England in 1539. This book would then be revised by Miles Coverdale and used until 1571.

It was a case of "my way…or else!" while Henry VIII was on the throne. Nevertheless, despite the establishment of the Anglican Church with the king as its head, there was little departure from the Catholic faith. Henry had never been in sympathy with the *Protestants,* so the English Reformation initially didn't enforce much doctrinal change. This change would take place during the reign of Henry's heir, Edward VI. In the meantime, extremists and perceived extremists on both sides were persecuted.

Palace Parlance
During the 16th century, **Protestants** were reformers who attacked the principles of the Roman Catholic Church and demanded separation from it. Inspired by revolutionary theologians John Calvin and Martin Luther, they largely divided into Calvinists and Lutherans.

Protestant martyrs were many, as were those who participated in a series of armed demonstrations in the north of England between October 1536 and January 1537. Known as the Pilgrimage of Grace, the rebellion came about because of discontent among the clergy, the nobles, and the peasants in that part of the country over the dissolution of the monasteries. Lord Thomas Darcy and Robert Aske led the rebellion, and they and others marched with crucifixes and sacred banners. Evidently, not everyone despised the monks. This demonstration was basically open revolt against the reformist policies of Henry VIII and his ministers. Surely I don't have to tell you what happened next: Darcy and Aske were arrested as traitors and executed without mercy. This same fate was shared by some of Henry's marital partners.

Crimes and Punishments: The Six Wives

Henry VIII is the Mickey Rooney, Zsa Zsa Gabor, and Liz Taylor of British royalty, holding the record as the most married monarch. Of his six wives, only two outlived him. Two others had their lives cut short by their associations with the king. The first three marriages were for mostly the right reasons: love, as well as a desire to produce a male heir to the throne. Once that had been achieved at the expense of his third wife's life, the other three unions were really marriages of convenience. The women's main purpose was to serve as the king's companion and, ultimately, his nurse. Henry really wasn't suited to marriage, although he believed he was. The following sections introduce you to Henry's wives.

Catherine of Aragon (1485-1536)

Before marrying Henry, Catherine was the wife of his brother, Arthur. This first marriage was thanks to the conniving of Henry VII and Ferdinand of Spain, who saw mutual benefits in an alliance between their two countries by way of an arranged marriage between their offspring. Arthur ruined that first attempt by dying young, so the fathers then decided to try again, pairing Catherine off with Prince Henry. Still, being that she was 16 years old and he was only 10, she had to wait. Why she had to wait is a mystery to me; remember the example of Richard II and his eight-year-old bride?

A Right Royal Tale

During his marriage to Catherine of Aragon, Henry VIII had other mistresses (surprise, surprise) besides Anne Boleyn. One of them was Anne's sister Mary, and another was Bessie Blount, one of Catherine's ladies-in-waiting, by whom he had a son but not an heir. At the age of six, this son was made Duke of Richmond, and St. James' Palace was built for him. Meanwhile, according to contemporary reports, when Catherine of Aragon died in 1536, her former husband showed his immense grief by staging Mass, throwing a banquet, and holding a jousting tournament. Dressed from head to toe in bright yellow, the King celebrated the ex-Queen's passing in fine style.

It wasn't until Henry's accession eight years later that they married, and initially it appears that they hit it off. As time wore on, however, and a male heir became an unlikely prospect, Henry turned toward Anne Boleyn. His 24-year marriage to Catherine was annulled in 1533. Deeply religious and very loyal, Catherine retired as Princess Dowager of Wales but refused to endorse her husband's other marriages. She also wouldn't swear to the Act of Succession, which meant that her daughter, Mary, would be passed over in favor of the king's son. That kind of stubbornness proved fatal to others, but Catherine got away with it and on her deathbed she dictated a letter of forgiveness to Henry.

Anne Boleyn (1507-1536)

Only two years old when Henry married for the first time, Anne was the daughter of Sir Thomas Boleyn and, at the age of 15, maid of honor to Catherine of Aragon. She first attracted the lecherous king's eye when he was having secret rendezvous with her sister, and it wasn't long before he transferred his affections to Anne. Following their marriage, she became queen at what was, in true Henry style, a magnificent coronation ceremony. Sadly, things soon turned sour.

Anne was already pregnant when she and the king married and the daughter born, Elizabeth, was a profound disappointment to the expectant father, as were the subsequent stillbirths and miscarriage. Henry's interest cooled, and with people at court criticizing the queen's arrogance and "frivolity," he wasted little time in finding a new love, Jane Seymour, and charging Anne with having been unfaithful to him. His accusation was never proved, but in Henry's eyes unfaithfulness by a wife amounted to treason. When it was committed by himself, on the other hand, it amounted to a lot of fun. You know where this is heading—or should I say beheading—don't you?

May 15, 1536: Anne Boleyn pays for upsetting King "Hal." (Picture courtesy of Corbis-Bettmann)

"Anne of the Thousand Days" hadn't been dead more than a day when Henry married Jane Seymour. The ceremony took place in the same room as his marriage to Anne had taken place three years earlier.

Jane Seymour (1509-1537)

Henry's third wife was of royal stock thanks to her decendency from Edward III, and, as with Anne, Henry didn't have to look far to find her. Jane had been a lady-in-waiting to both Catherine of Aragon and Anne Boleyn, but she wouldn't succumb to his physical charms, such as they were, until after their marriage.

Far more timid than either Catherine or Anne, Jane nevertheless went out of her way to befriend the King's daughters, 20-year-old Mary and three-year-old Elizabeth. Henry regarded Mary as Catherine's daughter, while others regarded Elizabeth as illegitimate. Thanks to Jane's efforts, these perceptions changed a little.

Eighteen months after the wedding, Jane Seymour finally presented Henry with the legitimate son he'd longed for. Naturally he was overjoyed and, even more naturally, he arranged for major celebrations in honor of the boy, Edward. Only 12 days later, however, Jane died from complications arising from the birth. For once in his life, Henry was truly aggrieved at the death of a wife. He wore suitable mourning clothes and, on his own death, would be buried alongside her at Windsor.

Anne of Cleves (1515-1557)

This marriage really was a disaster, although Henry ensured that it was short-lived. Anne was the daughter of John, Duke of Cleves, a leading light in the Protestant movement of western Germany. Thomas Cromwell, in his capacity as right-hand man to the King, believed that a Protestant alliance would be a great salvo to fire at the Catholic powers in Europe, and being that a portrait of Anne showed her to be fair-haired and "attractive," he went ahead and arranged the marriage. For his part, Henry wasn't enthralled at the prospect of having a wife who couldn't speak English, but as the date of her arrival neared he started to get excited.

His palaces and ships were redecorated and he spent lavish amounts on gifts for his new bride. She too was thrilled at the prospect of becoming England's Queen, so imagine the gaping mouths and skipped heartbeats when they first laid eyes on one another. Anne's portrait, you see, had been, well, let's just say complimentary to her.

Thin and pock-marked, she was—to put it kindly— plain, and her boring personality didn't help matters. On the other hand, by this time Henry VIII wasn't exactly an oil painting either; he was more like a giant billboard poster. He was already grossly overweight and his sparkling repartee appeared to desert him on seeing his wife-to-be. In fact, he was so shocked that he couldn't even bring himself to give her the lovely gifts that he'd bought. Breaking off the marriage at this advanced date would have been a diplomatic night-mare, however, so the couple somehow went through with the formalities and the result was a diplomatic nightmare.

Hear Ye, Hear Ye
"Wishing myself (specially an evening) in my sweetheart's arms, whose pretty dukkys [breasts] I trust shortly to kiss. Written with the hand of him that was, is, and shall be yours by his will."
—*Henry VIII's sign-off in a letter to his great love, Anne Boleyn*

Charmingly describing his bride as the "Mare of Flanders," Henry refused to consummate the relationship…and what a blessed relief that must have been for her. Then he did what he did in situations that weren't to his liking: He looked for someone to blame. As you might expect, the scapegoat was none other than the man who'd arranged this fiasco in the first place, Thomas Cromwell. Accusing Cromwell of hatching "The Plot" against him, Henry had his faithful servant arrested without warning and beheaded on a trumped-up charge of treason.

In July 1540, seven months after the wedding, the marriage was annulled on the grounds that the king hadn't given his full consent to the marriage. Isn't that a beauty! Relieved at having escaped so lightly, he then gave his latest ex-queen a fabulous settlement of 4,000 pounds per year and a couple of stately homes. As for a union with the Protestant League, all bets were off.

Catherine Howard (1522-1542)

Catherine Howard, the youngest of Henry VIII's wives—she was 18, he was 49—was described by the King as "My rose without a thorn." A small bundle of fun, she represented all that he wanted for his later years. A much larger bundle of "fun," he represented a massive climb in wealth and social status for a girl from a poor branch of a leading Catholic family of the English nobility. They married on July 28, 1540, the same month Henry obtained his divorce from the "Mare of Flanders" and on the same day that Thomas Cromwell was beheaded. What the King didn't know, however, was that his "rose without a thorn" had a few notches on her stem. One of these was the pre-marital affair she'd indulged in with a young nobleman named Francis Derham. Another was the extra-marital affair she immersed herself in with one of her husband's courtiers, Thomas Culpepper.

The Howard family had previously assured Henry of his sweetheart's purity, but now their enemies came forward and informed the monarch about her indiscretions. Initially, he didn't want to believe what he was hearing. (And the people who were telling him these stories didn't want to be lying!) Then, when the charges were proved, he wept publicly. Still, Catherine wasn't making any excuses. She and Culpepper were in love, and had been even before she'd married the King. And that was that. Henry really wasn't left with very much choice, was he? Can't you just envisage the words "high treason" forming in his mind?

Hear Ye, Hear Ye
"I die a queen, but I would rather die the wife of Culpepper."
—*Catherine Howard as she knelt before the chopping block*

Catherine Howard lost her head in February 1542. Her two beaus, Derham and Culpepper, were hanged until they were half-strangled, then cut down alive, quartered, and beheaded. The moral to this story: Don't mess with the wife of a king.

Katherine Parr (1512-1548)

Henry VIII gave marriage the cold shoulder after his horrible experience with Catherine Howard. In fact, he waited *a whole year* before getting wed again! Morbidly obese, jaundiced, and suffering from gout as well as an ulcerated leg, His Grumpiness looked far older than his 54 years. He was lonely, however, and in much the same way he always had room to fit in just a little more food, he probably thought, "Oh alright, let's go for another young wife."

His choice was Katherine Parr, the 31-year-old, twice-widowed daughter of Sir Thomas Parr, and a woman of solid aristocratic stock and royal ancestry. At the time of her courtship with the king, she was already in love with one Thomas Seymour, but before you roll your eyes and groan, "Oh no, not again, Henry!", relax.

Following their wedding in 1543, Katherine became the model wife for the ailing monarch. She'd married him out of a strong sense of duty, and her kindness, compassion, and intelligence helped see him through his last years while also bringing him closer to his young son and two daughters. Not that she didn't risk a quick beheading, either.

Tens of thousands of people had lost their lives in the name of religion, and troubled by the ongoing persecution, Katherine tried to persuade Henry to tone down his policies. *Big* mistake. Henry had an order drawn up for her arrest but then canceled it. Do you think he may have been mellowing in his old age? During Henry's last year, he decided to put on one more show of bravado by undertaking an expedition against France, even though he was in no fit state to do much of anything, let alone ride a horse. Still, while he was away, he named Katherine as Regent, before returning to England and dying in January 1547 at the age of 55. Several months later, Katherine married her true amour, Thomas Seymour, an uncle to the new King Edward VI. The following year she died giving birth to their first child.

The Least You Need to Know

➤ Henry VIII reigned from 1509 to 1547, and anyone who crossed him was threatened with execution.

➤ In 1534, after being excommunicated by the Pope for divorcing Catherine of Aragon and marrying Anne Boleyn, Henry severed all ties with Rome and established himself as head of the Church of England.

➤ Thousands of Catholics and Protestants died during the English Reformation, although the changes initially weren't doctrinal.

➤ Henry VIII was married six times. Two of the marriages ended in divorce, one wife died after giving birth to a son and heir, two wives were beheaded, and the last one outlived him.

Blood and Guts—That Feminine Touch

It's been pretty clear in recent times that women who become their nations' leaders can't always be counted on to display warmth and compassion any more than their male counterparts. In fact, in certain cases—and I'm not naming names—they appear to be even more ruthless. This observation is nothing new. Said national leaders have to be tough just to claw their way to the top of the political ladder, but what about the first British women who actually inherited supreme power?

Until the untimely death of young Edward VI in 1553, no woman had ever acceded to the throne. Many had the right to, but it was a given that the women would be passed over in favor of the "superior" male heirs. When the females finally got their chance to take the Crown, not only did they grab it with both hands, they gave the guys more than a run for their money. Mary I, the eldest daughter of Henry VIII, was among the most callous of British monarchs, having people slaughtered *en masse* in what could be aptly described as the execution of her royal duties. One of these unfortunates was her immediate predecessor, Lady Jane Grey, the first woman to ever ascend to the throne as well as the sovereign who reigned for the shortest period of time. I'll now tell you about these characters who stepped into the limelight at a crucial stage in England's history.

Poor Boy: Edward VI

After becoming king in 1547 at the age of nine, Edward VI continued to be raised by his stepmother, Katherine Parr. Within months, she married Thomas Seymour, the brother of Edward's late mother, Jane, and immediately there was family friction—not between the king and his stepmother, but between Uncle Thomas and his brother Edward Seymour.

As the leader of a party of extreme Protestants that had quickly taken charge, Edward Seymour had made himself Duke of Somerset and Lord Protector of England. Renewed attacks were launched against Roman Catholics and the remainder of Church property was seized. The next year, without papal guidance or leadership to control the conflict, saw more riots and uprisings than in all of Henry VIII's reign.

Katherine Parr died in 1548, and the following year Thomas Seymour was caught trying to kidnap the king and was summarily executed. At around the same time, the Roman Catholic Mass was declared illegal and the first *Book of Common Prayer* was issued, written by Thomas Cranmer and changing the Church service from Latin into English. Cranmer was a *Puritan*, ideologically opposed to those people who still wanted the old Roman Catholic-style services. The doctrinal Reformation was well under way, supplementing the political and constitutional one of Henry VIII's reign.

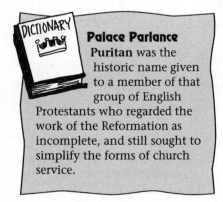

Palace Parlance
Puritan was the historic name given to a member of that group of English Protestants who regarded the work of the Reformation as incomplete, and still sought to simplify the forms of church service.

Still, Henry's will had created a distinct problem. In it, he'd named Edward as his heir and if he died without children, then Edward's sister Mary—a devout Catholic—would ascend to the throne. Then, if she died without children, her sister Elizabeth would succeed her. If all of that were to happen (and as you'll soon see, it did, save for a temporary hiccup) was the country supposed to flip between one form of religion and another? A lot of people weren't happy about the prospect.

These people included the nobles involved in the power struggle within the king's court. Having seen off his own brother Thomas Seymour, Edward the Duke of Somerset was now at loggerheads with John Dudley, Earl of Warwick. England was in a state of chaos, with looters running riot under the guise of religious protest and the country's economy totally depleted. In 1550, Warwick overthrew Somerset and proclaimed himself Earl of Northumberland and England's new protector, eventually rising to become Lord President of the Privy Council.

Northumberland's promotion was achieved partly with the king's support, and soon Northumberland began to increase his own power by playing on Edward's enthusiasm for the Protestant religion, while simultaneously isolating him from other influences. Edward was far from stupid; he was well read, used Latin as his second language, and had a very sharp mind. Even in his early teens he was able to see through a lot of what was going on at court, but the wily Northumberland undoubtedly held sway over him.

In 1552, convinced by the Lord Protector that the Duke of Somerset had been conspiring against him, Edward had a second Seymour uncle executed. Soon, however, the young monarch's illnesses began to overtake him, and, as it became clear that he wasn't going to recover, Northumberland realized he'd have to act quickly. He didn't want the staunchly Catholic Princess Mary ascending to the throne, so he now embarked on the second phase of his game plan.

Royal Rebuttal
Edward VI is often portrayed as having been a frail, sickly child, yet all evidence points to him having been quite healthy up until the last year of his life. At that point, he contracted measles and/or smallpox, which severely weakened his constitution and led to tuberculosis. Some of the toxic medicines then being administered only worsened his condition.

Nine Days of Reign: Lady Jane Grey

After the Princesses Mary and Elizabeth, the next in line to Edward VI's throne was his older cousin Frances, Duchess of Suffolk. Her 16-year-old daughter was Lady Jane Grey. John Dudley, Lord Protector, Duke of Northumberland, and all-round wheeler-dealer, easily persuaded the mother to relinquish her claim in favor of the girl, while proposing a deal that would benefit both sets of parents. In return for Lady Jane marrying his son Guilford Dudley, Northumberland would see to it that neither Mary or Elizabeth would make it onto the throne.

Lady Jane wasn't at all happy about marrying that obnoxious brat Guilford Dudley, but her parents, sensing that the throne was firmly within the family's grasp, forced her into the marriage in May 1553. Northumberland then used all his guile to talk the dying King into ensuring the Protestant succession, by making a will in which he named Lady Jane Grey as his heir. The Privy Council was cajoled into accepting this scheme, and four days after Edward's death on July 6, Lady Jane Grey was proclaimed as the new queen of England.

"No! No! The crown is not my right," Lady Jane reportedly cried out. "The Lady Mary is the rightful queen!" That, of course, could all have been a load of hogwash just to give the impression that the usurper was a loyal subject to the rightful heir; a sort of insurance scheme in the event of Mary seizing back the throne. Whatever the truth, Lady Jane and Guilford Dudley traveled in state to London and there she reigned for a grand total of nine days.

Princess Mary had evaded the attempts to seize her and had taken refuge inside Framlingham Castle in Suffolk, to the northeast of the capital. From there, she rapidly built up support, and when Northumberland advanced on Suffolk with an army, his men started to desert him. He was captured and taken to the Tower of London, at which point this sleazy operator turned yellow, pleading for his life and even renouncing the Protestant faith! He was quickly executed.

On Her Majesty's Service

The prayer book that Lady Jane Grey carried to her execution is now in the British Museum. And although most beheadings that took place at the Tower of London were carried out in public, a privileged few were decapitated in private. These included Lady Jane, as well as Henry VIII's wives, Anne Boleyn and Catherine Howard.

Lady Jane, meanwhile, had also been imprisoned. The new queen, Mary I, acceded on July 19, 1553, and was crowned in Westminster Abbey on October 1. Her advisors warned that, with Jane alive, there would always be plots to snatch back the throne, but Mary initially didn't want to do away with her unwitting cousin; she might even persuade her to become a Catholic! Jane, however, refused the offer and in so doing signed her own death warrant.

Lady Jane Grey and her husband were both beheaded for treason on Tower Green in 1554. England was now at the mercy of a fanatical and virulent Catholic.

Not Such a Fine Romance: Bloody Mary and Philip the Cad

There was plenty of popular support for Mary when she seized the throne in July 1553, but by the following year, the widespread enthusiasm was fading fast. If the execution of Lady Jane Grey didn't win the queen many friends, then her announcement that she would marry her cousin, the future Philip II of Spain, gained her a legion of enemies.

The nation was horrified that a Catholic foreigner would become king of England and Parliament begged Mary to reconsider, but she wasn't going to be denied her chance of real love as well as the national consolidation of the Catholic faith. In plain defiance of her Council and her people, Mary married Philip in a glittering ceremony at Winchester Cathedral on July 25, 1554. Yet, as things turned out, the marriage was more of a disaster for the queen than for her country.

To start with, she had to deal with a revolt to depose her led by Sir Thomas Wyatt. The plot very nearly succeeded until London's citizens, aware that the capital was about to fall into the hands of the rebels, rallied around Mary. Wyatt was duly executed, as were more than a hundred others who were taken captive, and even Princess Elizabeth was accused of complicity and imprisoned. Meanwhile, back at court, all was not well between the newlyweds.

At 27, Philip was 11 years younger than his new bride and he was not nearly in as much of a rush as she was to have a child. He'd already sired an heir by his deceased first wife, and while he always treated Mary with reverence, he didn't smother her with Spanish warmth and affection. In due course, and on two separate occasions, it was announced that the queen was indeed pregnant, but whether these were real or imagined, nothing ever came of either pregnancy.

Furthermore, if Philip didn't appear to be all that interested in his wife, he positively couldn't stand living in England. The people there may have been worried that he was thinking of taking over, but they could keep the climate *and* their lousy food! After only 14 months of marriage, he left to become king of Spain. He would never return and, but for a few weeks in 1557, he also wouldn't lay eyes (or anything else) on Mary again.

This steel engraving from a painting by Sir Antonio More depicts Philip II of Spain and Mary Tudor. (Picture courtesy of Corbis-Bettmann)

To say that this entire episode was embarrassing for England's sovereign would be a gross understatement. After the stir Mary had caused to marry the cad, the union had come to nothing. What's more, there wasn't even a Catholic heir to show for any of it! This issue was very close to the queen's heart, for the preservation of her faith as England's faith was the burning issue of her reign—and I don't use the word "burning" without good reason. You see, she *earned* the title of "Bloody Mary."

Papal Supremacy and Public Persecution

Before getting straight to the atrocities committed in the name of Bloody Mary, let's first look at the background that gave rise to her strong convictions and narrow-minded bigotry.

Following the divorce of her parents, Henry VIII and Catherine of Aragon, Mary had been subjected to a horrible childhood. Henry wouldn't allow her to see her mother, not even when she was dying, and following Catherine's death in 1536, Mary was declared illegitimate by an Act of Parliament. As if all that wasn't enough, during the reign of her small brother, Edward VI, she was persecuted as a Catholic, harangued to renounce the Mass, and expected to adhere to customs such as kneeling several times before the infant King before even sitting down in his presence. And, when she did sit down near the king, she was only permitted to be on a bench or cushion, not an armchair. Add to that the unfairness and indignity of having her brother sign away her right of succession, and you can see why Mary had cause to feel a little bitter.

Nevertheless, after her ascension to the throne, England's first properly crowned queen did start off by showing some leniency toward Protestants. If they didn't wish to live by her rules, they were allowed to leave—which a number of them did, forming their own Church of England while in exile. Those who stayed, however, didn't get off lightly. In 1553 Thomas Cranmer, the Protestant Archbishop of Canterbury who had been responsible for the *Book of Common Prayer*, was accused of complicity in Northumberland's plot against Mary's succession, and he was consequently imprisoned.

Hear Ye, Hear Ye
"Be of good cheer and play the man, brother Ridley. We shall this day light such a candle, by God's grace, in England as I trust shall never be put out!"
—Bishop Latimer to Bishop Ridley, as both men burned at the same stake, 1555

Soon afterward, Parliament passed the first Statute of Repeal, resulting in the restoration of Catholic bishops and doctrines. This in turn prompted a formal pardon from the Pope's ambassador and Mary's cousin, Cardinal Pole, for the split with Rome during the preceding Tudor years. In 1554, England once again found itself under papal authority, and it was now that the persecution of Protestants began in earnest.

The heresy laws were revived and enforced against anyone who didn't accept the Catholic doctrine. In other words, Mary was determined to oversee the wholesale conversion of her nation and in this atmosphere of rampant fanaticism, those who weren't willing to comply were liable to be burnt at the stake.

The first to die in this barbaric manner were John Rogers, the editor of Tyndale's Protestant version of the Bible, as well as several bishops. By the end of Mary's reign, nearly 300 other people—mostly lower-class citizens, 60 of them women—would follow in their footsteps. Among them was Thomas Cranmer, who, after spending nearly three years in confinement, had actually recanted for his "crimes" and taken full responsibility for all the misery and woe that had been brought upon the church. As he went to the stake, the 67-year-old Archbishop made a point of thrusting first into the flames "that unworthy hand" that had signed the confession.

Indeed, by trying to impose Catholicism in such a brutal way on the English people, Mary I and Cardinal Pole were simply ensuring its ultimate rejection there in favor of the Protestant faith. In 1558, while waging war against France, England lost its last French territory, Calais, which had been in its possession since the reign of Edward III. That same year, at the age of 42, the queen died of dropsy. Just before her death, she said that if her heart were opened after her death the word Calais would be found written on it. Such touching compassion!

The Least You Need to Know

➤ During the six-year reign of Edward VI, the Roman Catholic Mass was banned and Protestant doctrine took over.

➤ In order to ensure the Protestant succession, Edward was persuaded to name Lady Jane Grey, third in line to the throne, as the next queen instead of his sisters Mary and Elizabeth.

➤ After just nine days, Lady Jane Grey was overthrown by Mary I, who then lost the support of the English people by marrying Philip of Spain, reasserting the Catholic faith, and brutally persecuting the Protestants.

➤ In 1558, the year of Mary's death, England lost Calais, its last French territory.

Like a Virgin—Shrewd Queen Bess

In This Chapter

➤ Elizabeth I instigates another break with the Church of Rome

➤ The Virgin Queen's romantic escapades

➤ The treacherous, tragic life of Mary, Queen of Scots

➤ English acumen overcomes Spanish might

It wasn't exactly a great start, having a mother forced to lose her head and then being imprisoned by her big sister. However, Elizabeth I proved that she was not only a survivor but also one of England's most capable monarchs.

In an age when religious warfare and the threat of foreign invasion intermingled with the works of writers such as Ben Jonson and William Shakespeare, Elizabeth I was very much the right woman in the right place at the right time. She was brave, level-headed, sharp-witted, and extremely popular with the people of England. She could also be vain and overbearing, but these were minor flaws when compared to the character traits of most of her predecessors.

We'll now take a look at how "Queen Bess" always navigated a steady course, whether she was dealing with touchy issues relating to the Church of England, ambitious male suitors, troublesome relatives, or aggressive foreigners. Elizabethan England was undoubtedly an exciting place to live, but I'd still rather just write about it.

Welcome Back: Elizabeth Revives the Protestants

From the outset of Elizabeth's reign, it was clear to most people that they weren't going to be persecuted according to their religious beliefs. The queen was neither as cruel as her father or as fanatical as her sister, and, although she had Protestant leanings, she was well aware that an extreme bias against the Catholics could lead to a bloody rebellion or foreign invasion.

A Right Royal Tale

The coronation of Elizabeth I took place at Westminster Abbey on January 15, 1559, and the service wasn't without its awkward moments. Parliament hadn't yet resolved the nation's religious dilemma, so during Mass the queen withdrew to a concealed pew when Bishop Oglethorpe insisted on performing Roman Catholic rituals that she'd objected to. Still, this incident wasn't as embarrassing as the behavior of certain guests when Elizabeth first entered the Abbey. Luxuriant blue carpeting had been fitted especially for the occasion, and as the sovereign walked along it with great solemnity several souvenir hunters started snipping off pieces that she'd just trodden on. Walking behind the queen, the Duchess of Norfolk nearly tripped.

Nevertheless, even though people of all persuasions would be left alone as long as they didn't start causing trouble, in 1559, the year of her coronation, Elizabeth became head of the Church of England. Really she didn't have much choice in the matter, being that Pope Paul IV had ordered her to give up the throne on the grounds of her "illegitimacy," resulting from Henry VIII's "unlawful" marriage to Jane Seymour.

Well, Elizabeth was hardly going to go along with that line of reasoning, was she? Neither for that matter was Parliament, especially the House of Commons, which advised her to tell the Pope to clear off. This she subsequently did, establishing the Anglican Church and issuing a new *Book of Common Prayer*. England has been a Protestant nation ever since.

No Marriage, No Successor, but Mucho Male Interest

Of all Britain's adult monarchs, Elizabeth I was the only one since William II ("Rufus") in the 11th century not to marry. Being that he was probably gay, Rufus had good reason not to wed—although that apparently wasn't excuse enough for several of his successors. In the case of Elizabeth, on the other hand, she's been plagued down the years by her portrayal as the "Virgin Queen"—a frosty, frustrated woman who had eyes for several male suitors but a bed made strictly for sleeping in. The truth, however, is not quite so easy to nail down.

All her life Elizabeth was surrounded by handsome young men who would profess their love and proclaim her beauty. The admiration continued even when she was old, ugly, and caked in make-up. In a court of law, these ambitious admirers would have been charged with perjury, but at the court of the queen they were rewarded with titles and riches and encouraged to keep up the good work. So they did, and Elizabeth loved it. The only problem was, Parliament was forever pressuring her to get married and produce a Protestant heir, and she evidently wasn't prepared to follow its wishes. Possibly she couldn't.

ELIZABETH.

The frustration's in the eyes: A less than complimentary portrait of "Queen Bess." (Picture courtesy of Corbis-Bettmann)

Still, regardless of her ability to conceive, this shrewd woman took her role as queen extremely seriously, so the last thing she wanted was someone who would distract her from her duties or try to share in her power. Then again, she also knew that if she married a Catholic the Protestants would be up in arms, and if she wed a Protestant the Catholics would probably rebel. As her sister had learned, a foreign husband wouldn't necessarily be welcome, and an English or Scottish lord could stir up jealous rivalries among the nobility. No, in all likelihood Elizabeth never fully intended to marry, yet she also teased the French and Spanish with marital possibilities in order to stave off their aggressive instincts. Here now are some details about her main English suitors.

The Earl of Leicester

Princess Elizabeth and Lord Robert Dudley were childhood friends, and they were probably more than that when they reached maturity. During the early years of her reign there was plenty of talk about them getting married. He proposed, she refused—a game that she would play with men throughout her life.

At a young age, Robert Dudley had married an heiress named Amy Robsart, who broke her neck and died after falling down a flight of stairs on September 8, 1560. Following Amy's death, the gossips began asking some pointed questions: Did she fall or was she pushed? If she was pushed, who gave her the fatal shove? After all, Lord Dudley wasn't at home when the tragic accident took place, but did this mean that he was innocent, or could he have arranged the fall in order to free himself for marriage to the queen? There again, what if Elizabeth had accidentally-on-purpose bumped into Lady Dudley at the top of the stairs? It could even have been suicide. Oh yes, the tongues were really wagging over that little incident!

Royal Rebuttal
At the time of Amy Robsart's death, a rumor began to circulate that the queen was pregnant with Lord Robert Dudley's child. Anyone caught spreading this filthy lie was promptly arrested and tried in secret session to prevent the story from spreading, yet years later it was still making the rounds. Accordingly, some of the gossipmongers had their ears cut off as punishment.

In all probability, Amy Robsart had slipped accidentally, yet after the accident Elizabeth's Chief Secretary of State, William Cecil, had to convince the queen that it *really* wouldn't be a good idea for her to go ahead and marry Lord Dudley. Elizabeth saw the wisdom in this advice, but she was then furious when Dudley went and married someone else. In any case, she made him the first Earl of Leicester in 1564, and they sustained their friendship—whatever that amounted to—until his death in 1588.

Sir Walter Raleigh

Sir Walter Raleigh was the seafaring adventurer who, according to legend, gallantly spread his cape across a muddy puddle so that Elizabeth I could traverse it. This is the kind of charming anecdote one likes to associate with the England of a bygone and more romantic age, and in a book full of betrayal and torture, I'm doing my level best to dig up a few such stories for you!

Educated at Oxford, Raleigh built his reputation by exploring and colonizing unknown East Coast territories of what is now North America, and thus keeping them out of Spanish hands. In fact, Virginia was so-named in honor of England's "Virgin Queen," and she in turn was instantly charmed by the tall, handsome, witty, and extremely courteous Walter. As time went on, he was showered with property, money, and honors, including a knighthood in 1584, and he played a leading role in defeating the Spanish Armada (which you'll read about later in this chapter).

However, as the queen also started to have eyes for the Earl of Essex (more of whom in a moment), Sir Walter Raleigh began to fall out of favor. Then, in 1592 he really ruined things by having an affair with and marrying the queen's maid of honor, Elizabeth Throckmorton. For that misbehavior he was banished from the Royal Court, an action that would turn out to be the first installment in his slide down the slippery slope, ending with his imprisonment and execution during the reign of James I.

The Earl of Essex

I can't help it: Whenever the name of Elizabeth I is mentioned, I immediately think of Bette Davis. To all intents and purposes she *was* Elizabeth I, wasn't she? At least Hollywood thought so, casting her in the title role in *The Virgin Queen*, which detailed her conflicts with Sir Walter Raleigh, and opposite the dashing young Errol Flynn in *The Private Lives of Elizabeth and Essex*. Of course, these movies offered the less-than-authentic Tinsel Town versions of events, but they were colorful entertainment nonetheless, so who cared?

Robert Devereux, the second Earl of Essex, was actually the stepson of Elizabeth's former beau, Robert Dudley. During the 1590s, Essex was clearly the queen's favorite, yet being that, in his early twenties, he could have been the grandson of the monarch in her sixties, the whole scene played out as some sort of daft romantic comedy. After all, what did he think he was *doing*, writing her notes such as, "When I think how I have preferred your beauty to all things...I wonder at myself what cause there could be to absent myself from you..."

Did he ever take the time to actually *look* at her? (She herself couldn't bear to, having all of the mirrors removed from her residences.) Or, there again, do the words "ruthless gold-digger" spring to mind?

Elizabeth and Essex would often engage in lovers' quarrels, many of them pretty nasty, and during one of their kiss-and-forget sessions she presented him with an extra special ring. If they ever had a really bad spat, she told him, then all he had to do was send her that ring and she would forgive him no matter what. Now, wasn't that sweet? Unfortunately, Essex took her a bit too literally.

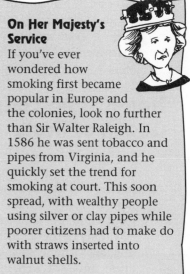

On Her Majesty's Service

If you've ever wondered how smoking first became popular in Europe and the colonies, look no further than Sir Walter Raleigh. In 1586 he was sent tobacco and pipes from Virginia, and he quickly set the trend for smoking at court. This soon spread, with wealthy people using silver or clay pipes while poorer citizens had to make do with straws inserted into walnut shells.

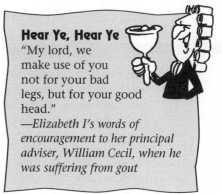

Hear Ye, Hear Ye

"My lord, we make use of you not for your bad legs, but for your good head."

—*Elizabeth I's words of encouragement to her principal adviser, William Cecil, when he was suffering from gout*

After leading a pathetic attempt to overthrow the government, the unethical earl was arrested and thrown into the Tower of London. So he sent her the special ring, and was then shocked and hurt when she didn't reply. "I had put up with but too much disrespect to my person," Elizabeth later explained, "but I warned him that he should not touch my sceptre."

Non-Kissing Cousins: Elizabeth and Mary, Queen of Scots

Remember Bloody Mary's husband, Philip of Spain, who had absolutely no interest in England's people or their culture? Well, as King Philip II he slightly revised that opinion, poking his nose into the nation's affairs and insisting that the English Church should have remained Roman Catholic. This was a point of principle, yet the English really did needle him, not least for their recent habit of sending explorers to the New World that, according to the Spanish and Portugese, was strictly their domain. Then there was England's interference in other issues, such as Elizabeth's military assistance to the Dutch Protestants who were fighting for their independence from Spanish rule.

Aware that England's current queen didn't have the same vindictive temper as that of his late wife, Philip started hatching a plot to overthrow Elizabeth and replace her with that good Catholic girl, Mary Stuart, Queen of Scots. The problem was Mary hadn't been too good of late in the eyes of her own subjects.

The daughter of Elizabeth I's first cousin, James V of Scotland (a grandson of Henry VII), Mary ascended to the Scottish throne in the first week of her life. At the age of five, she was betrothed to the French dauphin, Francis, son of Henry II, and spent the next 10 years in France, where she was raised a Roman Catholic while her French mother, Mary of Guise, served as Scotland's regent.

In 1558 Mary finally married the dauphin, and that same year her cousin, Elizabeth, became queen of England. However, as Catholics all over Europe considered Elizabeth's birth to have been illegitimate, they insisted that Mary was the rightful heir. It was a divisive issue, and matters weren't helped when Henry II died and Francis II ascended to the French throne, making Mary the queen of France as well as queen of Scots. The threat to Elizabeth appeared to be growing.

In Scotland, the fiery Protestant reformer John Knox had returned from the continent—where he'd fled during the reign of Mary I—and he was making quite an impact. Protestant support spread like wildfire, and, with the astute military assistance of Elizabeth I, the regent, Mary of Guise, was killed and the French were driven out of Scotland. Without the consent of the absent queen of Scots, a new Parliament was called, resulting in the proclamation of the Protestant faith and immediate suppression of Catholicism.

Mary, Queen of Scots' troubled love life led to a tragic end. (Picture courtesy of Corbis-Bettmann)

Meanwhile, after Mary's husband, Francis II, died suddenly, it was made pretty clear to her that the French no longer wanted her in their country. Therefore in 1561, at the age of 18, she returned to Scotland for the first time in 13 years, and she thought that she would be pleasing everyone by promoting absolute freedom of belief: Protestants and Catholics would each be entitled to observe their own religions. This religious acceptance wasn't what an extremist like John Knox wanted to hear. Worse than that, he was positively foaming at the mouth when the Scottish queen then married her Catholic cousin, Lord Darnley, in 1565. The relationship turned out to be disastrous for all concerned.

Soon growing tired of Darnley's arrogant, self-possessed attitude, Mary ensured that her husband could play no part in ruling her kingdom. Her move didn't please Darnley, and his rage was compounded by the increasing time Mary was spending with her Italian secretary, David Rizzio. With her own eyes, Mary saw Rizzio being murdered by Darnley and a bunch of thugs, and after a son, James, was born to the queen in that same year of 1566, Darnley refused to attend the baptism. Did he know something that we don't?

Still, no sooner had her Italian stallion been done away with than Mary found herself a new lover, the Earl of Bothwell, her chief adviser and commander of her armed forces.

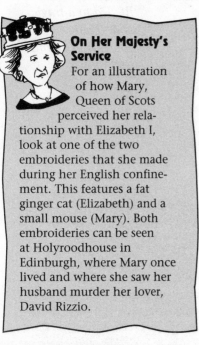

On Her Majesty's Service

For an illustration of how Mary, Queen of Scots perceived her relationship with Elizabeth I, look at one of the two embroideries that she made during her English confinement. This features a fat ginger cat (Elizabeth) and a small mouse (Mary). Both embroideries can be seen at Holyroodhouse in Edinburgh, where Mary once lived and where she saw her husband murder her lover, David Rizzio.

Hear Ye, Hear Ye

"What a valiant woman... It is a pity that Elizabeth and I cannot marry. Our children would have ruled the whole world."
—*Pope Sixtus V*

Together, they planned revenge. In 1567, Lord Darnley was murdered, and, although Bothwell was charged and then acquitted of the crime, documented evidence exists of the plot that he and the queen had hatched. Most citizens weren't fooled by the cover-up. In fact, they were appalled at the behavior of their monarch and her boyfriend, yet incredibly, just three months later, the couple got married. The nuptials were too much for the Scottish lords.

While Bothwell managed to run away, the queen was imprisoned in Lochleven Castle and forced to abdicate in favor of her infant son, James VI. Soon afterward, she managed to escape and with nowhere else to run, fled to England and asked cousin Elizabeth for asylum. Her request was pretty rich, considering that only a short time before she'd been staking her own claim to the English throne; Elizabeth was placed in an embarrassing and potentially dangerous situation. If she handed Mary back to her captors, the Catholics would be outraged. If she helped Mary regain the Scottish throne, the Protestants would rise up. And if she enabled Mary to go abroad, then she would be playing right into the hands of troublemakers like King Philip II of Spain.

The solution that Elizabeth and her advisor, William Cecil, came up with was to do none of the above. Instead they opted to imprison her, and for the next 19 years, while "Queen Bess" refused to see her cousin, that cousin spent her time in various northern castles plotting ways in which to escape and regain power. All the while, Elizabeth's spies kept her informed about Mary's plans and after repeated pleas from William Cecil to remove the threat, the English queen finally consented to have her cousin tried for conspiring against her. Mary was found guilty, and on February 8, 1587, she was beheaded at Fotheringhay Castle.

Of course, a major player in all of the plotting had been good old Philip of Spain. When Catholic uprisings in the north of England had been countered with executions and widespread persecution, he'd been incensed. Now that the former Queen of Scots had also been deprived of her head, he felt compelled to overthrow Elizabeth I once and for all. Besides, he had a good excuse: in her will, Mary had left her claim to the English throne not to her son, James VI of Scotland, but to...yes, you guessed it, King Philip. The Spaniards were on their way.

The Defeat of the Spanish Armada

Even in the days before there were spy planes or radar, it was pretty difficult to complete a mass build-up of arms and forces without the enemy learning about it. That was what Philip of Spain learned in 1587 when, in the middle of constructing warships with which to invade England, he lost no fewer than 37 of them in a surprise attack by Sir Francis Drake on Cadiz Harbor.

While England was desperately trying to build its own fleet and assemble the necessary forces, Drake tried to stall for time by way of his daring offensive. Nevertheless, in July 1588, the *Spanish Armada*, led by the Duke of Medina Sidonia and comprised of 130 ships carrying a total of 10,000 crewmen and 20,000 soldiers, moved into action. The English were facing the most powerful fleet in the world, but with 190 ships, they weren't outnumbered and they weren't about to be outclassed.

> **Palace Parlance**
> Armada is a term that describes a fleet of warships. The most famous was the **Spanish Armada** dispatched by King Philip II to invade England in 1588.

After the invasion force was first sighted off the Cornish coast in the southwest corner of England, Elizabeth's main fleet set sail from Plymouth. Under the command of Lord Howard, with Drake, Hawkins, and Frobisher each commanding their own squadrons, they went onto the attack and succeeded in disabling a number of galleons. The Spanish defenses were even stronger than expected, however, so the English spent a lot of ammunition without doing the kind of damage that they'd envisioned.

While Medina Sidonia regrouped his fleet off the French port of Calais and pondered his next move, 55-year-old Elizabeth I put on armor and rallied her army at Tilbury with a famous speech. "I know I have the body of a weak and feeble woman," she began, "but I have the heart and stomach of a king." (Fortunately, she didn't have the stomach of her father.) With their queen's battle cry still ringing in their ears, the English dispatched fireships for a midnight attack on the crowded fleet that was still anchored at Calais. The surprise tactic worked and in the confusion that followed, the Spanish ships collided with each other as they tried to set sail in the darkness and lost their formation, enabling the English to unleash a full-scale offensive.

The Spanish Armada took a battering, and soon it was retreating counterclockwise up England's east coast. As it happened, by this point the English had blown all of their ammunition, but the Spanish didn't know it. As the Armada rounded the north of Scotland it ran into severe gales that wrecked even more vessels along the rocky coastline. By the time it returned to Spain in the autumn of 1588, only 54 ships were left out of the original 130, while at least 11,000 men had been lost at sea.

Back in England, of course, it was party time, yet the celebrations were perhaps a bit premature. The English had won the battle, but they hadn't completed the war. Drake, Frobisher, and Hawkins all died in subsequent sea battles as the cocky English tried unsuccessfully to attack Spanish strongholds and bring back untold riches. Both sides would finally give up and sign a peace treaty in 1604.

The Least You Need to Know

➤ Elizabeth I returned the Church of England to the Protestant faith, yet she was a religious moderate.

➤ The Earl of Leicester, Sir Walter Raleigh, and Robert Devereux were three favorites at the court of "Queen Bess."

➤ Banished by her subjects for immoral behavior, Mary, Queen of Scots fled to England, was imprisoned by her cousin, Elizabeth I, and was eventually beheaded for plotting to overthrow Elizabeth.

➤ In the summer of 1558, Elizabeth's forces scored a famous victory when repelling an attempted invasion by the Spanish Armada.

Headaches in Parliament— The Turn of the Stuarts

> **In This Chapter**
>
> ➤ Relying on favorites and ruling without Parliament
>
> ➤ Will sparks fly as a result of the Gunpowder Plot?
>
> ➤ Conflicts and conquests surrounding the New World
>
> ➤ Another royal brainteaser to test your knowledge

Just before her death on March 24, 1603, Elizabeth I surprised quite a few people by bequeathing her throne to James VI of Scotland, the son of her nuisance of a cousin, Mary, Queen of Scots. That made him James I of England, and he now inherited a country in which industrial advances had benefited the rich while putting numerous other people out of jobs. The Poor Law of 1601 had been passed to relieve poverty courtesy of funds raised by local property taxes, yet there was still great disparity between the rich and the poor, as well as the unresolved conflict between Catholics and Protestants. With the transference of power from the House of Tudor to the House of Stuart, there would be added problems.

James I was a well educated man, but, as you're about to see, he was ill-equipped to run a country that was now used to a more modern and democratic style of rule than that of his native Scotland. I'll fill you in on the dramatic attempt to blow up King and Parliament, as well as James' role in the exploration of the New World, before ending with an exploration of your newfound knowledge regarding British royalty. Yes, at the end of this chapter it's once again quiz time!

James I: The Wisest Fool

James was used to ruling by the Divine Right of Kings. That meant he'd been appointed by God and, as such, wasn't answerable to mere mortals. He could use his subjects "like men at chess," and, while they always had to obey him, any rights or privileges that came their way would depend on his own generosity. That was in Scotland. It was a very different story in England. The nation had come a long way since the days of Henry VIII and Bloody Mary. During the steady, 45-year reign of Elizabeth I, both Parliament and the people felt a much closer bond with the monarch. The defeat of the Spanish Armada had been a joint effort, and in return for being treated with respect, the English people showed admiration and affection for their queen. Imagine their reaction, therefore, when a Scot assumed the throne and proceeded to behave like the autocrat he was.

A Right Royal Tale

Some historians believe that James I suffered from porphyries, the same disease that later afflicted George III, resulting in symptoms of madness. Indeed, James may have introduced it to England's royal line. Regardless, he was a very sick man with pronounced physical defects. For one thing, his tongue was too big for his mouth, causing him to drool incessantly. Then there was the rotund body that his legs weren't able to support, making it necessary for him to lean on his courtiers even on good days. On bad ones, such as the four months in 1619 when he lost all use of his lower limbs, he had to be carried around in a special chair.

For a start, there was James' foreign policy, which ranged from sensibly making peace with Spain in 1604 to thoughtlessly trying to pair off his son, Charles, with the daughter of the King of Spain. This latter folly took place from 1619 to 1623, by which time Charles was heir to the throne as a result of his elder brother Henry's death from typhoid. The problem was that the Spaniards were then playing a significant role in crushing the Protestant movement in Germany, so the English Protestants were up in arms to see their own King not only going easy on the Catholics, but trying to make a deal that would result in a Catholic queen on the throne and, after that, possibly a Catholic heir.

As it happens, the Spanish deal fell through, but this was all part of James I's ongoing policy to keep peace with Catholic Europe and thus avoid war. War was expensive, so to wage it he would need to ask for Parliament's help, which was the last thing he wanted to do. For long spells of his 22-year reign in England (he reigned in Scotland for all 58 years of his life) he ruled totally without Parliament, raising whatever money he needed by way of questionable taxes and turning for support to his favorite young males of the moment. His wife, Anne of Denmark, with whom he had nine children, was apparently fairly understanding in this respect.

Robert Ker, for instance, who was appointed Earl of Somerset and a member of the Privy Council, encouraged James to make a pact with Spain and played a role in the imposition of unpopular taxes. Adored by the king, he wasn't exactly a hero to the English. Then there was George Villiers, who was made Earl of Buckingham, and to whom James once wrote, "God bless you, my sweet child and wife, and grant that ye may ever be a comfort to your dear dad and husband, James R." (All of the monarchs sign their first names followed by the initial "R." This stands for *rex* or *regina*, the Latin words for king and queen.) Just in case anybody else missed the point, the starry-eyed sovereign also once said, "You may be sure that I love the Earl of Buckingham more than anyone else...Christ had his John, I have my George."

Which was all well and good, except that there were also numerous other hangers-on at court who the king misguidedly preferred to trust instead of his parliamentarians. To this rag-tag collection of opportunists, he would hand out titles and properties as if they were going out of fashion. Of course, all of this generosity cost plenty of money, which, when added to the expenses accrued as a result of James and his wife's lavish lifestyle, forced him to do exactly what I've said he wanted to avoid: summon Parliament for help. In the end, the entire situation merely strengthened Parliament's hand.

Meanwhile, another sore point with the House of Commons as well as many of the king's subjects was his religious conventionality. Soon after his ascension to the English throne he announced a policy of opposing the growing number of Puritans, those extreme Protestants who wished to eradicate all remnants of Catholic practices from church services. James, determined to retain absolute power, insisted on running the Church through the bishops and effectively told the Puritans to go along with this or else. Consequently he made enemies of many of the country's most influential men, even though the publication of the authorized King James Version of the Bible in 1611 met with widespread approval.

Royal Rebuttal

Scotland's House of Stuart took over the English throne in 1603, yet the family name had originally been spelled differently. The Scottish spelling is *Stewart*, but this spelling was amended when James V, the grandfather of James VI of Scotland/James I of England, took French nationality in 1537, prior to marrying Mary of Guise. Thereafter Scotland's royal family had a French surname.

The intellectual monarch was out of touch with the times and with his people. Not for nothing was he known as "The Wisest Fool in Christendom."

Guy Fawkes and the Gunpowder Plot

So you've now seen how James I managed to annoy the hard-line Protestants. Well, believe it or not, he also succeeded in alienating the Catholic fundamentalists, except that in this case his misinformed actions very nearly cost him his life.

On first becoming king of England, James actually tried to court popularity and create unity by showing leniency toward all Christians. He even thought he would spread a little happiness by abolishing the system of fining people who didn't attend the Anglican Church, but when that resulted in most people staying away, he restored the fines. Many Catholics took this as a personal affront, especially when 5,000 of them were prosecuted in the spring of 1605. There had been unsuccessful attempts to remove James from the throne a couple years earlier; now one man, Sir Robert Catesby, decided that it was time to take action.

The vain, conceited, but deeply religious James I of England and James VI of Scotland. (Picture courtesy of Corbis-Bettmann)

Catesby gathered together a band of like-minded hotheads and between them they plotted to assassinate the king and the country's leaders, blowing them up when they were assembled for the opening of Parliament on November 5, 1605. To that end, one of Catesby's recruits was Guido Fawkes, a Protestant who had converted to Catholicism and fought with the Spanish army against the Dutch Protestants. Guy Fawkes, as he was better known, would be the explosives expert.

The 12 conspirators began by renting a house near to the Houses of Parliament and digging a tunnel toward the House of Lords. Fawkes then discovered that they could hire a large storeroom right underneath the House of Lords, and so this room was used to stash 36 barrels of gunpowder, concealed by lumps of coal, planks of wood, and iron bars. Next, while Fawkes stood guard over all the goings-on, the other conspirators set about collecting the necessary arms in order to follow through on their *coup d'etat*. At this point, however, one of them lost his nerve and made a fatal mistake.

Francis Tresham knew that his brother-in-law, Lord Monteagle, would be attending the opening of Parliament, and so he sent him a note advising him to "retire into the country", as his fellow lords would be on the receiving end of "a terrible blow." Monteagle immediately passed the note to the Secretary of State who passed it onto the king, and, on November 4, the day before the proposed explosion, the Lord Chamberlain carried out a quick tour of inspection. On arriving at the storeroom, he asked Guy Fawkes who owned the suspicious amount of fuel in the room, and Fawkes coolly supplied the name of Thomas Percy, one of the conspirators. Obviously he hoped the bluff would work, because he was still standing at his post when soldiers arrived later that night and arrested him.

Taken straight to the king, Fawkes expressed no regret other than that the plot hadn't succeeded. "A dangerous disease requires a desperate remedy," he asserted, and, rounding on some of the Scottish courtiers, admitted that he'd intended to "blow the Scots back to Scotland." James VI/James I wasn't amused by that kind of talk, but Guy Fawkes obviously knew that his number was up and so he wasn't mindful of what he said. What he perhaps hadn't bargained for, however, was the treatment that awaited him prior to the inevitable hanging, drawing, and quartering. After all, there were 11 other conspirators to round up and the king wanted to know who they were. Fawkes wasn't about to betray them, so…yes, I'm afraid it was time to dust off the old stretching-rack!

Withstanding terrible torture in the White Tower of the Tower of London, Fawkes refused to disclose any names until he learned that some of the plotters had been arrested and others had been killed. In the end, he was so badly crippled that he couldn't even walk to the gallows. You can rest assured that he was given all the help that he needed to make it there.

On Her Majesty's Service

Whereas fireworks displays help Americans celebrate the country's independence every July 4, in Britain they are seen annually when people "Remember, remember the 5th of November." This is in commemoration of the Gunpowder Plot, as are bonfires on top of which Guy Fawkes effigies are burned. Children often make these effigies and try to raise money "for the Guy" in order to buy the fireworks.

Coming to America: Escaping from James in the New World

Early in James I's reign, Sir Walter Raleigh was imprisoned on a charge of treason. Instead of heading straight for the chopping block, however, he was allowed to lead a privileged life in the Tower, where he wrote his monumental *History of the World*. Fortunately the history was no small project, because Raleigh spent the next 13 years in captivity. Thereafter he was released in order to lead an expedition to El Dorado in search of hidden treasure, but when that trip ended in disaster James I decided that he was more trouble than he was worth. In 1618 Sir Walter Raleigh was executed.

Nevertheless, you may recall that on one of his trips of exploration to the New World during the reign of Elizabeth I, Raleigh had colonized some land on the East Coast and named it Virginia after the "Virgin Queen." The people who settled in Virginia soon learned that farming and felling trees for themselves wasn't very easy, so the colony failed. In 1607, however, while Raleigh was still in the Tower, another collection of explorers set out for America and built an entirely new settlement in Virginia. Also named after the reigning monarch, this was called James Town. (Original, weren't they?) Unfortunately, James Town quickly looked as if it would be heading the same way as Raleigh's Virginia, but then, just as the population was on the point of starvation, Captain John Smith came to the rescue.

This colorful adventurer took over the leadership of the settlement and soon began to organize it into some semblance of an ordered society, where people did a day's work and were expected to conform to local law. Early on, he got into a spot of trouble when he was captured by Red Indians and sentenced to death, but a certain princess named Pocahontas ensured that he survived and was able to return to Virginia. Eventually, thanks in part to the exporting of tobacco, the colony prospered, and over the next few years more and more people decided to leave England in search of a new life in America.

Hear Ye, Hear Ye
"A custom loathsome to the eye, hateful to the nose, harmful to the brain, dangerous to the lungs, and in the black, stinking fume thereof, nearest resembling the horrible Stygian smoke of the pit that is bottomless."
—*James I, writing about smoking tobacco*

Among them were some of the Puritans, who were sick and tired of the English and Scottish king's pedantic insistence on how they worship God. If they were able to join the expatriates in the New World, they reasoned, then they should be able to do things according to their own more easygoing rules. They'd already tried to settle in Holland but it hadn't worked out, so now Virginia was the place to be! The only problem was, they never quite made it there.

Setting sail on the *Mayflower* in 1620, the "Pilgrim Fathers," as they came to be known, got lost in the stormy Atlantic crossing. After ten harrowing weeks they managed to drop anchor near Cape Cod—hundreds of miles away from Virginia. What to do? Name the place New England! Obviously when naming land, those settlers didn't know the meaning of originality!

Now, at this point I could go into a lengthy dissertation about the history of the American colonies, but that isn't why you bought this book. Instead, I'll just end by saying that the Pilgrim Fathers weren't the only people to be fed up with King James I of England by the time that he died in 1625. Nothing that he ever did met with much approval (not that he cared), and, worse still, the country was far weaker than when he had ascended to the throne some 22 years earlier. I hope, however, that his distinct lack of success won't be reflected in your own performance as we now come to...

Are You a Complete Royal Idiot? Quiz #3

By now you should know the rules, so do your best and, if the results aren't up to scratch, suffer the consequences.

1. Who was the first Tudor monarch?

2. What special court was revived in 1487 to curb the powers of the barons?

3. What part of North America did John Cabot probably discover in 1487?

4. Who did Henry VII marry in order to unite the Houses of Lancaster and York?

5. Who did Henry VIII first appoint as lord chancellor to govern England?

6. What name was given to the lavish summit meeting between Henry VIII and the French king, Francis I, in 1520?

7. Name, in the correct order, all six wives of Henry VIII.

8. Which royal divorce caused the English Church to break with Rome?

9. Which of Henry VIII's wives were executed?

10. What was the nickname by which Henry VIII referred to Anne of Cleves?

11. Which heirs to the throne did Edward VI bypass when naming Lady Jane Grey as his successor?

12. How long did Lady Jane Grey reign for?

13. What was the name of Bloody Mary's foreign husband?

14. Which Protestant Archbishop of Canterbury did Mary I have burnt at the stake?

15. Lost in 1558, which was England's last French territory?

16. During whose reign did England become a Protestant nation once and for all?

17. Who discovered the American colony that was named Virginia?

18. Who introduced tobacco smoking to England?

19. Which regal cousin did Elizabeth I have executed after 19 years of imprisonment, but never meet?

20. In what year did the Spanish Armada attempt to invade England?

21. What was James I of England's other regal title?

22. What does the initial "R" stand for and mean when signed after the monarch's first name?

23. Who was in charge of the Gunpowder Plot?

24. On what date did the Catholic conspirators plan to blow up the king and Parliament?

25. Where did Sir Walter Raleigh lead a disastrous expedition to shortly before his execution?

As you'll remember from the previous quizzes (or this one if you've been cheating), the answers appear in Appendix G. Here's how to rate your performance:

➤ 20 or more—Maybe *you* should be next in line to the throne.

➤ 13-19—Good, but take a voyage of discovery through some of the pages you missed.

➤ 6-12—A quick session on the stretching-rack might sort you out.

➤ 5 or fewer—Even beheading wouldn't make much difference to *your* memory!

The Least You Need to Know

➤ King James I of England/King James VI of Scotland ruled for long periods without Parliament, instead placing his trust in a court of his favorites.

➤ The King James Version of the Bible was published in 1611.

➤ Guy Fawkes and his fellow conspirators planned to blow up James I at the opening of Parliament on November 5, 1605.

➤ The Pilgrim Fathers set sail for America in the hope of pursuing a more Puritan form of worship.

Part 5
Anarchy in the U.K.—Monarchy Under Siege (1625-1837)

All in all, no one could say those kings and queens hadn't been asking for it. Disaster strikes the British monarchy in this part of your Complete Idiot's Guide *and very nearly wipes it out.*

Charles I charged headlong into the abyss thanks to his insistence on doing what he wanted while ignoring everyone else, and he also plunged England into civil war. Then, after a rude interruption during which an upstart by the name of Oliver Cromwell turned the nation into a republic, the royals returned. (And thank goodness for that, otherwise what else would I have to write about?) Still, things would never be the same. The supreme power enjoyed by despots such as Henry VIII was a thing of the past; from now on British sovereigns would have to conform far more to Parliament's wishes.

James II was the only dissenter and, as you'll see, he paid the price. Even though the royals did make an effort to reform their ways, however, most of them still didn't get it. As Britain's domestic wealth and overseas power increased, its monarchs were steadily losing their own authority. So what, you may well ask, was the cause of all turmoil? Read on and find out.

"The Firm." A group shot of the Royal Family together with Princess Diana's relatives on the day of her 1981 wedding to Prince Charles. (Corbis–Bettmann)

Buckingham Palace, built in 1703 as a town house for the Duke of Buckingham, has been the official London residence of every British monarch since George III. (Corbis–Bettmann)

King Richard I ("the Lionheart") bids farewell to the Holy Land after a successful crusade that guaranteed Christians a safe pilgrimage to Jerusalem. (Corbis–Bettmann)

June 15, 1215: Barons and the clergy force King John to endorse the Magna Carta, but he doesn't look too happy about it. (Corbis–Bettmann)

An engraving depicting the Battle of Agincourt (1415), at which Henry V and 10,000 men defeated three times that number of French. (Corbis–Bettmann)

Gold paint and plastic or the real thing? (Corbis–Bettmann)

Henry VIII with his son Edward VI and daughter Elizabeth I. Although their combined reigns amounted to 89 years, that of young Edward only accounted for six of them. (Corbis–Bettmann)

One of the more spectacular British royal parades, Trooping the Colour takes place each year on the monarch's official birthday. (Corbis–Bettmann)

An aerial view of the June 2, 1953 coronation of Queen Elizabeth II in Westminster Abbey. (Corbis–Bettmann)

St. James' Palace. Constructed on the site of a leper hospital in the 16th century, it was once George III's main London residence and today serves the same purpose for Prince Charles. (Corbis–Bettmann)

September 6, 1997: Prince Charles, Prince Harry, Earl Spencer, Prince William, and Prince Philip stand as the coffin of Princess Diana is carried into Westminster Abbey. (Corbis–Bettmann)

"The People's Princess" as many will prefer to remember her—reaching out and spreading warmth and happiness. (Corbis–Bettmann)

Chapter 17

Absolute Power— The King and Mr. Cromwell

In This Chapter

➤ Charles I tries to rule without Parliament

➤ Civil war results in the removal of the monarchy

➤ The rise of Cromwell and execution of a king

➤ The Lord Protector who rules like a monarch

In the last chapter, I described how James I's belief in the Divine Right of Kings resulted in a highly unsuccessful reign. His second son, Charles I, clearly learned nothing from his father's mistakes, and his determination to also rule solely according to his own wishes resulted in civil war, his untimely death, and the removal of the monarchy. All of which went to prove that, in an increasingly democratic society, it didn't pay to govern like an autocrat.

Nevertheless, there were other lessons to be learned, too—for example, it's often easier to destroy a system of rule than to agree on a new one. Oliver Cromwell, the self-styled "Protector" who assumed the leadership role, soon discovered this lesson to his detriment. In the end, with no one able to agree on a better alternative, a simple solution was reached: Bring back the monarchy! Whoever said that the old recipes aren't the best?

Charles I—He Did it His Way

Charles I was very much his father's son. Not only did he share James I's belief that the king knew best and so there was little need for Parliament, but he also shared one of his father's companions. Do you remember George Villiers, whom James made Duke of Buckingham and addressed as "my sweet child and wife"? Well, by the time of the elder Stuart's death, Buckingham had already transferred his affections to young Charles. In fact, he had the new king totally under his spell, which was unfortunate for Henrietta Maria, 15-year-old sister to the king of France, who married Charles just a few months after his accession in 1625.

Then again, the partnership was also unfortunate for the government and the country. Buckingham was pulling all the strings, and it was thanks to him that England found itself with a Catholic queen and engaging in disastrous battles with the Spanish (in Holland) and the French (in France). In fact, within a year of Charles coming to the throne, Parliament tried to impeach the duke, but the king simply turned around and dissolved Parliament instead. This act illustrated the pattern of his early reign, dismissing Parliament whenever it tried to intervene in his hair-brained schemes, but also turning to it in times of crisis, particularly financial crisis.

In 1628, shortly after the Duke of Buckingham had been conveniently assassinated, Charles called Parliament to help him raise money for his overseas exploits by way of taxes. Parliament agreed to his plan, but in return he had to accept the Petition of Right, a declaration that not only rejected the Divine Right of Kings but also asserted Parliament's authority over the monarch. Under this Petition, it was illegal for the sovereign to force civilians to provide accommodation for his troops (a favorite way of saving money), to use military force during peacetime, or to tax and imprison people in order to satisfy his own political ends.

A Right Royal Tale

Under the terms of her marriage to Charles I, Henrietta Maria was permitted to continue her Catholic worship while raising their children until the age of 13. Such terms, however, were in direct contravention of an agreement between king and Parliament, and when the details leaked out there was widespread suspicion. In no way would the country tolerate Charles' successor being raised as a Catholic. Within a year of the queen arriving at court with her entourage, the king had dispatched her bishop, 29 priests, and 410 attendants back to France. Nevertheless, after Buckingham's death, she would be her husband's closest ally, forever encouraging him to rule without Parliament. They would have nine children together.

Charles reluctantly agreed to the Petition of Right but then went and broke the rules. Parliament therefore refused to supply him with the funds he needed, and he in turned dissolved Parliament and set about ruling without it—for the next *11 years!* And what a disaster. Without the necessary funds, he couldn't support an army that would do England justice abroad, while at home he imposed heavy taxes on upper-class landowners and businessmen. This meant the hapless king was alienating the very people he should have been taking care of, yet he still wasn't bringing in enough money to support an army.

Should there be a rebellion, then, he probably wouldn't have the means with which to defend himself. Remember, however, that we're dealing with Brits here, not hotheaded Latins who'll cry "Revolution!" at the drop of a hat. In other words, the citizens in his kingdom were relatively cool, calm, and collected individuals who would much sooner have a really good moan about their plight than take to the streets to do something about it. Without Parliament, they didn't even have any representation, so Charles was basically able to get away with his unfair and unlawful rule…unless you accept that he was the law.

At the same time, having squeezed the people economically and politically, the king also sought to eradicate their means of religious and spiritual expression. With the monarch's blessing, the traditionalist Archbishop Laud waged war on the Puritans, expelling all moderate clergymen from Anglican churches and outlawing any religious meetings that didn't have the approval of the hand-picked church authorities. The strictest rituals now had to be adhered to, and the net result was that a growing number of Puritans uprooted and moved to the New World. Meanwhile, those who remained in England started to combine their religious and political grievances into a single, cohesive form. In short, they hated Charles I and wanted to see him overthrown. However, it was their neighbors "north of the border" who were more accustomed to feisty rebellions.

In 1637, Charles and Archbishop Laud tried to force the *Book of Common Prayer* on the Scots, thus replacing the traditional Presbyterian form of service with the Anglican one. That was like waving the red rag at the bull. The Scots rose up and swore their allegiance to a National Covenant defending their form of religion, and, when Charles and his threadbare army marched north to enforce the king's law, they were more than ready for him. The two "Bishops' Wars" of 1639 and 1640 resulted in defeat for the English and bankruptcy for the king.

After 11 years, Charles decided that maybe it was time to call another Parliament. He needed money to flatten those stubborn Scots (who, it might have shocked him to recall, were his own subjects), but Parliament's attitude was "Why should we help you when you're not doing anything to help the English?" Fair enough. The *Short Parliament* was quickly dissolved. Charles had gone it alone before and he was perfectly capable of doing so again. Or so he thought.

> **Palace Parlance**
> The **Short Parliament** was called by Charles I in April 1640 when he needed supplies for his battles with the Scots. Parliament refused to comply, so the king dissolved it within three weeks.

The Scots were now pouring over the border and not only claiming their right to remain Presbyterian, but also demanding a huge amount of money in order to remove themselves. All sides were closing in on the king. However, the great irony of the situation was that this latest piece of Scottish opposition would soon have the English at each other's throats.

Cavaliers, Roundheads, and Civil War

Charles' back was against the wall. With no money to stave off the Scots and bitter enmity toward him from both sides of the border, his only option was to call yet another Parliament. This must have been like torture to Charles, not only because it flew in the face of the Divine Right of Kings, but also because he knew that going cap-in-hand to Parliament severely diminished his own power. He'd always had to make heavy compromises in return for some much-needed funds; this time he'd be a sitting target.

You've just read about the Short Parliament. In October 1640, Short Parliament was followed by, yes, the Long Parliament, so-called because it would last in one form or another for the next 20 years. That, however, would be just about the only thing that would last. Led by the Puritans in general and John Pym in particular, the House of Commons proceeded to systematically strip the king of his powers. To start, it dealt with his two main ministers, sending Archbishop Laud to the Tower and the even more powerful Earl of Strafford to the chopping block. Then, after steps had been taken to ensure that Parliament would meet regularly, some drastic measures were enforced. The Court of Star Chamber, revived by Henry VII as a means of providing fair hearings for all but used by Charles I to prosecute anyone who opposed him, was abolished along with the Court of High Commission. The illegal taxes he'd imposed were also abolished.

Palace Parlance
Roundheads was the nickname given to the mostly Puritan Parliamentarians who sported cropped hair at the time of the Long Parliament. Their coifs distinguished them from the king's swaggering, longhaired courtiers, who were dubbed **Cavaliers**.

Up to this point, there was virtually unanimous agreement in Parliament, but then, buoyed by their success, Pym and his followers got a little carried away. They threatened to get rid of all church bishops because of their Catholic leanings and tried to claim powers over the army and the king that would have amounted to the Divine Right of Parliament. In so doing, these Puritans were now casting themselves in the role of religious fanatics and making traditional Anglicans look moderate. England's ruling class started to divide down the middle. On one side were the Puritans and other Parliamentarians who grouped themselves into *Roundheads* and opposed the king, and on the other side were the royalists and religious moderates known as *Cavaliers*. Throughout the land, feelings were running high and war was in the offing.

In January 1642, Charles tried to arrest five Members of Parliament (hereafter referred to as MPs) whom he'd identified as leading opponents. Among them was John Pym, and, even though the attempt failed, the writing was now firmly on the wall. The

House of Commons, which consisted mainly of Roundheads, took immediate—and unconstitutional—measures to raise an armed force. This in turn prompted the king to flee London with the Cavaliers who made up most of the House of Lords and part of the Commons. They set up base in Nottingham, and throughout the summer both sides girded themselves for battle. It wasn't long in coming.

With a superior army and the cavalry command of Charles' German nephew, Prince Rupert, the royalists defeated the Parliamentary force at Edge Hill in 1642 and then Chalgrove Field the following year. However, the Parliamentarians had a couple of aces up their sleeve. One was the support of wealthy townspeople and businessmen who, angry at Charles' autocratic taxation schemes, now enabled Parliament to spend more money on its army than the king could spend on his. The other was a military genius from Huntingdon named Oliver Cromwell.

> **Hear Ye, Hear Ye**
> "I will rather choose to wear a crown of thorns with my Savior than to exchange that of gold, which is due to me, for one of lead."
> —*Charles I, holding firm in his beliefs, January 10, 1642*

Oliver Cromwell and the Bad King on the Block

Born in 1599, Oliver Cromwell came from a fairly comfortable family background and was an impassioned Puritan by the time he entered Parliament in 1628. There his passionate speeches made a considerable impression on his fellow MPs, and, even though he'd never had any military experience, when Civil War broke out in 1642 he threw himself into the front line of battle with typical enthusiasm.

Guided, as he saw it, by God's will, Cromwell led a cavalry force and, thanks to his sharp and disciplined mind, played a major role in the Parliamentary army's first victory over the royalists. That was at Marston Moor in 1644, and it proved to be a turning point in the war.

The following year, taking over from overly conservative generals, Cromwell formed the New Model Army, comprising a 15,000-strong troop of well-armed, highly trained, and extremely fervent Protestants ("Independents"). Prince Rupert's Cavaliers were no match for this army. Half the size of the New Model Army, the royalists put up a spirited fight at Naseby, but in the end they were soundly defeated by the force led by Cromwell and Thomas Fairfax. Then the king did a very stupid thing. Suddenly rediscovering his roots, he rushed north and surrendered to his "allies," the Scots. Now, maybe he'd forgotten his history with the Scots or perhaps he was hoping to win them over, but the Scots certainly weren't his allies, and they promptly handed their dastardly King to Parliament.

Charles subsequently escaped, only to be recaptured and imprisoned on the Isle of Wight in 1647. Still, most people really didn't want to get rid of the monarchy. For better or for worse, it was part of the national fabric, although which kind of fabric, I really don't want to say. The question was, could this king be trusted? He'd reneged on his agreements so many times in the past and now he was still extremely slippery in his negotiations with Parliament. This, of course, was partly due to Charles' unflinching belief in the absolute rule of the monarch, but it was also fuelled by his interest in seeing how another situation would resolve itself. You see, shortly after his surrender, the civil war had flared up all over again, except that this time the sides weren't quite the same. Instead, victors were fighting victors, with the losers joining in for good measure.

So, how did that ridiculous mess arise? Well, back in 1645 Parliament had won the Scots firmly over to its side by agreeing to make the English Church Presbyterian. Hey, Protestant, Presbyterian, what was the difference? Actually, one was English and the other was Scottish, but, now that they were friends, who cared? Cromwell's New Model Army, *that's* who cared! Remember, this army consisted of fervent Protestants who wanted religious freedom, not a state-run church. Therefore, when the Presbyterian Parliament decided to persecute the "Independents" and announced that it would also be disbanding the New Model Army and withholding its back pay, the Civil War Part 2 started up.

Now it was the Independents versus the Parliamentary Presbyterians, the Scots, and, curiously, the royalists. Talk about losers! Parliament had also started persecuting Anglicans, yet although the royalists were angered by this persecution, they still chose to fight on Parliament's side. The Independents had been the deciding factor in the Civil War Part 1, so there are no prizes for guessing who won Part 2. In 1648 the Scots were routed at Preston in northern England, and by December of that year, Cromwell and his cronies had purged Parliament of the Presbyterian MPs. The result was a "Rump Parliament," consisting of the more trustworthy 53 members who remained.

Meanwhile, clearly less than trustworthy was Charles I. While the Independents had been fighting for their freedom, he'd been conspiring on the side of his Scottish "allies." This would prove to be the last of his less-than-intelligent decisions. Like his grandmother, Mary, Queen of Scots, he'd obviously never stop stirring up trouble and plotting a comeback, so, in the view of those who now held power, he was better off dead.

Between January 20 and 27 of 1649, about 50 MPs tried the monarch for waging war against Parliament and his kingdom. The verdict and sentence were never in any doubt, but to the end Charles refused to recognize the trial's legality, portraying Oliver Cromwell as a murderer and himself as a martyr. He was executed on the morning of January 30.

This is what can happen when you wage war on your kingdom. Charles I learns the hard way. (Picture courtesy of Corbis-Bettmann)

Between Reigns: Republic and Protectorate

In 1650, and again in 1651, Scots royalists were defeated at Dunbar and then Worcester (pronounced "Wooster"), and Cromwell simply made it clear that toleration of other Protestant sects was obligatory. (So, apparently, was persecution of Catholics.) However, at that Worcester confrontation, those supporting the cause of Charles II were led by…Charles II. Escaping the clutches of the victors, he immediately decided to take a trip abroad.

In the meantime, while England was waging a successful war against its chief international trade rival, Holland, all was not well with the English republic. The Rump Parliament wasn't being nearly as cooperative as Cromwell had hoped, so in 1653 he abolished it and

On Her Majesty's Service

Oliver Cromwell was originally buried at Westminster Abbey. When the monarchy was restored in 1660, however, his body was exhumed, hung on gallows, and decapitated. His head was then stuck on a pole outside Westminster Hall, where it remained for 20 years until it blew down in a gale. If you wish to visit Cromwell's final resting place, the body's at Tyburn and the head is in Cambridge.

introduced a new constitution. England was now a Protectorate and Oliver Cromwell was its lord protector. The following year a new Parliament was very carefully selected to facilitate legislation, and all in all it was just a new form of the same old dictatorship. (Free elections were still way off in the future.) Before long, however, there were further disagreements, so the first Protectorate Parliament was dissolved, to be succeeded by two others in the years leading up to Cromwell's death.

There's no pleasing some people—Oliver Cromwell, Lord Protector of England, in a less-than-pleasant mood. (Picture courtesy of Corbis-Bettmann)

During that time, he would refuse Parliament's offer to become king—that's what he was anyway, bar the title—and wage another highly successful war against the Spanish, capturing Jamaica and once again improving England's standing in Europe. Yet, even though the country's economic affairs had been vastly improved, its people were growing increasingly frustrated with an administration that was just as oppressive as that of the deposed monarchy. When Oliver Cromwell died at age 59 in 1658, the role of lord protector was passed on to his son, Richard, yet it soon became clear that Richard was far too weak to follow in his father's footsteps.

It was 1660 and Charles II was residing in Holland. Had it been the modern day, he would have been waiting for the phone to ring.

The Least You Need to Know

➤ Charles I didn't learn from the mistakes of his father, James I, and insisted on ruling according to the Divine Right of Kings.

➤ In 1642, England was plunged into Civil War between the king and Parliament. Charles surrendered in 1646 and was executed three years later.

➤ The deciding factor in the Civil War was Oliver Cromwell's New Model Army, a highly trained force comprised of Protestant extremists.

➤ Between 1649 and 1658, under the rule of Oliver Cromwell, England became first a republic and then a Protectorate.

Chapter 18

Come Back, All Is Forgiven: Return of the Monarchy

In This Chapter

➤ Charles II initially bends to Parliament's rules

➤ Treacherous schemes and dirty deals

➤ Religious conflicts and abdication for James II

➤ A husband-and-wife team takes over the English throne

The monarchy returned in 1660, but the wide-ranging powers that it had once enjoyed didn't. Charles II initially had to work with Parliament, but gradually this craftiest of English kings found a variety of ways in which to do precisely as he pleased. I'll tell you about some of the sexual escapades and cutthroat transactions of the "Merry Monarch" in this chapter, and you'll surely appreciate just how ingenious Charles was when comparing him to his brother, James II.

Like Charles' deeply religious Stuart predecessors, James didn't know the meaning of terms such as "compromise" or "give-and-take." This in turn led not only to his overthrow and replacement by a Dutchman and his English wife, but also to constitutional changes that finally placed the main power tools in the hands of Parliament rather than the monarchy. Yes, future sovereigns would have much for which to thank the Stuarts.

Charles II Plays by the Rules

On May 29, 1660 Charles II ascended to the throne that had technically been his since the execution of his father, Charles I, back in 1649. A lot of water had run under the bridge during those 11 years. The uncrowned king had been in exile and seen several unsuccessful attempts to overthrow the rule of Oliver Cromwell. The nation, on the other hand, hadn't fared any better as a republic or Protectorate than as a kingdom. Now there would have to be some give and take on both sides.

In return for assuming what he certainly considered to be his rightful place as monarch, Charles II agreed to limitations in his power while vowing to summon Parliament regularly. Just as importantly, he wouldn't levy taxes or institute religious changes without Parliament's approval. At least, that's what he said. As to whether or not he would actually keep those promises; well, you be the judge.

Hear Ye, Hear Ye

"Here lies our sovereign Lord the King, Whose word no man relies on; Who never said a foolish thing, And never did a wise one."

—*Lord Rochester, when asked by Charles II to write his epitaph*

To start with, let me make something perfectly clear. Charles was a Catholic and he believed in the absolute power of the monarchy—he simply didn't let on that this was his belief. He knew the elected Parliament he had to deal with comprised mostly of Anglicans and the landed gentry, so for much of his reign this crafty, conniving monarch kept his views to himself. All the while, however, he was conspiring and cutting deals behind Parliament's back in order to realize his own ends with regard to personal power and a Catholic succession.

In 1661 Parliament passed the Corporation Act, which banned all Non-Conformists to the Anglican faith from holding posts in municipal government. Then, in 1662, the Act of Uniformity presented Puritans with an ultimatum to either accept the doctrines of the Church of England or face expulsion. (Two thousand Puritan clergymen were expelled as a result.) Two years later, the Conventicle Act decreed that anyone who attended Non-Conformist services was liable to be imprisoned or deported. As you can imagine, Charles II was none too pleased with this form of persecution, yet for now he thought it best to keep a sealed mouth on the subject. Besides, he had other, far more pleasurable activities to attend to.

In 1662 Charles had married Catherine of Braganza, daughter to the king of Portugal, and gained not only a wife but also a 300,000 pound dowry together with the naval bases of Tangier and Bombay. In spite of this attractive package, however, the "Merry Monarch," as he came to be known, was rarely sticking to his husbandly duties. Instead, he was off gallivanting with his steady stream of mistresses. At least 13 mistresses have been accounted for, along with 14 illegitimate children. Today, a number of England's nobles are descended from these offspring. Princess Diana was one of them.

Still, although Charles loved bed-hopping from one good-time girl to the other and often even kept two or more company at the same time, he knew better than to let them encroach on or influence the way in which he ruled. Gifts and huge sums of money were lavished on favorites such as Nell Gwynne and Lucy Walters, yet the king always ensured that while they could toy with his physical charms they couldn't tamper with his mind.

The Merry Monarch, Charles II, devoted his life to the pursuit of pleasure. (Picture courtesy of Corbis-Bettmann)

In June 1665, the bubonic plague hit London, wiping out more than 100,000 people in just three months. Then, on September 2, 1666, a fire that broke out in a central London bakery spread rapidly among the many wooden properties, and within three days four-fifths of the city had been destroyed. That accounted for more than 13,000 houses and public buildings. Unbelievably, fewer than a dozen people actually died. The same, fortunately, couldn't be said for any plague-carrying rats that had still been doing the rounds, yet right there in the thick of things when the flames were at their height was none other than the dashing sovereign.

Charles and his brother James both joined in the desperate effort to douse the fire, including helping to block it by pulling down buildings in its path. This kind of selfless courage, documented at length by contemporary observers such as the famous diarist Samuel Pepys (pronounced "Peeps"), gained the king much popularity among many people. To others, however, he was less than a hero. Those Puritans who blamed him for the way in which Parliament persecuted them also disapproved of the Merry Monarch's well-known philandering and they saw the Great Plague and the Great Fire as God's punishment for the corruption and debauchery at court.

That, of course, was the corruption and debauchery that they knew about. What they weren't so aware of, however, was the double-dealing that the king was doing behind not only their back, but also Parliament's back.

Grand Deception by the Closet Catholic

In 1670, Charles signed the secret Treaty of Dover with King Louis XIV of France, promising to aid the French in a preemptive strike against the Dutch, while agreeing to eventually restore the Catholic faith in England and come out about his own Catholicism. This was in return for covert financial subsidies that would enable the English king to do without parliamentary grants. Thus, like his father and grandfather before him, Charles II was carving out his own independence, only he was doing so in a far less conspicuous way.

To his mind the pact against Holland made sense. The Dutch were avid colonialists and England's main trade rivals, and following the war between the two nations during Cromwell's rule there had been a second conflict in 1665-1667. (In 1664 the English had captured New Amsterdam and renamed it New York, thereby ending Holland's colonial aspirations in North America.) Throughout his reign, Charles felt a close affiliation with the French, so it was only natural that they and the English should gang up on the Dutch in yet another trade war (commencing in 1672). Natural, that is, to Charles' way of thinking, but not to that of his fellow countrymen.

On Her Majesty's Service
During Charles II's reign there were notable changes in style and decoration thanks to the influence of his Portuguese wife, Catherine of Braganza. Her dowry included the trading rights to China, so silks, ivories, and imported porcelain became all the rage in England. If you see a Charles II artifact, it might be adorned with intricate Chinese figures.

The English, let's not forget, were hardly bosom buddies with the French, as the number of wars between the two nations would testify. During the 17th century there was, once again, rising anti-French sentiment in England. At the same time, with their own power shrinking and the dual threat of the English at sea and the French on land, the Dutch had to do some quick thinking if they didn't want to be swallowed up. Supported by the English, the French invaded Holland in 1672. By 1674, however, Holland had made peace with England and there was little that Charles could do about it. He was playing a treasonous game and had to tread very carefully.

Throughout the 1670s there were a number of rumors about Catholics planning to usurp the English throne, culminating in 1678 when an Anglican parson named Titus Oates claimed to have discovered a "Popish Plot." Supposedly, the idea here was to murder Charles II and replace him with his Catholic brother, James, courtesy of assistance from the French. Oates was lying, but of course his testimony tuned right into national fears and resulted in government-endorsed persecution of the Catholics. Many were executed and it was Charles II who signed their death warrants, even though he himself didn't believe Oates' story. That's right, as a closet Catholic he had to assume the role of an angry Protestant! Talk about a low-down double-crosser.

All of this persecution heightened tensions, and for a time a second civil war wasn't out of the question. In 1679, two distinct political parties came into force in England. The *Tories* stood by the monarchy and the authority of the Anglican Church, and the *Whigs* wanted to limit royal powers while showing tolerance toward religious dissenters.

In the elections of 1679 the Whigs scored a landslide victory, and the new Parliament wasted no time in proposing an Exclusion Bill that would prevent Charles' openly Catholic brother, James, from ascending to the throne. Being that he hadn't sired a legitimate heir (with special emphasis on the word "legitimate") Charles wouldn't stand for the bill. He immediately dissolved Parliament, but then a second Whig Parliament was duly elected and passed the Exclusion Bill, only for it to be rejected by the House of Lords, which has the right of veto after the Commons votes for something.

The Whigs were in a fury. They'd successfully managed to curb some of the king's power by way of the 1679 Habeus Corpus Act, preventing him from imprisoning people without a fair trial, but now they could see that he was as conniving as his grandfather in trying to ensure the Catholic succession. Charles, of course, denied the accusations. After all, he was just a good "Protestant" who was being loyal to his brother! However, when he refused to summon another Parliament after 1681, opting instead to rule on his own, the Whigs' worst suspicions were confirmed. He was a Stuart like all the rest.

Subsequently, in April 1683 a plan to assassinate both Charles II and his brother, James, was uncovered. Known as the Rye House Plot, because the murder was

Palace Parlance

Tory was an Irish term for a royalist outlaw, whereas **Whigs** had been Scottish Presbyterians who opposed royal power. During the late-17th century, England's chief political parties applied these names derisively to each other.

On Her Majesty's Service

Coffee houses became very fashionable during the reign of Charles II. By 1683 there were more than 2,000 of them in London alone, and while people sat in them, talking and drinking, they would often put coins in wall-boxes marked "T.I.P.S." This was "To Insure Prompt Service," something you may wish to consider next time you reward a waiter or bartender.

set to take place at Rye House in Hertfordshire (pronounced "Hartfordshear") just north of London, the intention was to replace Charles on the throne with one of his illegitimate sons, the Duke of Monmouth. The plan was foiled when the two Royals left Rye House earlier than expected, and the conspirators were betrayed and arrested. Comprising the principal Whig leaders, they were either sent into exile or, in the case of Algernon Sidney and William, Lord Russell, executed.

Hereafter, with the support of the happy Tories and a subsidy from Louis XIV of France, Charles II was able to rule virtually as he pleased. I say virtually, because the Tories, in helping to stifle any thought of an uprising in the country, drew a guarantee that he wouldn't convert England to Catholicism, and this time he was true to his word. After all, Charles' double-dealing had finally resulted in him being able to rule unopposed without Parliament, and it looked odds-on that his Catholic brother would succeed him, so why blow it?

As it turned out, Charles didn't have all that long to live. On February 6, 1685, he passed away at the age of 54. Guess what he did on his deathbed? (No, he wasn't with a woman.) That's right, he stopped breathing, and, just beforehand, he officially *converted* to Catholicism!

James II: Trying to Indulge Himself

Charles' brother did ascend to the throne in February 1685, yet his was a short reign that was doomed to failure from the start. The majority of English people didn't want a return to Catholicism and all that it would entail, and within months James II was having to fend off overthrow attempts. He had the support of the Anglican and royalist Tories, but the depleted Whigs were another matter. Some wanted to see James' Dutch nephew, William of Orange, on the throne. Married to his first cousin, Mary, William was the leading exponent of the Protestant cause in Europe. Meanwhile, another Protestant contender was Charles II's illegitimate son, the Duke of Monmouth, and, with popular support behind him, he wasted little time in making his move.

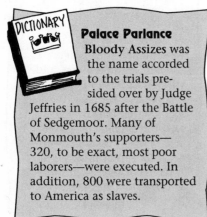

Palace Parlance
Bloody Assizes was the name accorded to the trials presided over by Judge Jeffries in 1685 after the Battle of Sedgemoor. Many of Monmouth's supporters—320, to be exact, most poor laborers—were executed. In addition, 800 were transported to America as slaves.

In June and July 1685, there were rebellions in Scotland and England designed to place Monmouth on the throne. The Scottish rebellion, led by the Earl of Argyll, was crushed and Argyll was executed. Monmouth himself led the charge at the English Battle of Sedgemoor, but, in spite of having a larger army than the king, he too was defeated, arrested, and executed as part of the *Bloody Assizes*. To date, this was the last war to be fought on British soil. (That is, if you discount the battles between soccer hooligans.) So, it was a victory to the king in the short term, but in the long run he was really helping to seal his own fate. Many people were sickened by the slaughtering of poor farmers and clothworkers who had supported Monmouth, while those who had already opposed

James II now found themselves with little choice but to get behind the campaign to install William of Orange and Mary on the throne.

At this point you might think that James would have toned down his zealous behavior and done everything in his power to unite his subjects. You'd be wrong. If nothing else, James was just another Stuart monarch who thought he had the divine right to do as he pleased. (Apparently that family never learned their lessons.) So, what did he go and do? To begin, he set up a 13,000-strong standing army at Hounslow to intimidate the nearby Londoners. At the same time, he set about ensuring that Roman Catholics gained prominent positions within the army, government institutions, and the Anglican Church. Then, in 1688, what he probably thought was an act of goodwill turned into a disaster.

The Declaration of Indulgence enabled all of James II's subjects to pursue their different religions without persecution. This meant that nonconformists to the Anglican faith would be left to worship as they pleased; the Puritans still weren't happy, however, because the document also meant that Catholics would be free from persecution! When the clergy were duly ordered to read the Declaration of Indulgence during their church services, seven bishops—including the Archbishop of Canterbury—petitioned the king against doing so. James II's response was to have them arrested and sent straight to the Tower, but, believe it or not, they were all acquitted at trial. Everyone, including the royal army, celebrated the verdict. None of this would have happened in the old days.

At this point, James must have seen the writing on the wall, yet in June 1688 he still had one last mistake to make, even though it probably dated back about nine months. After the death of his Protestant first wife, Anne Hyde, with whom he had two daughters, the king had married Mary of Modena, a Catholic. They subsequently had 10 children who all died as infants, but when it was announced around the start of 1688 that Mary was pregnant again, plenty of Protestants were concerned about her producing a Catholic son and heir. On June 10, she did produce a Catholic son and heir, also called James.

Hear Ye, Hear Ye
"Don't worry, Jamie. They'll never kill me to make you king."
—*Charles II, after his brother James had disapproved of the Merry Monarch's lack of personal security precautions*

Now, I said that James II's mistake in this regard *probably* dated back to about nine months earlier. That's because those same Protestants who had feared the birth of a Catholic heir now believed that the baby was an orphan that had been smuggled into the royal bedchamber! Among the disbelievers were the king's own daughters, Mary and Anne. Mary, the wife of William of Orange, had been first in line for the throne, and so political leaders from both the Whig and Tory parties now moved quickly to secretly invite William to take over. This behavior was high treason, but it was an appealing proposition for the Dutch leader. By uniting the Protestant powers of Holland and England he would have the resources to stave off any attacks by his archenemies the French.

On November 5, 1688, William's invasion fleet landed at Brixham in the south of England, and, with his own support hemorrhaging by the hour, James II was soon packing his bags and running for his life. At first, some over-eager captors thwarted his escape, but William had no intention of imprisoning or harming his wife's father. So, James was allowed to "escape" again, and this time he made it to France, which was ruled by his Catholic cousin, Louis XIV, and to where his wife and baby son had already fled. He would die there in 1701 at the age of 77.

An Orange Package: William and Mary

It was clear from the start that William and Mary came as a package, and so, in 1689, a freely elected Parliament made the unique concession of allowing them to be joint monarchs. What it wasn't going to allow, however, was for England to ever again be placed in the hands of power-crazed autocrats.

A Right Royal Tale

Although Mary II was deeply in love with her fairly cold and physically unattractive husband, William III, she had initially married him against her own wishes and wept throughout the wedding ceremony. At one point, that Merry Monarch uncle of hers, Charles II, had tried to cheer her up by cracking a joke. A number of coins had been symbolically spread out on a prayer book as William said, "With all my worldly goods I thee endow." "Gather it up and put it in your pocket while you've got the chance," Charles whispered in his niece's ear, but instead of giving her a fit of the giggles it merely caused her to blubber even harder.

The husband-and-wife team therefore had to accept something known as the Declaration of Rights, which Parliament had drawn up and would incorporate into the Bill of Rights later that year. In a nutshell, while proclaiming that James II's "escape" from England amounted to his abdication, the Bill decreed that the monarch couldn't suspend or dispense with laws, levy taxes, or maintain a standing army without Parliament's consent; that people accused of crimes couldn't be refused a jury trial or punished cruelly; that a freely elected Parliament should meet frequently and be allowed open debates; and that no Catholics could ascend to the throne.

William III and Mary II agreed to the terms and thus started the "Glorious Revolution." The monarchy was now constitutional, meaning that the sovereign was chosen by Parliament instead of being "divinely ordained," and so the power struggles between the two factions were largely at an end. Nevertheless some contentious issues remained, such as Parliament's control of the purse strings, how much influence the monarch's ministers should have on Parliament, and what part, if any, Parliament should play in the selection of said royal ministers.

In 1689 the Toleration Act granted freedom of worship to all religious denominations *except* Catholics and Unitarians. As things turned out, the government would no longer persecute, imprison, or deport any of these people on religious grounds. Yet, not too surprisingly, the Catholics were more than a little miffed with the Act, and in Ireland this served to heighten the sharp divisions that already existed.

Ever since Henry VIII had declared himself king of the "Emerald Isle" in 1541, the Anglican monarchs had ensured the settlement there of English Protestants. This was mainly in the province of Ulster (in what is today Northern Ireland), and it caused a lot of resentment among the nation's mostly Catholic population. That, however, was nothing compared to how they felt when Oliver Cromwell handed over much of their land to the Protestants. James II intended to right that wrong, and so when he was forced to "escape" England, the Irish Catholics quickly rose in his support. James responded by sailing over from France to lead the rebellion and, he hoped, invade England with a combined Irish and French force.

In 1689, after about 30,000 Irish Protestants had taken refuge within the walled confines of Londonderry, James' forces laid siege to the city. The starving population held out until English help arrived, at which point the ex-monarch and his army moved south to the banks of the River Boyne near Drogheda, just north of Dublin. William III knew that Louis XIV would love to get a foothold in Ireland and use it as a stepping stone over to England, so the Battle of the Boyne, fought on July 1, 1690, was of major importance. William's superior forces won the day, and the fate of Ireland was sealed.

Hereafter, Protestants would dominate the Irish Parliament and the Catholics would be second-class citizens in their own land. It was an injustice fueled by England's fear that its near neighbor could align itself to aggressive foreign causes. Suppression, subordination, and exploitation would eliminate that threat. (In some ways there are parallels between England's attitude toward Ireland and that of the United States toward Cuba.) Meanwhile, even though Scotland was somewhat easier to win over, James still had his supporters there. Such clans were given the opportunity to make peace with William III and swear their allegiance to him, but some were slow to come around and in February 1692, one in particular paid a terrible price. The Macdonalds of Glencoe were virtually wiped out when the rival Campbell clan attacked them on the king's orders. In all, 38 Macdonalds died, and the Massacre of Glencoe would go down in infamy.

Hear Ye, Hear Ye
"Madam, your countrymen have run away."
—*James II to Lady Tyrconnel after he had lost the Battle of the Boyne and fled to the safety of Dublin, prompting her to reply: "Sire, Your Majesty seems to have won the race."*

These were the battles close to home, while abroad there was a totally inconsequential conflict with France between 1691 and 1697. This war was followed by the War of Spanish Succession in 1701, which was caused by Charles II of Spain, who had died the previous year without leaving an heir. Greedy Louis XIV of France considered the Spanish throne up for grabs, so his grandson Philip quickly staked his claim to it. This in turn prompted an alliance between England, Holland, and Austria to prevent a union of the French and Spanish crowns, yet it couldn't stop hostilities from breaking out. The war would lurch from one bloody battle to the next and well into the next chapter of this book, by which time both William III and Mary II would be long gone.

Mary died of smallpox on December 28, 1694, at the age of 32. Thereafter the crown was solely in William's hands, and, being that he had no children, Mary's sister Anne was next in line to the throne. All of Anne's children had died young, however, so there was growing concern that if she were to die prematurely, James II's son James "The Pretender" (more of whom later on) would seize the throne. The last thing Parliament wanted was another Catholic monarch, and it was Parliament that now reserved the right to choose the sovereign. Consequently, in 1701 the Act of Settlement was passed, decreeing that in the event of Anne's death the succession would pass to her nearest Protestant relative, the Electress Sophia of Hanover.

This was a touchy issue. The idea of having a German on the English throne appealed to no one, and besides, what about the principle of succession being based on hereditary right? The 1689 Bill of Rights had decreed that no Catholic could become king or queen, yet despite that decree, or perhaps because of it, some people supported the claim of James III. The whole messy matter would not find a quick resolution.

On March 8, 1702, William III died after being thrown from a horse while hunting at Hampton Court. So began the reign of Queen Anne.

The Least You Need to Know

➤ Charles II was a Catholic who pretended to be Protestant in order to hold onto the throne.

➤ The Great Fire of London followed the Great Plague of 1665 the very next year.

➤ The late 17th century saw the emergence of English political parties, the Tories, who supported the monarchy and the Anglican Church, and the Whigs, who wanted to limit royal power and show tolerance to religious nonconformists.

➤ In 1689, the Bill of Rights transferred power from the monarchy to Parliament.

➤ On July 1, 1690, the Battle of the Boyne sealed the fate of Irish Catholics as well as that of James II.

➤ The 1701 Act of Settlement provided for the succession to pass to the House of Hanover in the event of Anne Stuart's death.

Power Plays and Empire Building

Good Queen Anne is how she was known, and her 12-year reign proved to be extremely good for her country. An amiable woman, Anne mixed patriotism with innate common sense to not only repair much of the damage done by her Stuart ancestors, but also help England become one of the richest and most powerful nations on earth. Unfortunately, however, the queen's private life wasn't quite so successful. Devoted to her dim-witted husband, Prince George of Denmark, Anne was pregnant 18 times, suffered 13 still-births, and lost her remaining children during their youth. She also suffered from weight problems, went through agony with gout, had a falling-out with her closest friends, and by the end of her life was an emotional and physical mess.

In this chapter I describe how trading opportunities and territorial gains laid the foundations for the British Empire, while closer to home England and Scotland were finally united under one Parliament. This was also the era when party politics came into their own, with the Tories and Whigs squabbling in a manner that we've now come to expect from those in public office. For her part, Anne got caught up in a spot of Palace intrigue that her ministers didn't necessarily expect from their queen. Yet, all in all, I think you can now see the royals' transition into something approaching normal human beings, compared to the thugs and murderers of a few chapters ago.

Anne and the War of the Spanish Succession

Queen Anne inherited from her brother-in-law, William of Orange, a situation that almost amounted to a world war. The Spanish Empire that was up for grabs then included what is now known as Belgium, as well as large parts of Italy, North America, and South America. The prospect of Louis XIV's Catholic grandson, Philip, controlling that much territory in addition, eventually, to France itself, was frightening to contemplate, so England and Holland sided with the other claimant to the Spanish throne, Archduke Charles of Austria. A couple of months after Anne's March 1702 accession, England declared war on France. At this point, John Churchill, the 1st Duke of Marlborough and a direct ancestor of Britain's legendary World War II prime minister Sir Winston Churchill, made a name for himself as one of England's greatest soldiers.

By the time the Duke was made commander-in-chief of the allied forces against Louis XIV, he had already distinguished himself in a number of wars. The armies under his control were small, neither the Dutch nor Austrian generals were easy to get along with, and initially there was much maneuvering but little progress. Then, in 1704, Churchill's military genius manifested itself in the form of a stunning victory at the Battle of Blenheim. The French had been heading across the Rhine toward the Austrian capital of Vienna when the Duke engineered a brilliant interception at Blenheim (pronounced "Blen-em") on the River Danube. A total of 28 French regiments surrendered, and their commander-in-chief, Tallard, was taken prisoner.

Back in England the victory was hailed as the nation's greatest since Henry V thrashed the French at the Battle of Agincourt. In gratitude, Queen Anne gave Marlborough the royal estate at Woodstock, and Parliament voted to build him and his wife the appropriately named Blenheim Palace. For the first time, but not the last, a Churchill was a national hero. Between 1704 and 1709, Churchill masterminded another three famous victories in the War of the Spanish Succession: The French were kicked out of Holland in the Battle of Ramillies (1706); the French again suffered heavy losses in the Battle of Oudenarde (1708); and both English and French blood was spilled copiously at the Battle of Malplaquet (1709).

Hear Ye, Hear Ye
"It means I'm growing old when ladies declare war on me."
—*King Louis XIV of France, May 4, 1702*

On Her Majesty's Service
Blenheim Palace is well worth a visit. Designed by John Vanburgh, erected between 1705 and 1722, and landscaped in the mid-18th century by Capability Brown, the Palace near Oxford is the nation's largest private home. It was while attending a party at Blenheim that Winston Churchill's mother gave birth, in a closet, to the future prime minister. He's now buried in nearby Bladon.

Still, although the French were on their knees, they still wouldn't give up; for John Churchill, their perseverance was very convenient. At the height of his powers, he was in great demand while the war continued. Contrary to what he thought, however, he wasn't indispensable. In 1713 the Treaty of Utrecht between England and France ended the War of the Spanish Succession and secured Gibraltar, Newfoundland, Nova Scotia, the Hudson Bay territory, and trading rights in Spanish America for Queen Anne's realm. Churchill, however, was no longer around, having been dismissed in disgrace two years earlier. The official line was that the 1st Duke of Marlborough had been misappropriating military funds for his own use, but in truth trouble had been brewing behind the scenes for quite some time in the lead-up to this event. It's a story that can't be properly told in a couple of sentences, for it involves Anne's sexual leanings, broken friendships, and political backstabbing. In fact, it'll take the next couple of sections to explain it fully.

The Marlboroughs Push Their Luck

As a couple, John and Sarah Churchill were well suited. Intelligent and overtly ambitious, they operated as a team when making their power plays at the court of Queen Anne.

Before marrying Churchill in 1677, Sarah Jennings had been a childhood friend of Anne's. Four years older than the Princess and far more attractive, Sarah exerted a great deal of influence over Anne from the start, and this influence continued well into adulthood and into Anne's ascension. In fact, it was often suggested that the Churchills, who became the Duke and Duchess of Marlborough in the year of Anne's ascension, were the ones who were running the country, and this belief was supported by the derisory manner in which Sarah sometimes talked to the queen. Previous sovereigns would have had Sarah beheaded for such behavior, but Anne almost encouraged it, even suggesting that she and Sarah should address each other with play-names in all written correspondence to stress the equality of their relationship. So it was that the Duchess of Marlborough was Mrs. Freeman and the queen was Mrs. Morley!

Maybe it would be wise to point out at this stage that some psychiatrists have indicated Anne suffered from porphyria. This is the "family illness" that probably afflicted James I and George III, producing symptoms of madness that were more likely delirium. Whatever the truth of that theory, Anne's behavior in relation to "Mrs. Morley" was childlike—or at least odd. Nevertheless, when Sarah got a little too pushy for her liking, the queen stood her ground.

The two women were diametrically opposed in terms of their political views. As a devout Protestant, Anne favored the Tories, whereas Sarah was a staunch supporter of the Whigs. Their differences were fine, except that Sarah wouldn't leave the subject alone, haranguing Anne for being ungrateful to the political leaders whom she owed everything while asserting that

Palace Parlance
Jacobites were the people who supported the claim to the English throne of James II, as well as that of his son and grandson. The word derives from *Jacobus*, which is Latin for *James*.

all Tories were *Jacobites*. This needling soon placed considerable strain on the relationship, so to lighten the atmosphere Anne showered the Marlboroughs with gifts and numerous other perks.

Obviously Anne was more concerned than the Churchills about keeping the friendship alive, yet perhaps the Marlboroughs were just playing a cruel and manipulative game to get what they wanted. No matter what the queen did for them, it was never enough. When John Churchill was made supreme commander of the armed forces, the couple claimed the appointment should be for life. Then, when he was given a colossal pension of 50,000 pounds per year, they insisted this should also be paid to all subsequent generations of Churchills. Soon, they were also meddling in affairs of state.

In 1706, the Marlboroughs demanded that Anne replace her Tory Secretary of State, Sir Charles Hedges, with their Whig son-in-law, Sunderland. This time, however, the queen refused, citing that it was her right to hire and fire as she chose, regardless of her Ministers' political allegiances. I'm sorry to reveal that ultimately Sunderland was subsequently installed as Secretary of State.

This kind of concession encouraged Sarah Churchill to view Anne as a soft touch and treat her badly. In August 1708, following England's victory at the Battle of Oudenarde, the two women had a row in the royal carriage as they were traveling to a Thanksgiving service at St. Paul's Cathedral. "Be quiet!" Sarah ordered the queen, before following up with a letter in which she stated, "Your Majesty chose a very wrong day to mortify me." Can you imagine what would have happened if these words had been spoken to Bloody Mary?

Party Poopers: Tories and Whigs

Sidney Godolphin, a Whig whom the queen had made Lord High Treasurer in 1702 as one of her many concessions to the Churchills, was a loyal supporter of the Duke of Marlborough. Both men wanted to strengthen the Whigs' representation in the House of Commons, and so as part of their ongoing plan they approached Anne in 1704 and suggested that she replace Nottingham, a High Tory, as Secretary of State. The man who they wanted to take over was a solid Whig named Robert Harley. Anne naturally complied. However, things wouldn't all be going the Whigs' way.

As the public grew tired with the incessant wars against France, support began to swing away from the Whigs towards the Tories. The queen's pro-Tory views reflected the general mood, as did those of Robert Harley, who himself became a Tory moderate and a close political ally to the monarch. The Marlboroughs and Sidney Godolphin (whose name makes him sound like a Miami football fan) weren't happy.

In the meantime, Sarah Churchill had wanted Anne to secure a job for a poor cousin of hers by the name of Abigail Hill. Well, being that Abigail was neither a man nor a politician, she certainly wasn't able to enter Parliament. Instead, Abigail was made a royal bedchamber woman. Soon she and the queen were as thick as thieves, and as Anne's friendship with the Duchess of Marlborough turned sour, she increasingly turned to Abigail for a little warmth and understanding.

Plump and prone to severe attacks of gout, Queen Anne had a taste for elegant, well-proportioned furniture. (Picture courtesy of Corbis-Bettmann)

Sarah had probably been counting on Abigail to do some spying on her behalf, but she hadn't counted on her cousin and the queen becoming close buddies. So, when Sarah subsequently discovered that Abigail had secretly married someone with the romantic name of Mr. Masham and that Anne had known about the union, she flew into a rage. Sarah accused the queen of betraying their friendship, and, sensing that there was "some mystery in the affair," decided to do a little detective work.

Within a week, she'd come up with the answer. For some time now, whenever Anne's lazy, drunken husband, Prince George of Denmark, fell asleep, the queen and her bedchamber girl would spend a couple of hours bonding with each other!

In the meantime, Anne had started to play hardball with the Marlboroughs. Aware that she was more in touch with public opinion than they were, she stopped giving in to their demands. They, in turn, couldn't figure where this soft touch of a woman was suddenly getting courage. Then the duke and Sidney Godolphin came up with the answer: Robert

197

Harley had been influencing the monarch behind the scenes. In February 1708, Marlborough and Godolphin both offered their resignations rather than work with "so vile a creature," but they soon changed their minds when Anne decided that it would be easier for now to just dismiss Harley.

The queen, you see, had been pushed to her limit, but while she was intent on getting rid of the Churchills she was also aware of the duke's vital role in the War of the Spanish Succession. Peace, therefore, was one answer. Another was to hold her nerve as the Whigs' public support continued to crumble and, taking strength from the continuing support of Robert Harley, start to weed out the troublemakers. In 1710, Marlborough's son-in-law, Sunderland, and his right-hand man, Godolphin, were the first to go.

A Right Royal Tale

Queen Anne's husband, Prince George of Denmark, cut a rather pathetic figure. Never playing a significant part in affairs of state, he apparently occupied himself by making model ships, gorging himself, and drinking like a fish. Quickly turning to fat, he became a popular butt of Court jokes. An erstwhile admirer of the queen suggested that George's asthma attacks were just a means of ensuring that he wasn't mistaken for dead and taken away for burial. In addition, her uncle, Charles II, quipped, "I have tried him drunk and I have tried him sober, but there is nothing in him." In 1708, Anne personally cared for George on his deathbed.

That same year the rising tide of anti-war sentiment resulted in a landslide Tory victory in the general election. Then, at the start of 1711 and following some unpleasant scenes, Sarah Churchill was dismissed from all her public office positions. Still the duke didn't budge. He and his supporters were holding out hope that he could deliver a knockout blow to the French. At the same time, aware that the allies didn't have the strength to place Austria's Archduke Charles on the Spanish throne, Robert Harley was negotiating a peace treaty with the French. This treaty amounted to Prince Philip ruling Spain and the Indies in return for a guarantee that the French and Spanish thrones would never unite. All the while, Harley was also spreading the word about Churchill having embezzled army funds.

In December 1711 the peace proposal was rejected by the House of Lords. Three weeks later, the Duke of Marlborough was dismissed on embezzlement charges. At this point, Harley turned to the queen and convinced her that, in order to get the peace treaty approved by the House of Lords, she would need to create 12 new peers who were sympathetic to the Tory cause. She did so and, after protracted negotiations at Utrecht, the pact was signed. Unfortunately, the creation of peers for strictly party purposes represented a significant weakening of the royal prerogative.

England, Scotland, and the Act of Union

Although the 1603 accession to the English throne of James I had effectively united the thrones of England and Scotland, both countries still had separate parliaments and their own religious and legal systems when Anne became queen. As you've already seen, these close neighbors were used to being the best of enemies down the centuries, and since the Glorious Revolution of the House of Orange, the relationship had once again slithered into the gutter. Episodes such as the massacre of Glencoe hadn't helped matters. Still, while the Scots knew that they could no longer match England's resources on the battlefield, the English had enough problems dealing with Louis XIV of France.

Consequently, William III proposed uniting the kingdoms in his last message to Parliament, and Queen Anne's first message had echoed this sentiment. Negotiations to that end broke down, however, and in 1704 the Scottish Parliament passed an Act of Security decreeing that, on Anne's death, the Scots wouldn't choose the same monarch unless he or she agreed to recognize their country's total independence. In February of the following year, the English Parliament's response was the Aliens Act. This document stated that, unless by December 1705 the Scots had either accepted the succession of the House of Hanover or were negotiating for a union with England, they would be treated as aliens and, as such, all trade between the two countries would be prohibited. The Scots decided it was time to enter into talks.

April 1706 saw swift negotiations, and the upshot was that the Scottish Parliament ceased to exist and 45 of its MPs were transferred to the British House of Commons, while 16 elected peers would take their places in the Lords. There would also be a common flag, common coinage, and common monarchy, yet both countries would retain their own religious, legal, and educational systems. The same guidelines apply today.

It was on May 1, 1707, that the Act of Union unified the kingdoms of England and Scotland. For Queen Anne it was one of the major achievements of her reign. For the English and the Scots it was a marriage of convenience rather than a love match made in heaven.

Hear Ye, Hear Ye
"I believe sleep was never more welcome to a weary traveler than death was to her."
—*Queen Anne's doctor, August 1, 1714*

The Least You Need to Know

➤ The War of the Spanish Succession was fought between 1702 and 1713 and pitted the English, Dutch, and Austrians against the French.

➤ John Churchill, 1st Duke of Marlborough and a direct ancestor of legendary prime minister Sir Winston Churchill, was one of England's greatest military leaders.

➤ Queen Anne was controlled for much of her reign by the Duke and Duchess of Marlborough. The duchess was her childhood friend, Sarah.

➤ The Act of Union, which came into effect on May 1, 1707, unified the kingdoms of England and Scotland, thus creating Great Britain.

Chapter 20

A Spell of German Domination— The Hanoverians

In This Chapter

➤ Unpopular rule by indifferent George I

➤ Family feuds for George II

➤ The Jacobite rebellion of Bonnie Prince Charlie

➤ Britain builds its Empire

➤ The loss of the American colonies and victories over Napoleon during the reign of "Mad George III"

➤ The over-active love life and disastrous marriage of George IV

➤ The ineffectual reign of "Silly Billy"

After all of the trouble caused by the Stuarts, the Catholics were *persona non grata* as far as the British monarchy was concerned. The 1701 Act of Settlement had decreed that James I's Protestant granddaughter, the Electress Sophia of Hanover, would succeed Anne on the throne. The Electress died a couple of months before the British queen, however, so on August 1, 1714, Sophia's son, George Ludwig, became king.

As emphasized by this chapter, the wisdom of that decision is open to debate. For one thing, the Brits were not at all happy about having foreigners on the throne, and, for their part, the first two in the Hanover series, the Georges I and II, weren't very interested in Britain, either. Still, the same period did see the advent of the first prime minister, the onset of the Industrial Revolution, and the rapid expansion of the British Empire, only for the American colonies to be lost during the reign of the unfortunate George III.

At a time when figures such as Napoleon Bonaparte, Lord Horatio Nelson, and the Duke of Wellington all rose to prominence, I suppose the best that can be said about the Hanovers is that they improved as they went along. So did the stories, from the deranged behavior of George III to the royal romances of George IV. And, oh yes, just to break the pattern, we also have a William thrown in for good measure toward the end. He was known as "Silly Billy," but he wasn't a complete idiot.

George I: Do You Speak English?

Although not nearly as barbaric as some of his royal predecessors—he wouldn't have gotten away with it if he'd tried—George I really comes across as one of the lesser attractions among those who have ascended to the English or British throne.

George didn't have a lot going for him. For starters, he was unable to speak English and totally disinterested in Britain, the British, the arts, religion, or any intellectual studies. In addition, he was lazy, indifferent, and pretty stupid—and that was on a good day! What's more, there was no little woman around to help shape up his ideas.

George had married Sophia Dorothea in 1682. Although they couldn't stand each other from the start, they amazingly had two children together. George naturally had a number

Hear Ye, Hear Ye
"I hate all boets and bainters."
—*George I decrying poets and painters in his broken English*

of women on the side, but when his wife fell for a Swedish diplomat named Philip von Koenigsmark, he was unable to bear her unfaithfulness. The affair made headlines in Germany, so in 1694 George did the decent thing and had Koenigsmark killed. Sophia Dorothea, meanwhile, was imprisoned in Ahlden Castle, and she was still there when George I ascended to the British throne in 1714. She would remain imprisoned until her death in 1726. So much for the happy home life of Britain's first German king.

In addition, George's public role was quickly threatened by those who still wanted to see the Stuart "Pretender," James Edward, take over as monarch. In 1715, while James was in France, a Jacobite uprising took place in Scotland in his honor. The disruption was easily crushed by George I's forces, and then when James landed in Britain, another rebellion arose and was squashed in the northern English town of Preston in Lancashire. The leaders were subsequently executed and James himself set sail for France.

Thereafter, George was free to spend more time in his beloved Hanover. Charles Townshend and Robert Walpole were running the Whig government that had been elected in 1714, and, being that they could speak better English than he, the king entrusted Britain into their capable hands. The move was quite convenient for George, who hated to argue with his ministers in broken French and crumbling Latin. In 1717, however, he did argue with Charles Townshend, resulting in Townshend being dismissed from the government and Walpole resigning in sympathy. George was distraught. He admired Walpole and relied on his assistance, yet the minister wouldn't return to the government for another four years, and when he did it would be as the result of an embarrassing financial crisis.

In 1711 the South Sea Company had been set up to do trade with South America. The national debt, which amounted to just 50 million pounds, was then transferred to the company and people were invited to buy stock. Being that this get-rich-quick scheme was endorsed by the monarchy, many citizens believed it to be a sure-fire winner, which it wasn't. Initially, the world and his brother invested in the South Sea Company and as the stock climbed rapidly, those who got out fast made a killing. Others, however, didn't sell; soon they wished they had. In 1720, the "South Sea Bubble" burst and with it went the investments of countless people.

George I had to interrupt a very pleasant vacation in Hanover to return to Britain and reassure everyone that, "We're doing all we can to sort the problem out." His English wasn't good enough to competently speak the comforting words, and besides, no one was going to take any reassurances from him anyway! Enter Sir Robert Walpole. Having previously forecast that all of the speculating would lead to trouble, he'd sold his South Sea shares while the going was good. Now he set about calming down the country and the House of Commons, and in the process designed a bill that would restore public credit. It was passed by a large majority and in 1721 Walpole was appointed First Lord of the Treasury, the same post that he'd relinquished a few years earlier.

Since the reign of William and Mary, the government had been run by a "cabinet" of ministers drawn from the political party that had the most MPs in the House of Commons. The sovereign would preside over the weekly meetings of this cabinet, yet, being that George I was often away in Hanover, he generously delegated this task to Sir Robert Walpole. In effect, therefore, Walpole was the king's first minister, or, to give him a slightly grander title, prime minister. He set the standard for those to follow.

On Her Majesty's Service

As First Lord of the Treasury, Sir Robert Walpole worked from an office in Downing Street, a London cul-de-sac situated close to the Houses of Parliament. Today, the nation's chief accountant, the Chancellor of the Exchequer, resides at No.11 Downing Street, while the prime minister lives next door at No.10. Due to security precautions, the general public can no longer enter the street.

Walpole would remain in office until his resignation in 1742, by which time George I had been dead for 15 years. (He was, of course, in Hanover when he passed on.) The king had never had much time for his son and heir, George II. In fact, he hated him. But then, as you'll see, parental love wasn't a Hanoverian trait.

George II: The Last Sovereign Soldier

Okay, so having thoroughly trashed the character of Britain's first German monarch, let's see what I can do with regard to his successor! As it happens, George II did have several redeeming features. He was brave, he had kind words for his British subjects, and he didn't imprison his wife. At the same time, he was also an ugly little womanizer with a bad temper who was widely criticized for being rude, arrogant, vain, and selfish. I'm glad I got *that* off my chest.

George II was well served by both Prime Minister Walpole and Queen Caroline. For the first 12 years of the king's reign, Walpole managed to steer Britain clear of all foreign conflicts. Caroline, on the other hand, not only tolerated her husband's incessant love affairs—many of them conducted in the royal palace—but she also fed him with political ideas and watched as he made them his own. Yes, between Walpole and Caroline, the king was in good hands. Then they both deserted him.

Caroline died in 1737, and five years later Britain's first prime minister resigned. By then, Britain was at war, and at the age of 66 Sir Robert Walpole knew it was time to step down. The first conflict, known as the War of Jenkins' Ear, had broken out in 1739. In short, the scuttle was a result of the Spanish getting sick of the English contravening the Treaty of Utrecht by shipping more than mere slaves to Spanish South America. Captain Jenkins had been caught doing some contraband trade, and he lost an ear as a result. Now, if he'd have taken that punishment like a man it's possible that nothing much would have happened. But Jenkins bleated on and on about how he'd been made to suffer and soon the English were chomping at the bit to have a go at the Spanish.

Royal Rebuttal
Certainly Lady Diana Spencer was unique, but, when he was Prince of Wales, George II nearly married someone of the same name. As the granddaughter of the Duchess of Marlborough, that Lady Di was offered to George along with a 100,000 pound dowry. He gladly accepted and a date was set for the secret wedding, but when Sir Robert Walpole learned of the arrangement, all bets were off.

The War of Jenkins' Ear dragged on for two years and served to drag England into the War of the Austrian Succession in 1740. England became involved in the war because France was an ally of Spain and, in conjunction with Prussia, was attempting to overthrow the Austrian throne. England rushed to Austria's aid and, at the age of 60, King George II became the last British monarch to lead his troops into battle. That was at Dettingen in Bavaria in 1743, where the English succeeded in driving back the French. The war itself would last another five years, but following Dettingen the King returned to England a hero.

Unfortunately, when the king reached the palace, there were no happy slaps on the back for his eldest son, Frederick, Prince of Wales. Frederick was the original kid who could never get it right, and both parents despised him. In fact, on her deathbed in 1737, Queen Caroline had been consoled with the thought that she would "never see that monster again."

In the meantime, there was also plenty of trouble for George II just beyond his doorstep. The Jacobites, who had failed miserably in 1715 when trying to place James Edward Stuart on the throne, were rising again, and this time they meant business. In 1745, James was considered to be the "Old Pretender," being that his 25-year-old son, Charles Edward Stuart, had taken up the cause. The most charismatic of the Stuarts since Charles II—which was not exactly a great achievement—the "Young Pretender" left France with a handful of officers and arrived in Edinburgh in July.

Charles Edward Stuart, affectionately known as Bonnie Prince Charlie, when he was a young and sprightly 12-year-old. (Picture courtesy of Corbis-Bettmann)

Within a few weeks, a 3,000-strong army backed him. In September, "Bonnie Prince Charlie" led his men to victory over the English at Prestonpans, just east of Edinburgh. Having proclaimed his father King Edward III (a title already conferred on the Old Pretender by the Jacobite Scots in 1715), Charles now proceeded to revel in his victory and made the fatal mistake of allowing the English to regroup while assuming that numerous men from that country would rally to his cause.

The Jacobite forces didn't march south across the border until November, at which point they were met by an army of nearly 10,000 men under the command of William, Duke of

Cumberland and the second son of George II. Nicknamed "The Butcher" by the Scots, Cumberland proceeded to drive the Jacobites back into Scotland, and on April 15, 1746, Bonnie Prince Charlie and his brave but tired men suffered a resounding and decisive defeat on Culloden Moor. Of those who weren't slaughtered right there and then, the Jacobite prisoners were either shot, starved, or shipped off to America as slaves. Many of the leaders were taken to London and executed, among them 80-year-old Lord Lovat, who was the last person ever to be publicly beheaded in England. (What went on in private, as always, was another matter.)

Bonnie Prince Charlie managed to escape into the Scottish Highlands, at one point even dressing in women's clothes and adopting the name of Betty Burke. "Betty" eventually made his way to France, took to the bottle, and died broke in Rome in 1788 at the age of 68. The Jacobite cause had been dealt a death blow at the Battle of Culloden, yet for his part George II really didn't appear to be too bothered one way or the other.

A Right Royal Tale

Prince Frederick, known as Fretz in German, was reviled by George II and Queen Caroline. Once, in a show of typical motherly sentiment, Caroline exclaimed, "My God, popularity always makes me sick, but Fretz's popularity makes me vomit!" That may sound a little unkind, but consider her reasons for feeling such resentment: "Our first-born is the greatest ass, the greatest liar, the greatest canaille, and the greatest beast in the whole world, and we heartily wish he was out of it." Well, before he could ever make it onto the British throne, Frederick was indeed out of it, dying in 1751 and thus making his own son, George, the heir to the Crown.

The same could be said for his attitude toward the Seven Years' War with France (1756-63), for, as his reign approached its end, the grouchy old king sounded more and more like his father when expressing his disgust with England and the English. By then, however, his opinions really didn't matter all that much. In 1757, the same year William Pitt became Prime Minister, Robert Clive secured the Indian province of Bengal for the British, and a couple of years later James Wolfe captured Quebec and kicked the French out of Canada. The Brits were now flexing their muscles and expanding their Empire, and so when their German monarch passed on at the age of 76 in 1760, it really was a case of "goodbye and good riddance!"

George III: American Revolution in the Head

Son of the late Prince Frederick and grandson of George II, George III was the first Hanoverian monarch to be born and raised in England. For that matter, he was also the first of them to be liked and respected as a fair, sincere, and hard-working man. What's more, he was actually faithful to his wife, Queen Charlotte. He didn't get on with young George, his eldest son, however, which appears to be a family trait.

George III's nearly 60-year reign, the second longest in English history, encompassed great change in the country, famous triumphs, a notable loss, and, ultimately, personal tragedy. This last aspect was because for most of his adult life, "Farmer George" as he was fondly called due to his interest in agriculture, was dogged by mental illness. In his day, he and everyone around him accepted that he was psychotic, a madman, given to manic depressive fits and periods of complete insanity. Then, in 1969, English psychiatrists Ida Macalpine and Richard Hunter wrote a book entitled *George III and the Mad-Business*, in which they asserted that the monarch suffered from a disease called porphyria that simply displays *symptoms* of madness.

Either way, George was struck down by a series of fits in 1788, 1801, and 1804; although he managed to recover from each of these, around 1810 he suffered a permanent relapse. The following year, having at last managed a reconciliation with his father, Prince George was made prince regent and assumed the royal duties. That left George III, blind and deranged, to sit out the last nine years of his life, often clothed in a straitjacket or even tied to his bed.

A contemporary portrait of George III making toast mocks the king in later years. (Picture courtesy of Corbis-Bettmann)

Still, what a life it had been. On one hand was the loss of Britain's 13 North American colonies, all arising from the settlers' displeasure at the manner in which George's government constantly interfered in their affairs and then, to add insult to injury, started raising taxes. The whole topic of the War of Independence warrants its own book (perhaps a *Complete Idiot's Guide*), but suffice it to say that, at the war's conclusion in 1783, George III was no longer ruling Britain and its colonies actively. During the first third of his reign, he'd personally intervened in party politics, but now he handed over most of his ministerial power to William Pitt the Younger, son of former Prime Minister William Pitt the Elder. Pitt was also Tory Prime Minister from 1783 until his death in 1806, with a break from 1801 to 1804.

It was Pitt who guided England through the French Revolutionary and Napoleonic Wars of 1793 to 1815, which began when the revolutionaries who had overthrown the French monarchy next set about conquering Europe. Britain and other European nations naturally declared war on the French and initial losses on land were countered by victories at sea. By 1797, Britain found itself alone in a war against not only the French but the Spaniards and the Dutch, yet naval supremacy was turning the conflict decisively in favor of the Brits. This culminated in Lord Nelson's historic defeat of the combined French and Spanish fleets off Cape Trafalgar in 1805 and the Duke of Wellington's victory over Napoleon Bonaparte at Waterloo 10 years later. For the power-mad French Emperor, this defeat would prove to be the final blow. He was exiled to St. Helena, where he died in 1821.

So, what else took place during the reign of George III? Well, how about the king's purchase of Buckingham Palace ("Yours for just 28,000 pounds"), James Cook's first voyage around the world, the first publications of the *Encyclopedia Britannica* and Thomas Paine's *Rights of Man*, the invention of James Watt's steam engine, the introduction of income tax, the Act of Union with Ireland, and the abolition of the slave trade in 1807. (Slavery itself would continue throughout the British Empire until 1833.)

Hear Ye, Hear Ye
"Six hours sleep are enough for a man, seven for a woman, and eight for a fool."
—*King George III*

If all of that wasn't enough to pack into one era, let alone a few pages of this book, you're never satisfied—which is something that could have quite easily been said to George IV, a man for whom the pursuit of satisfaction appears to have been all-consuming.

George IV: Potent Lover, Impotent King

He acceded to the British throne on January 29, 1820, yet George IV had practically been the nation's King since taking over as Prince Regent nine years earlier. His was an era during which trade unions were legalized, the Stockton and Darlington Railway became the world's first train service, and the Metropolitan Police Force was set up by Robert Peel. Nevertheless, George's rule was mainly distinguished only by his patronage of the arts and his enabling Catholics to become members of Parliament. It's what he did *before* he came to the throne that's most worthy of our attention.

If the multi-married Henry VIII was the oversized Mickey Rooney of British royalty, then George IV was its Errol Flynn: a handsome and dashing young Prince of Wales who collected lovers as others collect coins, and whose heavy-drinking, hard-partying lifestyle eventually took its toll on his health and his looks. The Countess of Jersey, the Marchioness of Hertford, Lady Melbourne, The Marchioness of Conyngham, and the actress Mary Robinson were just a few of George's many mistresses. But his first big mistake was when he hooked up with Maria FitzHerbert in 1785.

Already twice-widowed at the age of 28, FitzHerbert was a devout Catholic who refused to have sex out of wedlock...so George married her! The problem was, according to the rules, British Royals were only supposed to wed other Royals who were also Protestants, and Madam FitzHerbert was neither. George therefore ensured that their wedding was a secret, in direct contravention of the Royal Marriages Act of 1772, which decreed that the King had to give his permission for all royal marriages. George III himself had pushed this Act through Parliament, and he wasn't now about to ask for another Act to repeal it. He believed that his wayward son's marriage wasn't legal and that was that.

For her part, Maria FitzHerbert still considered the prince to be her rightful husband, and when asked for his opinion, the Pope agreed with her. (But then he would, wouldn't he?) So, Maria and George continued to spend time with each other while he also pursued other women; this arrangement lasted until a day in 1795 when the prince's lavish lifestyle finally caught up with him. In debt up to his eyeballs, he reluctantly accepted Parliament's offer to pay off his creditors in return for him marrying a woman of the ministers' choosing. They chose his first cousin, Caroline of Brunswick, and a more disastrous decision they couldn't have made.

Plain and overweight, Princess Caroline was also, according to George, fairly dirty. Now, if there was one thing he liked in a woman it was a fresh scent and a ready smile, but it's amazing the lengths he would go to in order to square his accounts. April 8, 1795, was set as the day of the royal marriage, and just to show that he was going to give it his best shot, George turned up for the ceremony drunk as a skunk. He proceeded to cry throughout the service before being barred from the honeymoon suite that night. In the morning he was allowed in and, somehow defying the laws of physics, he bravely impregnated Caroline. The result of their passion was Princess Charlotte, who represented the start and end of Caroline and George's romance.

> **On Her Majesty's Service**
>
> One of George IV's great loves, apart from women, was the construction of expansive and expensive buildings, many of them during his time as prince regent. A prime example is the exotic-looking Brighton Pavilion, while, courtesy of great architects, much of what you'll see in Central London also dates back to the "Regency" era, including the buildings on Regent Street and in Regent's Park.

Because George didn't perform as a husband should, Caroline decided she would take her charms elsewhere. Unfortunately, she wasn't subtle about her paramours, and to make matters worse she also tried to claim her rights as queen once George had ascended to the throne. Poor George. He tried to divorce his disobedient wife at a public trial in which he actually had the nerve to accuse her of adultery (now wasn't *that* rich?), but without the assistance of, say, Alan Dershowitz, he didn't get far in that endeavor. Still, when he was crowned at Westminster Abbey on July 19, 1821, George did succeed in having Caroline barred from the ceremony. The indignity of it all! She'd turned up decked out in jewels and fancy clothes hoping to be crowned as well. Instead, she was left out in the cold and died just a few weeks later.

Hear Ye, Hear Ye
A courtier, giving George IV the news that Napoleon Bonaparte had just died in exile, May 5, 1821: "I have, Sir, to congratulate you; your greatest enemy is dead." To which George, thinking the courtier was referring to Caroline, responded: "Is *she*, by God?"

On the political scene, George IV was a fairly impotent regent and king because, during his days as Prince of Wales, he'd been an outspoken supporter of the Whigs. When the Tories came to power, they weren't in a very forgiving mood. George had a tough time with his prime ministers, the last of whom was Arthur Wellesley, the Duke of Wellington. He took over running the government in 1828, but by that time the king was virtually off the scene. Years of drinking and debauchery had taken their toll. George was sick and overweight (from Errol Flynn to Henry VIII in just a few short years!), and for the last months of his life he didn't emerge from Windsor. He died there, aged 67, on June 26, 1830.

William IV and the Great Reform Bill

Princess Charlotte, the product of George IV's single morning of passion with Caroline, died in 1817. Ten years later, George's eldest brother, Frederick, Duke of York, also passed away, and so that paved the way for the next brother in line to ascend to the throne as William IV.

William was 64 years old when he became king, and, as he was the third of George III's sons, had never been envisioned as a future monarch and was therefore unprepared and largely uneducated. He'd entered the Navy at the age of 13, and during a steady but unspectacular career, his royal blood helped him become Lord High Admiral. Nevertheless, while likable, William could also be excitable and argumentative, and some of his more ridiculous outbursts earned him the nickname "Silly Billy."

All the while he lived with his girlfriend, the actress Dorothea Jordan, with whom he had no fewer than 10 children. Yet Dorothea wasn't considered to be royal marriage material, so William eventually began to search around for a suitable wife. By that time he was into middle age and hardly a prize catch, so several likely lasses were lined up for him and several likely lasses turned him down. Finally, one agreed to accept William's request to become his wife—after all, he was third in line to the throne of George III—so on July 13, 1818, at the age of 53, the Prince married Princess Adelaide of Saxe-Meiningen. She was less than half his age.

As king, the best that could be said about William IV is that he was unobtrusive. The days of the busy-body monarchs were clearly at an end, and so, while there were several great reforms during his reign, he played little part in them. In 1831 the Whigs won the general election, and their leader, Lord Grey, was determined to push through a Reform Bill that would give an extra half million people the right to vote. The House of Lords didn't like the sound of extending democratic rights to the middle classes, so the Bill was rejected. Lord Grey therefore went to the king and asked him to create a few more Whig peers for the House of Lords. William did as he was told and the bill was subsequently passed in 1832.

The following year, slavery was abolished throughout the British Empire and 20 million pounds in compensation was extended to slave owners. Also in 1833, the Factory Act prevented children under the age of nine from working and those under 13 were limited to 48 hours a week, yet adolescents of 18 and under could still work 68 hours. Then, in 1834, the Poor Law Act created workhouses for the underprivileged. These were just some of the improvements to living standards instigated by Parliament during the William IV years, yet the king himself was obviously preoccupied with other matters—such as the over-eager mother of his niece, Princess Victoria!

Being that William and Adelaide's two little daughters didn't live even three months between them, the *heir presumptive* was Alexandrina Victoria, known as Drina and then just Victoria, and the daughter of William's late brother, Edward, Duke of Kent. Victoria's mother, the Duchess of Kent, was forever pushing her shy daughter into the limelight and, with the assistance of Sir John Conroy, controller of her household (and, many believe, her lover), trying to gain the Princess regal privileges. This kind of behavior got up the king's nose, especially as he and his wife hadn't yet given up all hope of siring their own heir. The last straw was when he discovered that, against his expressed wishes, the duchess and her daughter had taken over a suite of 17 rooms in Kensington Palace.

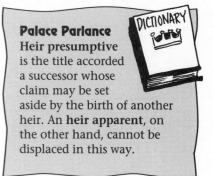

Palace Parlance
Heir presumptive is the title accorded a successor whose claim may be set aside by the birth of another heir. An **heir apparent**, on the other hand, cannot be displaced in this way.

In front of 100 guests at his own birthday dinner, William, who by now had taken to sporting a black wig and heavy makeup, launched into a furious tirade against the duchess. Shaking so badly that his wig nearly slipped off, he shouted that he would do all he could to live until Victoria was 18, just to ensure that her obnoxious mother would never get to rule as regent. It was an embarrassing scene to say the least, but Silly Billy wasn't about to have his authority undermined by an overbearing sister-in-law!

As it happens, William IV did get to see Victoria reach her 18th birthday, but he only managed it by four weeks, dying at Windsor Castle on June 20, 1837. He was 71 and was sadly missed...by some.

The Least You Need to Know

➤ George I couldn't speak English and spent plenty of time in his native Hanover. The task of running the British government was therefore handed to Sir Robert Walpole, Britain's first Prime Minister.

➤ In Dettingen, Bavaria, in 1743, 60-year-old George II became the last British monarch to lead troops into battle.

➤ George III probably suffered from an illness called porphyria that produced symptoms of insanity.

➤ Slavery was abolished throughout the British Empire in 1833, more than 30 years before it was banned in America.

Part 6
A Bunch of Posers—
The Figurehead Monarchy
(Since 1837)

It's funny how power slips away…The Stuarts really blew it big time for the British monarchy and afterwards nothing was ever really the same again. Many of the Hanoverian kings had little interest in being royal rulers, and by the time of William IV, the sovereign was little more than a puppet of Parliament.

In this final part of your Complete Idiot's Guide *you'll see how the royals completed their transition from despotic demons to nominal leaders and high-ranking envoys. Long-gone are the days of murder, torture, and treachery in the name of the throne, but the scandals are as prevalent as ever and many of the characters are just as colorful.*

Today there are constant questions as to whether or not the monarchy will survive, yet one thing's for certain: It's been a long and eventful trip from Egbert of Wessex to Elizabeth II of Windsor, confirming that, while those British royals may no longer have supreme power, they certainly have staying power!

Not Amused—
The Long, Long
Reign of Queen
Victoria

In This Chapter

➤ Queen Victoria and the men that she trusted

➤ Prince Albert and the Great Exhibition of 1851

➤ Albert's death sends Victoria into seclusion

➤ The amorous adventures and foreign friendships of Edward VII

Hanover became a kingdom in 1815 and its laws decreed that the throne could not be passed to a woman. Therefore, when William IV died in 1837 and Queen Victoria took over as the British monarch, it was Ernest, Duke of Cumberland and fifth son of George III, who became the Hanoverian king. In this way, England split from Hanover and the German arms were removed from the English royal arms.

Victoria reigned for a long time: just over 63 years, four more than George III (if you include the nine years in which his son served as Regent). To date, she holds the longevity record for a British monarch. During her reign, the queen experienced great personal highs and lows, as did the popularity of the monarchy, yet Britain flourished as an imperial and industrial power, and by the end of her reign, the 81-year-old queen was much loved and respected. Unfortunately, she didn't extend much of that love to her eldest son, Edward VII. Before and after he became king at the age of 59, however, he garnered female affection of another kind. I tell you, there's no end to the gossip!

Young Vic, Old Vic: Up Close and Personal

Queen Victoria's father, Edward, Duke of Kent, died when she was only eight months old, and she was raised by an overbearing, controlling mother. Therefore, as soon as she ascended to the throne, Queen Victoria was only too happy to escape from her mother's clutches and throw herself into her new role.

She was, however, a young queen—only 18 years old, naive and inexperienced, and in great need of a father figure to help guide her through the unknown terrain of presiding over the most powerful nation on earth. Sir John Conroy, the controller of her mother's household (and possibly more) wasn't that man. He was more intent on citing Victoria's inexperience as a reason for him to become regent. No, she needed someone far more trustworthy—and Lord Melbourne was the man.

As prime minister and leader of the Whigs, Lord Melbourne assisted Victoria by way of his solid political advice while also allowing for her own strong opinions and sometimes obstinate attitude. This side of her character showed itself early on during her reign, shortly after her beloved Melbourne had been defeated by the far-from-friendly Tory, Sir Robert Peel. Victoria didn't like Peel, and when he made the insensitive demand that the queen should fire her bedchamber women, many of whom were related to Whig ministers, and hire others with more tasteful Tory views, she refused.

Peel's request hadn't been unusual. It was customary for ladies-in-waiting to be changed when a new administration came to power. The new Prime Minister was outraged by Victoria's refusal. How could he work with such an arrogant young upstart? On that basis, there was no way he could form a government, which meant that Lord Melbourne could return as Prime Minister! So he did and certain disgruntled citizens showed their displeasure—and their disrespect for an increasingly ridiculed monarchy—by chiding Victoria with shouts of "Mrs. Melbourne!"

This type of disrespectful behavior could have resulted in a trip to the Tower a few years earlier, and indeed, Victoria was a woman of powerful enough convictions that, had she not been a *constitutional monarch*, she may well have resorted to strong-arm tactics in dealing with her opponents. Instead, she had to put up with being unpopular for a large part of her reign, until old age earned a special respect and turned public opinion toward her.

In the meantime, in 1840 "Mrs. Melbourne" actually became the wife of Prince Albert of Saxe-Coburg and Gotha. I'll be telling you more about him in the next section of this chapter, but for now I'll just say that, of all the men in Victoria's life, Albert was perhaps the one best able to get around her and along with her. After all, consider some of the Victorian values: A strictly ordered, male-dominated society in which the man worked and the woman stayed at

Palace Parlance
Constitutional monarch describes a sovereign who has to adhere to the laws and principles of the State. The 1689 Bill of Rights comprised a cornerstone of the British Constitution regarding Parliament's control over the monarchy.

home; a dress code that covered all parts of the body save the head and the hands; and a bevy of sexual taboos that amounted to the word hardly ever being mentioned (while plenty of repression-free activity took place behind closed doors).

These values reflected Victoria's own virtuous—some say self-righteous—beliefs, as well as her willingness to stand up for her convictions, and her no-nonsense approach often complicated issues. None of these traits made her particularly easy to live with. Things had to be done the queen's way. Whatever suited her best counted most, and while frowning on others who yielded to temptation, she was a stern taskmaster at home who always stood in judgment over her children, regardless of their age.

Queen Victoria, benefiting from the invention of photography, is captured in habitual pose in 1897. (Photo courtesy of Corbis-Bettmann)

On the political front, following Lord Melbourne, Victoria's next favorite was Tory Prime Minister Benjamin Disraeli, during whose term of office she became Empress of India. The queen made Disraeli Earl of Beaconsfield and was fully supportive of his imperialist policies, not the least of which saw Britain taking control of Egypt's Suez Canal and thus securing a convenient trade route to India. The Whig leader William Gladstone, on the other hand, was morally opposed to all of the empire building. His chief concerns were to allow Ireland to govern itself, improve educational standards, and provide more people with the right to vote—all policies that spoke of fairness and equal opportunities. In addition, all the policies were thoroughly despised by Queen Victoria, as was Gladstone himself.

Still, while Victoria's favoritism often provoked resentments at court, her friendship with a Scottish servant named John Brown inspired suspicion, exasperation, raised eyebrows, and not a small amount of gossip. Following Prince Albert's untimely death in 1861, Victoria was a queen in mourning for the remaining 40 years of her life. Yet somehow John Brown was able to bring her out of herself (at least by her own somber standards) and as his influence over the crusty monarch increased, so did his pay and status, along with all of the speculation. After all, what *was* it about this Brown character that had the queen so enthralled?

What the queen referred to as Brown's "forthright" manner others considered to be rudeness—a rudeness that was perfectly understandable considering that he was frequently drunk. So much for Victorian values! Could "Old Vic" be having an affair with her sloppy servant? Brown was often seen walking into her bedroom without first knocking. Perhaps they were secretly married!

Well, that was the sort of tittle-tattle that was doing the royal rounds. Yet, I have to say, you only have to look at those photos of Victoria in her later years, garbed all in black (as was her custom following Albert's death), and sporting the facial expression of a hippo with a bad case of heartburn, and it's pretty difficult to believe that she was frolicking with anyone. Still, she really did go overboard when Brown died, erecting statues in his memory and even attempting to publish a memoir that she'd written about him. She was fortunately persuaded otherwise, and when Edward VII ascended to the throne, he immediately tore down the statues of John Brown, servant of repute. (Whether that repute was good or bad is open to debate.)

Royal Rebuttal
Given Queen Victoria's stiff, unsmiling photographic poses, as well as all of the stories about how stern she could be, the quote most frequently attributed to her, "We are not amused," seems perfectly in character. However, there's no documented record of her ever having said these famous words. What she *has* been recorded as saying, on the other hand, is "I was very much amused."

When Queen Victoria died in 1901, she was survived by six children, 40 grandchildren, and 37 great-grandchildren. These descendents included four future kings: Edward VII, George V, Edward VIII, and George VI. Victoria herself outlived three other children, while her eldest and favorite, Vicky, died only six months after the old queen. The youngest, Princess Beatrice, died in 1944. The marriages of these children and grandchildren linked the British monarchy with the royal houses of Germany, Spain, Russia, Sweden, Norway, and Romania.

All in all, therefore, the 21-year marriage of Victoria and Albert was a fairly productive one—and not only due to the number of offspring. As I've already said, the Prince knew how to get around and along with the queen, and that considerable attribute paid off in more ways than one.

Paradise Lost: Prince Albert of Saxe-Coburg-Gotha

Intelligent, conscientious, and a devoted husband and father, Albert of Saxe-Coburg-Gotha made a couple of mistakes as far as the British people were concerned. One was that he was German and after the performance of some of the Hanoverian kings, German ancestry wasn't the greatest credential to have. The other was that he helped promote his wife's influence in affairs of state, when everyone knew that her designated role really amounted to little more than a figurehead. Nevertheless, thanks in part to Albert's efforts, the image of the British monarchy would rise to new heights of respectability, where it would remain until the scandals of recent years.

Made a British citizen yet never an English peer, Albert was given no official political position, the lowest possible precedence with regard to the line of succession, and only after 17 years of marriage to his first cousin, Victoria, (and four years before his death) was he made Prince Consort. The queen felt a great amount of bitterness toward Parliament for what she considered the shabby treatment of a husband whom she adored, yet Albert didn't allow this to jade his own interest in his adopted country. He encouraged and influenced Victoria's interest in domestic political issues, and he took an active interest in Britain's position as a world leader in terms of industrial development. This in turn led him to come up with an inspired idea.

With the Industrial Revolution in full force, Albert spent a lot of time visiting the nation's factories to see how the technological advances were being put into practice. He knew that, while Britain was becoming ever more powerful and wealthy, the benefits still weren't reaching all sections of society. Poverty was rife and he considered industry to be the means by which the lower classes could improve their lot in life. Therefore, to help that cause and to promote British achievement, what could be better than an international exhibition of industrial products that would be staged in London?

Hear Ye, Hear Ye

"Poor dear Albert, how cruelly are they ill-using that dearest Angel! Monsters! You Tories shall be punished. Revenge, revenge!"
—*An entry in Queen Victoria's diary, February 2, 1840, eight days before her marriage*

Initially, the answer to that question appeared to be "A lot of things could be better." At least, that seemed to be the government's attitude, so Albert set about publicizing his idea via the press, and it quickly gained popular support, leading to the raising of the necessary funds to launch the project. This in turn manifested itself in the form of a spectacular, 100,000-square-foot exhibition center in Central London's Hyde Park. Designed by

Joseph Paxton and consisting of more than 300,000 panes of glass supported by a cast-iron framework, the building was dubbed the "Crystal Palace" by the satirical *Punch* magazine. The name stuck. Meanwhile, the Exhibition of the Works of Industry of All Nations turned out to be a magnet to people from all walks of life.

On Her Majesty's Service

The Great Exhibition of 1851 earned a profit of 186,000 pounds, and today you can see the fruits of this work in the form of the science and arts buildings, founded during Albert's lifetime, that stand in Kensington, Central London. These buildings include the Victoria and Albert Museum, the Science Museum, the Natural History Museum, the Imperial College of Science and Technology, and the Royal College of Music.

The Great Exhibition took place halfway through Victoria's marriage, and it represented the pinnacle of Albert's achievements. Thereafter, he continued to exert a tremendous amount of influence over the queen while intervening behind the scenes in political affairs. Then, in 1861, he contracted typhoid (some retrospective diagnoses also state it was cancer) and on December 14 of that year, at the age of 42, the Prince Consort died.

Victoria was inconsolable. Without her greatest love, greatest ally, and most trusted advisor she was lost; she'd later confess to her daughter Vicky that she even contemplated suicide. Statues and monuments were erected in Albert's memory all over the land—the most notable being London's Royal Albert Hall, opened in 1871, and the nearby Albert Memorial—and for the rest of her life the queen would dress in black. For 13 years she would also withdraw from public life and conduct all affairs of state in seclusion, an act which, in itself, would only serve to fuel demands to abolish the monarchy.

63 Years on the Throne

"I will be good," Victoria had said on learning as a child that one day she would be queen and for many years she tried her best. Yet, there were a lot of years in which to try, so the results were a fairly mixed bag.

Although Victoria had her political favorites, chose ministers, and took an active interest in affairs of state, she was able to play little part in the political legislation that brought about tremendous social and economic change during her reign. These included acts that forbade women and children to be employed in underground mines, introduced compulsory elementary education in England and Wales, established a ten-hour working day, legalized Trade Unions, and extended the right to vote in national elections. All were implemented by the 10 prime ministers of the Victorian era.

At the same time, thanks mainly to territorial gains in India, Egypt, Afghanistan, Zululand, the Sudan, South Africa, Burma, and the Pacific, the British Empire doubled in size. Victoria particularly liked being made Empress of India in 1876—all future monarchs were also Emperors there, until India gained its independence in 1947—yet, again, she had done little in this respect other than lend her support and hire an Indian servant.

The queen's endorsement of British imperialism wasn't universally approved, yet that was nothing compared to the criticism that she attracted during her self-imposed withdrawal from public life and political meetings. Many people seriously questioned what need there was for a monarchy, and while an increasing number of them started to call for a republic, others pressed for Victoria's abdication and her replacement by Edward, Prince of Wales. These dissenters included quite a few Members of Parliament, yet one of them, Prime Minister Benjamin Disraeli, along with Royal Family members and friends, finally managed to persuade the queen to make a comeback. That was in 1874 and at first she trod carefully, but within no time at all she was making appearances around the country, riding in an open carriage, attending state balls, and even posing in front of that new-fangled device, the camera. No doubt if television had been invented she would have also turned up on several talk shows.

It's amazing what a little effort will do. By the time of her Golden Jubilee in 1887, "Old Vic" was Madam Popular, and all over the British Empire there were celebrations and church services to mark her 50th anniversary on the throne. Then, 10 years later, everybody was at it again, turning out in force for her Diamond Jubilee. Obviously it couldn't continue. Three and a half years later, on January 22, 1901, Queen Victoria passed on, and her many subjects mourned, yet perhaps one man wasn't quite as aggrieved as most. Edward, Prince of Wales, had been waiting around a long time to get on the throne and he didn't have many kind words from his mother to show for it. Now, at the age of 59, it was his time at last.

Royal Rebuttal

Queen Victoria's 63-year reign was longer than that of any other British monarch, and she also lived to the highest age, beating George III in the maturity stakes by three days. Don't assume, however, that she's the world record holder. That honor belongs to Louis XIV of France (1638-1715) who reigned for 72 years. The Austrian Emperor, Francis Joseph (1830-1916) reigned for 68.

Edward VII: The Uncle of Europe

Throughout his life Edward exulted in the pursuit of pleasure. He loved yachting, hunting, and horse racing, and he loved traveling abroad, but above all he loved women. Lots of them. Beautiful socialites, models, actresses, and all in the full glare of the public spotlight. It was a carefree lifestyle that made him popular with the public and a source of embarrassment and irritation to his parents. Even on his deathbed in 1861, Prince Albert was concerned about his eldest son's latest liaison with an Irish actress. Victoria resented Albert's libido and, considering Edward to be an irresponsible little layabout (actually he was short and stocky), she chose to freeze him out of all diplomatic and political affairs.

Now, if Edward had taken the time to do some quick research into his Hanoverian past, he would have seen that it wasn't at all unusual for the monarchs to hate their kids. He was too busy with his pastimes to take a course in family history, however, and besides, his mother never appeared to have any problems confiding in his sisters. The pain which that must have caused, together with his frustration at being excluded from affairs of state, only exacerbated Edward's desire to involve himself in affairs of an altogether more enjoyable nature.

Alexandra and Edward—She learned to live with his philandering ways. (Photo courtesy of UPI/Corbis-Bettmann)

On March 10, 1863, at the age of 21, the Prince of Wales married Princess Alexandra, the elder daughter of King Christian IX of Denmark. An elegant, sophisticated woman, she was also remarkably tolerant, as evidenced by the way in which she put up with her husband's incessant and brazen promiscuity. Indeed, being married didn't seem to discourage him one iota. The famous actress and model, Lillie Langtry, was among his most well-known mistresses, as were Lady Brooke and his last lover, Mrs. Keppel.

Still, as if all of this womanizing wasn't enough for Edward's poor wife and mother to bear, there were also other public humiliations, such as his involvement in a scandal known as The Baccarat Case. This almost sounds like a Sherlock Holmes murder-mystery, yet in truth it simply revolved around a game of cards in 1891 at the home of the Prince's society friend, Tranby Croft. (Aren't some of these names great?)

During the course of the evening, Edward heard that a fellow guest, Sir William Gordon-Cumming, had been caught cheating. Five players testified to his guilt, while Sir William, of course, denied the charge. Still, anxious to avoid the frightful indignity of having his good name besmirched, the accused man promised to never play cards ever again as long as this scandalous affair was kept quiet.

Now, what do you think happened? Was a prime piece of society gossip going to remain buried along with Sir William's chances of ever winning another game of Baccarat? No way! Soon the word of his *faux pas* began to spread, and so Mr. Gordon-Cumming, Esq. was left with little option other than to sue his accusers for slander. The story hit the papers and, of course, the Prince of Wales' name was dragged into the whole sorry mess—a case of guilt by association. The public was shocked and Victoria was appalled, yet the whole matter soon blew over. Such were the risks of living life in the fast lane.

Nevertheless, while many people shared Victoria's reservations about her eldest son's ascension to the throne, Edward VII would prove the doubters wrong. As a king, he took his royal duties seriously. He excelled at dealing with his ministers and, especially, overseas rulers. After all, he may not have been well read on the subject of foreign affairs, but as Prince of Wales he'd traveled the world: America, Canada, Ireland, France, Belgium, Germany, Italy, Spain, Denmark, Russia, Egypt, and the Holy Land were among the places he'd visited. In addition, he could speak fluent French and German, as well as adequate Spanish and Italian. Edward's foreign links were numerous and he helped pave the way for the *Entente Cordiale* of 1904 that settled all outstanding territorial disputes between Britain and France. Not for nothing was he known as "The Uncle of Europe," the perfect goodwill ambassador.

Hear Ye, Hear Ye
"I don't mind praying to the eternal Father, but I must be the only man in the country afflicted with an eternal mother."
—*Edward, Prince of Wales, while waiting to succeed Queen Victoria*

This was the era when the Wright brothers made the first flight and the horseless carriage—or motor car—came into its own. It was also a time of free state education and old-age pensions, as well as the violent protests of the Suffragette movement, in which women fought for their emancipation. The king's constitutional role meant that his ministers didn't really allow him to get involved in political matters. There were, however, approved activities: regularly opening Parliament, or raising the Royal Family to new heights of public esteem. Yet, when Edward VII died on May 6, 1910, at the age of 68, the country was in the throes of a constitutional crisis.

The previous year, the Chancellor of the Exchequer, Lloyd George, had introduced the People's Budget, which aimed to increase taxes on the rich in order to raise the money needed for the aforementioned social reforms. The House of Lords didn't like the tax and rejected the Budget, so in 1910 the House of Commons introduced the Parliament Bill, attempting to curb the powers of the Lords. As you can imagine, that didn't go down too well, either, so the result was a political mess—one that Edward's son, George V, would be forced to resolve soon after his ascendance to the throne.

The Least You Need to Know

➤ Queen Victoria reigned for 63 years, longer than any other British monarch.

➤ Victoria wasn't always popular, especially after her long seclusion following Prince Albert's death, but she staged a comeback in later years.

➤ Victoria was an avid imperialist and the British Empire doubled in size during her reign.

➤ Edward VII waited 59 years to become king and he was already a grandfather by the time he ascended to the throne.

Mass Media Monarchs—Those Radio and TV Windsors

In This Chapter

➤ George V changes the family name and rallies the nation at home and abroad

➤ Edward VIII's short reign and traitorous allegiances

➤ The model wartime leadership of George VI

➤ Domestic strife for Elizabeth II and her little sister

As the accession of Queen Victoria coincided with the separation of the British and Hanoverian thrones, her children took the Saxe-Coburg-Gotha family name of their father, Prince Albert. Edward VII therefore had that name, and so did his son, George V, while the British royals were still popularly equated with the House of Hanover. However, when anti-German sentiments were running high during the First World War, George did the diplomatic thing and changed the family name—as well as the royal house—to Windsor.

That name has survived to this day, and in this chapter I tell you more about how that change came about, as well as the reigns of all of the Windsor monarchs to date. The first and third of these each had to see their country through a world war, while the one in between abdicated before his coronation. Finally, we'll take a look at the first 25 years on the throne of the current queen—years not without their share of controversy, but relatively stable and peaceful years nonetheless.

Talk about the lull before the storm!

George V: Coping with Crises

The second son of Edward VII, George had to give up his flourishing naval career in 1892 on the death of his elder brother, Albert. As the new heir-apparent, he had to wait another 18 years before ascending to the throne just one month short of his 45th birthday, and then he assumed the role of king just as his country was in the middle of a constitutional crisis.

This crisis had come about as a result of the predominantly Tory House of Lords voting down the tax-the-rich budget of the Liberal Chancellor of the Exchequer. (The Liberal Party had succeeded the Whigs during the mid-19th century.) This vote was unprecedented, and the Liberals responded by trying to curb the powers of the House of Lords by way of the Parliament Bill. In 1910, for the first and only time, Britain had two general elections in the same year. George V was put under heavy pressure to counter the Tory majority in the Lords by creating some new Liberal peers who would ensure the safe passage of the Parliament Bill. The king really resented such an abuse of the few powers still remaining to him.

In the end, rather than see new Liberal peers flooding into the House of Lords, a number of Tories—now also known as Conservatives—decided to either stay away when the Parliament Bill was presented or even vote with the Liberals. The bill, then, become law, and as a result the House of Lords could no longer reject a money-related bill. Furthermore, any bill that the Lords blocked three successive times would automatically become law (so why bother with the third vote?), while the maximum length of a Parliament— the maximum time between general elections—was reduced from seven to five years.

Royal Rebuttal

George V's elder brother, Albert, Duke of Clarence, had, by most accounts, a severe learning disability. Had he lived, therefore, he could have been a problematic monarch—although probably not so bad as some of his predecessors. Despite several theories that have been advanced regarding a certain mystery murder, however, there's no conclusive proof that "Prince Eddy," as he was known, was Jack the Ripper.

So, the Liberals had gotten their way, yet the second general election of 1910 had raised another problem. In order to have a workable number of MPs on the government's side (a "working majority") in the House of Commons, the Liberals needed to gain the support of the Irish members. In return, those Irish MPs would be demanding Home Rule, something that would please the second-class Catholic majority but cause problems with the Protestant minority that, with British backing, had been enjoying the best of things.

The Conservatives were against this change, especially as both Irish factions appeared to be preparing for an armed conflict. The House of Lords was no longer able to indefinitely block a bill proposing Irish Home Rule, however, so the Conservative leader, Bonar Law, suggested to George V that he might want to use the royal veto. There again, he might not. After all, what if the use of such a veto resulted in an uprising? It could spell the end for the monarchy. One solution put forward amounted to separating the northern part of Ireland where the Protestants had settled from the

rest of the country. In 1914, the king hosted a confer-
ence on this issue at Buckingham Palace, but it met
with disapproval on both sides and the talks failed. At
that point, further negotiations had to be put on ice,
because suddenly there was a far more wide-ranging
problem: the outbreak of World War I.

Hear Ye, Hear Ye
"I look upon him
as the greatest
criminal known for
having plunged the
world into this ghastly
war."
—*King George V, following the
abdication of his cousin, Kaiser
Wilhelm II of Germany, 1918*

The British Royals obviously had many gallons of
German blood running through their veins, yet
George V fully supported the government's decision to
fight "the Hun" after the Germans invaded Belgium in
August 1914. The British king worked tirelessly for the
next four years, traveling back and forth between
England and France, monitoring progress and visiting
the troops. So did his wife and eldest children. In this modern war the monarch no
longer led his troops into battle, yet George did sustain an old-fashioned injury. While
out in the field, the horse of Field Marshall Sir Douglas Haig reared and toppled onto the
king's horse, knocking the monarch to the ground and breaking his pelvis. For the next
few weeks, he was pinning medals on soldiers while sitting in his hospital bed.

As a decidedly anti-German mood swept across Britain many people were suspicious of
their Royal Family's German allegiances. After all, what if certain members were colluding
with George's first cousin, Kaiser Wilhelm II? What the public didn't know was that,
behind the scenes, many of the British royals had never been all that crazy about the
arrogant kaiser. A few of them didn't even like the Germans, yet for the sake of diplomacy
the king wasn't about to announce his views. Instead, to avoid further upset and suspicion that would only undermine the nation's confidence and threaten the monarchy, he
made a gesture that clearly illustrated where the British royals' sympathies lay.

On July 17, 1917, he issued a proclamation declaring that he and all of the other descendants of Queen Victoria were changing their German surnames—be they Saxe-Coburg-
Gotha, Battenberg, Saxony, or Hesse—to Windsor. This was taken from the town where
the monarchy's main non-London residence is located. The "Great War" ended in 1918,
yet immediately there were problems on the home front that had been brewing for a few
years.

In 1916, there had been an Easter Rising in Dublin by the Irish Republican Army (IRA) in
an unsuccessful attempt to establish an independent state. Then, in the general election
of 1918, the IRA's political wing, Sinn Fein ("Ourselves Alone"), had 73 MPs elected to
Parliament. Instead of taking their places at Westminster, they tried to form their own
government. This move was thwarted by British troops, yet, following further armed
conflicts, by 1921 Ireland had been formally partitioned into the Catholic-controlled Free
State and the much smaller British province of Northern Ireland. The problems of that
troubled isle were far from over.

Neither were troubles over elsewhere, as the crippling General Strike of 1926 paved the way for the Stock Market crash of 1929. With unemployment going through the roof and the British economy collapsing through the floor, George V played a significant role in persuading the leaders of the nation's three main political parties—the Liberals, the Conservatives, and now Labour—to form a National Coalition government in August 1931. This same year the Statute of Westminster turned the subordinate British dominions into independent nations within the British Commonwealth.

On Her Majesty's Service

George V's wife was Mary of Teck, otherwise known as Queen Mary, whom he married in 1893. Mary had been engaged to George's elder brother, Albert, until he died the year before. An expert needlewoman and an authority on art and antiques, Mary organized the royal collection and rearranged all the palaces. You'll see her flair for design and composition if you visit Windsor Castle.

The times were rapidly changing, and as result, George V was the first British monarch to speak to his subjects via radio broadcasts. As with the newsreels that now captured the nation's first family, these really helped personalize the relationship between king and country and greatly popularized the monarchy. It was on Christmas Day 1932 that George's broadcast to the nation started an annual tradition; the script for that auspicious occasion was written by Rudyard Kipling, author of, among other things, *The Jungle Book*.

George V died on Jan 20, 1936, at the age of 70. Queen Mary followed him in 1953.

Edward VIII: The Playboy Prince and Uncrowned King

His full name was Edward Albert Christian George Andrew Patrick David Windsor, but his family called him David, and the nation knew him as the Prince of Wales and Edward VIII. He ascended to the throne on Jan 20, 1936, and abdicated on December 11 of the same year. Following his abdication he was also known by a few other choice names, "the Duke of Windsor" being the least offensive of them.

As the Prince of Wales, Edward cut a fairly dashing public figure: a snappy dresser who made popular official visits around the world. Yet the character flaws that would be his undoing were already evident to those who really knew the prince. When things didn't interest him he made little effort to disguise his boredom, whether at ceremonies of State, which he hated, or important meetings where he'd chat about his pastimes. The most notable of these was a hobby he shared with his grandfather, Edward VII: the pursuit of pleasure. Nightclubs, society friends, and fast women were always top of the prince's agenda, yet whereas Edward VII lived up to his regal responsibilities when he became King, Edward VIII did anything but.

"Spineless," "selfish," "stubborn," and "stupid" were all adjectives applied to Edward VIII with regard to his abdication; the next sections describe the events prior to and surrounding that momentous occasion in British royal history. However, in light of some his subsequent activities, it would also be apt to call him a traitor, which I'll also explain.

Abdication! The King and Mrs. Simpson

George V knew about it and the overseas press talked about it, but in those pre-tabloid days the British newspapers decided to turn a blind eye to the relationship between the Prince of Wales and Mrs. Wallis Simpson.

An American with aristocratic connections, the former Wallis Warfield was divorced and married to her second husband when she and Edward first met in 1930. Two years later she visited the prince's home, and by 1934 the couple was spending an increasing amount of time together. George V had always been concerned about his eldest son's private life getting in the way of his public duties, but this liaison smacked of the real thing: trouble.

Hear Ye, Hear Ye
"After I am dead the boy will ruin himself in 12 months."
—*George V talking about his son, Edward, Prince of Wales, to Prime Minister Stanley Baldwin*

In the summer of 1936, several months after Edward VIII's ascension to the throne, he and Mrs. Simpson vacationed in the Balkans together, where they were photographed by the press but still left alone by the British newspapers. Nevertheless, the word began to spread; the king was consorting with a twice-married, American divorcee who was also a commoner. The appropriately named Bishop Blunt of Bradford took it upon himself to allude to the relationship during one of his sermons, and when the *Yorkshire Post* tried to analyze his comments, the British press felt it had the green light to move ahead with the story. This was the opportunity the editors had been waiting for.

The newspapers had a field day, and when it emerged that Mrs. Simpson had filed for a divorce from her second husband, the Conservative Prime Minister, Stanley Baldwin, knew that he had a major crisis on his hands. It wasn't that Mrs. Simpson was an American, or that she was a commoner; no, the problem lay in the fact that she was twice-divorced. Back in the 12th century, Henry II had married the divorcee, Eleanor of Aquitaine, but times had changed. If Edward planned to marry his double-divorcee, not only would public morals be offended, but the Church of England, of which he was head, would object.

Baldwin therefore met with the king and, while pointing to the general attitude in the country toward the relationship, explained that he and the leaders of the Liberal and Labour parties didn't feel that Wallis Simpson would quite cut it as queen. Still, on October 27 she was granted her divorce and Edward made it clear that he did indeed intend to marry her. Now, if that happened the government would probably resign in protest, and, as the Cabinet's view wouldn't be opposed by the people or, consequently, the other political parties, where would that leave the monarchy? About 60 MPs were reportedly prepared to support a king's government, but that was hardly enough, and the news that Fascists and Communists were rallying to Edward's cause was hardly encouraging.

Any ideas that Edward may have had about making Wallis Simpson his queen were looking increasingly unattainable, and as British law didn't recognize *morganatic marriage,* he was really being presented with a straight choice: abdicate or dump his darling divorcee. The British public, suddenly distracted from relatively minor issues such as unemployment, the rise of Fascism, and the threat of Hitler, found it hard to believe that their king would choose a woman over his royal duties. They had a surprise awaiting them.

Palace Parlance
Morganatic marriage is a union between a man of high rank and woman of lower rank, whereby the wife and children can't claim his title or possessions. A king's wife in a morganic marriage would have no royal status.

On December 10, 1936, witnessed by his three brothers, Edward VIII signed the Instrument of Abdication, relinquishing the throne for himself and his descendants. The next day the abdication became official and Edward made a legendary BBC Radio broadcast to the nation in which he explained how he'd "found it impossible to carry the heavy burden of responsibility and to discharge my duties as king as I would wish to do without the help and support of the woman I love." Just before the broadcast, Edward had sat in his bedroom, drinking a whisky and soda while being treated to a pedicure. Immediately after the speech was over, he put his arm around the shoulder of a colleague named Walter Monckton and said, "Walter, it is a far better thing I go to."

The throne now passed to Edward's brother, Prince Albert, Duke of York, who, in the royal way of things, naturally became George VI. Meanwhile, Edward (David to his relatives) left England with the woman he loved. One of the new king's first acts was to make his predecessor the Duke of Windsor, and after said duke married Mrs. Simpson on June 3, 1937, she became a duchess. Yet she was never given the title of Her Royal Highness, a snub that would irk the duke for the rest of his life.

Did he do the right thing? Six months after his abdication, the Duke of Windsor looks hesitant when marrying Mrs. Wallis Warfield Simpson on June 3, 1937. (Photo courtesy of UPI/ Corbis-Bettmann)

Duke in Exile

Edward, Duke of Windsor, may have given up the throne and left his homeland, but his idiotic behavior continued to plague the Royal Family. Having openly expressed his admiration for fascist leaders such as Hitler and Mussolini, the duke and duchess paid a visit to the Nazi leader in October 1937, at a time when the Germans were girding themselves for an all-out assault on European democracy. It was wonderful propaganda for Goebbels, Goering, Himmler, and Hess to be seen socializing with British royalty, as well as for the smiling, happy-go-lucky fuehrer to be photographed shaking hands with

Edward and Wallis. Wonderful, that is, for the Germans. Hitler, tactful as ever, remarked on how the duchess "would have made a good queen." Meanwhile, back in England, George VI was appalled, and when he learned that his brother was also planning to meet with America's President Roosevelt in order to discuss Germany's peaceful intentions, the king intervened. The trip was cancelled, but the duke's other plans weren't.

World War II erupted in September 1939 and the following year, at the height of the Battle of Britain, the Duke of Windsor gave an interview in which he proclaimed the greatness of Hitler and the stupidity of the British if they thought they could defeat him. Basically, therefore, the country that Edward had once ruled should just concede to the Fuehrer's reasonable demands of controlling most of Europe…for the time being. At that time, the duke and duchess were residing in Spain and Portugal as guests of another charming Fascist leader, Generalissimo Franco. From there, Edward made it clear that he wouldn't return to England unless Wallis was accorded a proper royal title. Well, you can imagine how long George VI mulled over *that* tempting proposition.

Instead, the British government decided to get the troublesome duke out of the way by naming him Governor of the Bahamas. The Nazis (you'll love this) had been secretly planning to kidnap Edward and Wallis while they were in Portugal and, after the Germans had overrun Britain, install them on the throne! The duke and duchess had, in fact, already discussed that possibility with German officials, but the Bahamas assignment ruined Nazi plans.

It has since emerged that, while Edward was Governor of the Bahamas, he was passing top-secret British government information to the Nazis. That was high treason, for which he could have been executed. Instead he saw out the rest of the war, and then he and his lovely wife moved to France where, during the 1950s and 60s, they held court as leaders of the international jet-set. Edward died there in 1972. He was joined by his wife 14 years later.

On Her Majesty's Service

When the Duke of Windsor was greeted with *Heil Hitlers* during his 1937 German trip, he gave a modified Nazi salute; part wave, part the real thing. That's because royals never wave like ordinary people, flapping their hands vigorously. To wave like the Queen Mother, for instance, keep your fingers together, face your hand toward yourself, and twirl your wrist in a modest circular motion.

George VI: King of Hearts

George VI did share a couple of things in common with his brother, Edward VIII: He married a commoner, Elizabeth Bowes-Lyon, in 1923, who was the strong partner of the relationship; and, in the run-up to war, he favored a policy of appeasement to avoid conflict with Germany. There, however, the similarities end.

A sickly child who developed a nervous stammer at the age of eight, "Bertie," as he was affectionately known, grew up to be a good athlete and a fine king. During difficult times, he turned for support and inspiration to his cool-headed, hot-tempered wife (later to become the sweet little Queen Mother), who was descended from Scottish kings. Between them they rallied the nation during the dark days of war.

Staying in Buckingham Palace even after it was bombed, the king and queen gained the love and support of their people as they constantly visited those who had lost homes, limbs, and relatives during the blitz. George VI also made several morale-boosting trips abroad to meet with the troops, and he even wanted to accompany the invasion forces that were liberating France in 1944 but was persuaded by Prime Minister Winston Churchill not to risk his life. All the while, the king and his family survived on wartime rations as did their subjects, and when it was suggested that the young princesses, Elizabeth and Margaret, would be safer abroad than in their haven of Windsor Castle, the queen replied: "The children won't leave without me, I won't leave without the king, and the king will never leave."

Although just a figurehead monarch, George VI was entrusted by Churchill with top-level secrets. He was one of only four people to be informed in detail about the plans to deploy the atomic bomb. After the war, he was disappointed when Churchill was displaced by the election of a Labour government, yet he fell into line with the administration of Prime Minister Clement Atlee and helped put his victorious but war-ravaged nation back on its feet.

> **Hear Ye, Hear Ye**
> "I am glad we've been bombed. It makes me feel we can look the East End in the face."
> —*Queen Elizabeth, wife of George VI, relating to one of London's most damaged neighborhoods after Buckingham Palace had been hit by two bombs on September 12, 1940*

In 1951, on the centenary of the Great Exhibition, George VI played a central role in organizing the Festival of Britain, a celebration and promotion of the nation's trade. Arteriosclerosis and lung cancer were beginning to take their toll, however, and on February 6, 1952, while Princess Elizabeth and her husband Prince Philip were on a visit to Kenya, the much-loved king died in his sleep. He was 56.

The Young Ones: Elizabeth II and Princess Margaret

Princess Elizabeth and Lieutenant Philip Mountbatten first met at Dartmouth Naval College in 1939. She was 13, he was 18, and they corresponded throughout the war, during which time "Lilibet" eventually became a truck driver (her only known similarity to Elvis Presley) in the Auxiliary Transport Service. The couple married on November 20, 1947, at which point Philip was created Duke of Edinburgh and busied himself with various activities, nautical and otherwise. I tell you more about this royal marriage in Chapter 25—and if that isn't a teaser I don't know what is!

At the time of their 1947 engagement, Princess Elizabeth and Lt. Philip Mountbatten pose with Queen Elizabeth, King George VI, and Princess Margaret in the White Drawing Room of Buckingham Palace. (Photo courtesy of UPI/Corbis-Bettmann)

On June 2, 1953, 16 months after ascending to the throne, Elizabeth II was crowned at Westminster Abbey. She immediately asserted her independence by insisting that the ceremony be televised, which was against the expressed advice of Sir Winston Churchill (in the middle of a second spell as prime minister), the Cabinet, and the Archbishop of Canterbury. Still, citizens rushed out to buy TV sets and a then-massive British audience of 20 million watched the coronation, while 12 million listened in on the radio.

Nevertheless, in a country that was growing sick of the austerity of the post-war years, the hopes of a "New Elizabethan Age"—as promoted, of course, by the British press—soon began to dwindle. In 1957, the young queen was criticized for appearing dowdy and remote and for making speeches like those of a "priggish schoolgirl" according to Lord

Altrincham. She was also criticized by TV personality Malcolm Muggeridge for heading the cast of a "royal soap opera…a sort of substitute or ersatz religion." If only he knew then the script that would be written by the next generation of royals. Still, what Muggeridge was alluding to wasn't just the misplaced hero-worship courted by the monarchy, but also messy incidents such as that which had involved the queen's sister just a few years earlier.

In 1953, Princess Margaret told Elizabeth that she wanted to marry 39-year-old Group Captain Peter Townsend, a man who had seen distinguished service as a fighter pilot in World War II and controller of the Queen Mother's household. The Royal Marriages Act of 1772 required the 23-year-old princess to ask for the queen's permission to wed this upstanding citizen, but there was one hitch: he was divorced. As it happens, he was the innocent party—meaning that he'd been the one to seek the dissolution of his marriage on the grounds of his wife's behavior—yet, as far as the establishment was concerned, divorce was still a black mark. After all, there had been a long-standing tradition to not admit even the innocent party in a divorce into the royal enclosure at Ascot. As for the guilty party, well, he or she could forget being invited to any royal functions at all!

Of course, the Church of England wouldn't approve of a marriage between Townsend and someone who was so close to the throne and neither, in its official capacity, would the Cabinet. Privately, however, Churchill was all for the union. Therefore, even though no one really had anything against the gallant Group Captain, the queen denied her sister's request and Townsend was posted to Brussels as an air attache.

Townsend's reassignment was in the hope that the separation would serve as a kind of cold shower to the over-anxious lovers, but after two years Townsend was back and their passion hadn't cooled one bit. Again, the prospect of a marriage was raised and this time not only did the Cabinet and the Church disapprove, but the Establishment really closed ranks. At a time when a large proportion of British public opinion was on Princess Margaret's side, the traditionalist London newspaper *The Times* contrived to publish an editorial in which it asserted that, if she went ahead with her plans, would be embarking on something that "vast numbers of her sister's people…cannot in conscience regard as a marriage."

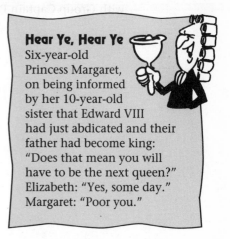

Hear Ye, Hear Ye
Six-year-old Princess Margaret, on being informed by her 10-year-old sister that Edward VIII had just abdicated and their father had become king: "Does that mean you will have to be the next queen?" Elizabeth: "Yes, some day." Margaret: "Poor you."

It was claptrap such as this that finally forced the poor princess to call off her marriage to—and relationship with—a man whom she truly loved. Of course, those guardians of the national conscience gave their complete blessing when Margaret wed a photographer named Anthony Armstrong-Jones in 1960; everything was squeaky clean and to their liking. Yet, their earlier interferences came back to haunt not so much them but the troubled princess when her marriage faltered after a few years, limping along until the inevitable divorce in 1978.

I'll fill you in on Margaret's further romantic problems in Chapter 25, but suffice it to say that the Peter Townsend episode was the only major piece of scandal during Elizabeth II's first quarter century on the throne. While the British Empire crumbled and the nation itself experienced the ups and downs of its longest period of peace, the figurehead monarchy trod a steady course. Back in 1952, Elizabeth had been pronounced queen in each of the self-governing countries of the Empire, and she was confirmed as Head of the Commonwealth in 1953. In 1977 her Silver Jubilee was celebrated on the grand scale throughout that Commonwealth as well as in her native Britain.

However, little did the 20th century's longest-reigning monarch—or her subjects—realize that the period of royal stability was about to come to an end. Her children were growing up and they would conduct themselves very differently than she had.

The Least You Need to Know

➤ On July 17, 1917 Britain's Royal Family changed its last name to Windsor.

➤ Edward VIII signed the Instrument of Abdication on December 10, 1936, and this was enacted the next day.

➤ Although just a figurehead monarch, George VI's wartime efforts greatly increased Britain's respect for its monarchy.

➤ In 1955, Establishment pressure forced Princess Margaret to end her relationship with Group Captain Peter Townsend.

Chapter 23

The Family Firm

If Queen Elizabeth II is still on the throne on December 12, 2007, at 81 years and 244 days she'll be the oldest British monarch in history. On the other hand, if she lasts until September 11, 2015, at 63 years and 217 days she'll also have had the longest reign. Queen Victoria presently holds both of these records.

Those are the facts and figures, and there are more facts and figures later in this chapter, as well as details of some of the things the queen and her family might be doing to occupy themselves during the intervening years. You see, in this chapter I give you some concise background information about several of the key players in the current British monarchy, as well as information about what they do at work and at play. I also explain where the money they receive comes from—as you'll learn, it certainly isn't all from the British taxpayers—and how in recent times they've been keeping the taxman happy like everyone else…well, nearly everyone else.

Who's Who: QE2 and the Original Seven

Back in the mid-1960s, it was so simple. There was the queen, her mother, her sister, her husband, and their four children. Sure, there were other relatives (including Margaret's family), but the main focus of attention was invariably on these eight members of Britain's royal household. Then, however, the children grew up and it all got very complicated. Their wives and husbands entered onto the scene, some in turn exited, and a whole new generation of royals was born.

The Royal Family in the Swinging '60s: (L-R) Prince Philip, Princess Anne, a royal corgi, Prince Edward, Queen Elizabeth II, Prince Charles, and Prince Andrew. (Photo courtesy of UPI/ Corbis-Bettmann)

Nevertheless, Elizabeth II is still on the throne and that core family is still around her. So, having already filled you in on the background of Princess Diana, I thought I'd now provide you with some details on "QE2 and the original seven." (Most of these people have numerous different royal titles, but I'm just using the ones with which they're most popularly associated.)

Queen Elizabeth II

Born: April 21, 1926

Educated at home with her younger sister, Princess Margaret, Princess Elizabeth became heir presumptive when her father, George VI, ascended to the throne in 1936. Thereafter, Elizabeth's education had to prepare her for her future role, so she studied, among other subjects, constitutional history, law, art, and music. As a child, she also learned to ride horses, enrolled as a Girl Guide, and, when she was 13, won the Children's Challenge Shield in a swimming competition at London's Bath Club.

Soon afterward, the future queen began to develop a public role. In October 1940, she made her first radio broadcast, sending a message to the children of Britain and the Commonwealth. Then, at the start of 1942, she became Colonel of the Grenadier Guards, inspecting the regiment as part of her first public engagement on her 16th birthday. More official duties followed as the princess became President of the Queen Elizabeth Hospital for Children in East London and of the National Society for the Prevention of Cruelty to Children. At the same time she started to accompany her parents on their tours around Britain, and just after her 18th birthday, she was appointed as Counsellor of State while the king was touring Italian battlefields. This meant that for the first time she was able to carry out some of the duties usually assigned to the monarch.

A Right Royal Tale

At 7:18 a.m. on July 9, 1982, the queen woke up to see a young man sitting on her bed. Michael Fagan had climbed through a Buckingham Palace window while a Palace police sergeant assumed he'd heard a faulty alarm bell. As Fagan described his troubled home life to Her Majesty, she pressed the alarm button. It didn't work. Her bedside bell went unanswered, the on-duty footman was exercising the corgis, and two "calm"-sounding phone calls asking for the police didn't cause concern. Finally, when Fagan asked for a cigarette, the queen exited the bedroom to "fetch some" and ran into her maid, her footman, and her corgis. Fagan was quickly arrested.

A Subaltern in the Auxiliary Territorial Service, Princess Elizabeth climbed to the rank of Junior Commander by the war's end. Her first official overseas visit was a 1947 tour of South Africa alongside her parents and her sister, during which Elizabeth celebrated her 21st birthday and made a radio broadcast dedicating herself to the Commonwealth. She would repeat this dedication on ascending to the throne in 1952.

Queen Elizabeth, the Queen Mother

Born: August 4, 1900

The Honourable Elizabeth Angela Marguerite Bowes-Lyon, descendant of the Royal House of Scotland and daughter of Lord Glamis, spent her early childhood in Hertfordshire, just north of London. Educated at home, Lady Elizabeth could speak fluent French by the age of 10. The First World War broke out on her 14th birthday, after which the family home, Glamis Castle, was used as a hospital. The house also accommodated royal visitors, for Elizabeth and her older sisters were childhood friends of George V's children.

In 1922, Lady Elizabeth was a bridesmaid at the wedding of the king's daughter, Princess Mary. The following January, Elizabeth became engaged to Albert, Duke of York, second son of the king and queen. On April 23 of that year they were married in Westminster Abbey. When, in 1936, Albert ascended to the throne as George VI, Elizabeth not only became queen but was also created a Lady of the Garter. At the coronation the following year she then became, as a Scottish queen, the first ever Lady of the Thistle.

Princess Margaret

Born: August 21, 1930

Christened Margaret Rose, the younger daughter of George VI and Queen Elizabeth was born at Glamis Castle, where her own mother had been raised. Along with her sister, Princess Elizabeth, Margaret was educated at home and as a child she was a keen horse-rider, swimmer, and gardener. In 1937, she joined the Brownies and later became a Girl Guide, maintaining links to this day: She is currently President and Chairwoman of the Council of the Girl Guides Association.

After the Peter Townsend debacle (which you can read about in Chapter 22), the queen consented to Princess Margaret's engagement to Antony Armstrong-Jones in February 1960. On May 6 of that year, they were married at Westminster Abbey, and in October, Armstrong-Jones was created Earl of Snowdon. The couple divorced in 1978, but their union produced two children: David Albert Charles, born on November 3, 1961, and now known as Viscount Linley; and Lady Sarah Frances Elizabeth, born on May 1, 1964.

Prince Philip, Duke of Edinburgh

Born: June 10, 1921

Originally assuming the title of Prince of Greece and Denmark, Philip was the only son of Prince Andrew of Greece (the grandson of King Christian IX of Denmark) and Princess Alice of Battenburg (daughter of Prince Louis of Battenberg and sister of Earl Mountbatten of Burma).

In 1868, Prince Louis was naturalized as a British citizen, and by 1914 he was First Sea Lord in the Royal Navy. During the First World War, he then Anglicised the family name by changing it to Mountbatten. In 1947, Philip adopted the name Mountbatten when he too was naturalized as a British subject and renounced his hereditary royal title. That same year he married Princess Elizabeth—both are great-great-grandchildren of Queen Victoria.

Initially schooled in France, Prince Philip then started attending Cheam Preparatory School in England at the age of seven. Five years later, he went to Salem School in Germany, and at the age of 13 attended Gordonstoun in Morayshire, Scotland, which he would later ensure all three of his sons attend. Philip stayed at Gordonstoun for five years, and on leaving in 1939, he joined the Royal Navy as a Cadet. Dedicated and industrious, he rose through the ranks very quickly, advancing to First Lieutenant when he was only 21. After seeing World War II service, the Prince continued his assignments. He was promoted to Lieutenant-Commander in 1950, and then Commander in 1952, but a few months later his career was cut short when, following the death of George VI, he had to assume his royal duties as husband of the new queen. To this day he still has strong naval, military, and aviation involvement.

> **Hear Ye, Hear Ye**
> "If…people feel it has no further part to play, then for goodness' sakes let's end the thing on amicable terms without having a row about it."
> —*Prince Philip, regarding the future of the British monarchy*

Lieutenant Philip Mountbatten married Princess Elizabeth on November 20, 1947, shortly after being created HRH Duke of Edinburgh, Earl of Merioneth, and Baron Greenwich. The Duke of Edinburgh is the title by which he is commonly known, and he also became a British Prince in 1957. Elizabeth and Philip had two children before she became queen and two after her ascension.

Charles, Prince of Wales

Born: November 14, 1948

Prince Charles Philip Arthur George was born at Buckingham Palace. On his mother's ascension he became heir apparent and Duke of Cornwall, and in 1958 he was also created Prince of Wales and Earl of Chester.

The two main schools that Charles attended as a youth were ones that his father had previously attended: Cheam and Gordonstoun. In 1966, he also went to the Geelong Church of England Grammar School in Melbourne, Australia, as an exchange student, marking the first time a Royal Family member had attended an overseas Commonwealth school. Thereafter, he went to Cambridge University, where he studied archaeology,

> **Royal Rebuttal**
> At a private dinner in his honor in 1978, Prince Charles told Prime Minister James Callaghan and members of his Cabinet about a conversation he'd had with an Air Quantess flight stewardess who had said, "God, what a rotten, boring job you've got!" When Callaghan and the others laughed on cue, Charles cried, "But no, you don't understand what I mean. She was right!"

anthropology, and history, appeared in a number of college theatrical productions, and was an active member of the polo team. Following a term at the University of Wales, Charles had his formal investiture as Prince of Wales in Caernarvon Castle on July 1, 1969. He then graduated with a BA (Honours) degree from Cambridge the following year.

Like his father, Charles has been strongly involved with all areas of the armed forces and currently holds the rank of Captain in the Royal Navy and Group Captain in the Royal Air Force. He married Lady Diana Spencer in St. Paul's Cathedral on July 29, 1981, and together they had two children: Prince William, born on June 21, 1982, and second in line to the throne; and Prince Henry (Harry), born on September 15, 1984, and third in line. Charles and Diana officially divorced in August 1996.

Anne, Princess Royal

Born: August 15, 1950

Princess Anne Elizabeth Alice Louise was born at Clarence House in London and baptized at Buckingham Palace, where she gained her initial education. She spent a year studying in France at the age of 12, and at 13 she moved to Benenden School in Kent. An extremely keen horsewoman, Anne won the individual European Three-Day Event Championship at Burghley, Lincoln-shire in 1971 and in 1976 was a member of the British Three-Day Event team at the Montreal Olympic Games.

Hear Ye, Hear Ye

"Only a moral imperative can persuade husbands and wives to be faithful to each other."

—*Prince Philip, regarding marital fidelity*

During the interim, she became engaged to Lieutenant (later Captain) Mark Phillips of the Queen's Dragoon Guards on May 29, 1973, and in best British royal tradition, married him in Westminster Abbey on November 14 of that year. Their first child, Peter Mark Andrew Phillips, was born on November 15, 1977, followed by a daughter, Zara Anne Elizabeth, on May 15, 1981.

The marriage of Anne and Captain Phillips was dissolved in April 1992, making her the first of three divorcees among the Queen's four children. On December 12 of that same year, she married Captain Timothy Laurence of the Royal Navy in a private ceremony at Craithie Church, near the royal retreat of Balmoral Castle in Scotland.

In recognition of her extensive charity work (more of which a little later), Anne was made Princess Royal by her mother in June 1987.

Prince Andrew, Duke of York

Born: February 19, 1960

Prince Andrew Albert Christian Edward was the first child born to a reigning monarch in 103 years. Initially educated at Buckingham Palace, Andrew went to Heatherdown Preparatory School in Ascot at the age of eight and, after five years, followed in the footsteps of his father and elder brother by attending Gordonstoun. Except for a couple of terms on an exchange program at Lakefield College School in Ontario, Canada, Andrew remained at Gordonstoun until he joined the Royal Navy in 1979. Like his father, the Prince has enjoyed an illustrious naval career, seen active service (as part of the Task Force that regained the Falkland Islands from Argentina in 1982), and has been involved with the Army and Royal Air Force.

On marrying 26-year-old Sarah Ferguson at Westminster Abbey on July 23, 1986, Andrew was created Duke of York, making Sarah the Duchess. Their first child, Beatrice Elizabeth Mary of York, was born on August 8, 1988, followed by Eugenie Victoria Helena on March 23, 1990. The duke and duchess were divorced in May 1996.

Prince Edward

Born: March 10, 1964

The youngest child of the Queen and the Duke of Edinburgh, Prince Edward Anthony Richard Louis was, like Prince Andrew before him, educated at Heatherdown Preparatory School in Ascot and Gordonstoun in Morayshire, Scotland. He then went to Jesus College, Cambridge, where he graduated with a BA in History in 1986.

At this point it looked as if Prince Edward would follow his father and brothers' well-trodden course of long and distinguished service in the armed forces. After only three years as a Second Lieutenant in the Royal Marines, however, it was agreed that this wasn't the life for him. Edward quit the marines and went into theater production, working for the Theatre Division and Sir Andrew Lloyd Webber's Really Useful Theatre Company. In 1993 Prince Edward formed the TV production company Ardent Productions Limited, where he is the Director of Production.

Keeping Themselves Busy—Royal Leisure Activities

In a moment, we'll come to some of the charitable endeavors that the queen and her family undertake in the line of duty. The royal life isn't, however, a case of all work and no play. Those royals really know how to have a good time when they get the opportunity, and they get quite a few opportunities.

The queen and Queen Mother, for instance, both like to spend much of their leisure time in the countryside. (When she was young, Princess Elizabeth predicted that one day she'd marry a farmer. Fortune-telling was never her strong point.) Believe it or not, the Queen Mother was also a keen and accomplished fisherwoman in her younger days, and she and her eldest daughter share a deep and abiding love for horse racing. Indeed, the queen goes in for quite a bit of horse breeding. Her horses have won many prizes and, by sheer coincidence, in the year of her Silver Jubilee she was named top British horse breeder of the year. On a number of occasions, Her Majesty has also made brief private visits to America in order to see stallion stations and stud farms in Kentucky.

Of course, this love of horses has been passed on to Princess Anne. A regular competitor at the Horse of the Year Show and Badminton Horse Trials when she was younger, Anne was nominated Sportswoman of the Year by the British Sports Writer's Association in 1971 and was voted the BBC's Sports Personality that same year. She has competed in countless events, won several prizes, and spent five years as President of the British Olympic Association. Anne was actually elected to the International Olympic Committee in 1988—a couple of years after having succeeded her father as the President of the International Equestrian Federation.

For his part, Prince Philip has found horses useful in some of his leisure activities, such as foxhunting and polo. He played polo regularly until 1971, and since then Prince Charles has followed in his father's footsteps. A keen pilot, Philip has represented Britain in a number of European and World four-in-hand driving championships, and he is also Admiral of the Royal Yacht Squadron. In addition, on two occasions he has served as President of the Marylebone ("Marry-le-bone") Cricket Club.

As you can tell, this is a sporting family. Both Charles and Andrew are happy whether they're flying, parachuting, or skiing. In addition, Andrew enjoys golf and squash. Charles, on the other hand, has inherited his mother and grandmother's love of the countryside, and his many other interests—ranging from the arts and architecture to conservation and the environment—overlap with his work. Much the same can be said for Prince Edward, of course, who has found a way of indulging his love for the theater and television by way of his professional career. There again, he too enjoys horse riding, sailing, skiing, and badminton. Meanwhile, Princess Margaret loves ballet and classical music. In 1957, she became the first President of the Royal Ballet, and in operatic terms, she has also served as President of the Sadler's Wells Foundation.

On Her Majesty's Service

You have plenty of opportunity to run into the royals. They're constantly opening hospital wards, making public speeches, and so on, and they also travel extensively. No sovereign has ever journeyed overseas as much as the present queen, who has made more than 60 State Visits to foreign shores. The royal schedules appear under "press releases" on the official monarchy Web site: www.royal.gov.uk.

Hear Ye, Hear Ye

"When I appear in public, people expect me to neigh, grind my teeth, paw the ground, and swish my tail."
—*Princess Anne*

Still, while the members of the Royal Family are often closely associated with their very public personal interests, some of their tastes and leisure activities are a little less predictable. I mean, it's one thing for the queen to like military brass band music, but how about the reports in years gone by that she enjoyed settling down in front of her TV set to watch a good bout of wrestling!

All in a Good Cause: Charitable Work

For all of their pastimes, sporting and otherwise, the royals dedicate a considerable amount of time to charity work. This charity work largely justifies and earns respect for the figurehead monarchy; it also promotes Britain overseas and lets the royals publicly get involved in issues pertaining to business, education, health, and the environment. After all, the queen and her relatives have to be seen making a definite contribution, or they'll be accused of living the life of the idle rich. (The accusation is still often flung at them, despite their charity work.)

As patrons or presidents of a wide range of charitable organizations, the Royal Family undertakes a huge number of assignments each year. Leading the field in this respect is Prince Philip, who, never given a specific role to play, has carved out his own niche by taking a special interest in British industry, scientific, and technological research and development, sport, young people, conservation, and the environment. The Patron or President of some 800 organizations, he carried out a staggering total of 619 public engagements in the UK and overseas in 1996, many in conjunction with the queen, and others on his own.

Meanwhile, Princess Anne ran her father a very close second in 1996 with no fewer than 609 public engagements in the U.K. and overseas. The Princess Royal is Patron or President of 222 organizations—she has been President of the Save the Children fund since 1970—and just behind her in terms of 1996 engagements was the queen, who undertook a grand total of 585 as Patron or President of more than 700 organizations. On the other hand, the Queen Mother, who is as old as the century itself, is Patron of some 350 organizations, and in 1996 she still managed to carry out 58 engagements.

Prince Charles, the future monarch, is president or patron of around 200 different organizations dealing with the young, the old, the unemployed, the disabled, education, medicine, inner city problems, the arts, national heritage, conservation, the environment, architecture, and sport. In 1996, he carried out 384 public engagements. As for Prince Andrew, 1997 sees him winding down his naval career, yet he has still managed to fit in official engagements: 129 for him in 1996 as Patron of more than 90 organizations. The same goes for Prince Edward, who in the same year managed to carry out 170 engagements on behalf of the queen and in support of the various organizations that he is involved with, mainly pertaining to young people, the arts, and sport.

Being that I'm not including the charitable work of other Royal Family members, this leaves us with Princess Margaret. Often taking on the engagements

On Her Majesty's Service

Considering how much Americans wanted to eliminate George III during the War of Independence, the current American fascination with Britain's Royal Family is ironic. If this attraction puzzles you, consider the words of a historian who once asserted, "It's the fairy stories that keep it going. Whoever heard of a girl kissing a frog and it turning into a handsome senator?"

that her sister, Elizabeth II, doesn't have time to fulfill, Margaret also has more than 80 organizations of which she herself is patron or president. Still, back in 1977 and 1978, when personal problems resulted in this troubled princess reducing her number of public engagements, large sections of the British public (led on by the British press) began to complain about what certain royals were doing for their money. Such complaints were based partly on a false assumption, yet eventually they resulted in some notable changes with regard to the financial arrangements of the monarchy.

The Taxman Cometh: Paying Those Dues

Once Princess Margaret had set the ball of public criticism rolling, other Royals also found themselves under fire in the value-for-money debate. At first, these members included "miserable" Princess Anne and "outspoken" Prince Philip, but by the early 1990s the epidemic had spread. With Britain suffering through another economic recession while many of the Windsors appeared to be having a fine old jet-set time, few were spared the diatribe.

Palace Parlance
The **Civil List** comprises the annual allowance by Parliament for the official expenses of the sovereign's household so that royal duties can be carried out. It's set for a period of up to 10 years.

The false assumption that many people were—and still are—making was that the *Civil List* amounts to the salary of the queen and her closest relatives. It doesn't. Dating back to the monarchy's restoration in 1660 and revamped on George III's accession a century later, the Civil List system amounts to Parliament (and therefore the taxpayers) picking up the tab for official expenses in return for the sovereign surrendering the revenues from the Crown Estates. Being that the Civil List is currently set at an annual rate of 7.9 million pounds ($12 million) while the annual revenue being surrendered by the Queen is about 95 million pounds ($143 million), that's not a bad deal for Parliament.

Around 70 percent of Civil List expenditure goes on the salaries of the queen's staff. These people deal with State documents and arrange public engagements, meetings, and receptions undertaken by Her Majesty. Furthermore, the Civil List also covers the costs of functions such as the royal garden parties, which are attended by more than 40,000 people every year.

The costs of maintenance and upkeep pertaining to palaces inhabited by the Royal Family and used for official purposes are met by Grants-in-Aid, as are those for travel. These are provided by Parliament, while the Privy Purse, which meets all official expenses of the queen not covered by the Civil List, is furnished by estate revenues from the Duchy of Lancaster. In all cases—the Civil List, Grants-in-Aid, and the Privy Purse—expense accounts are prepared for everything so that Parliament can ensure all is in order. Any surplus is offset against the grants of future years. Meanwhile, private expenditure is met by the queen's income from her personal investment portfolio.

All in all, this should give you some idea as to how much control Parliament exerts over the British monarchy. Still, back in the early 1990s, a lot of people were objecting to the fact that the queen, the "wealthiest woman in the world," didn't have to pay tax on her income or her profits (capital gains). Well, in 1992, with her family's image at what she then must have mistakenly considered to be a 20th-century low, the queen relented and agreed to pay these taxes on a voluntary basis, commencing the following year. The Privy Purse is part of the taxable income, yet the Civil List and Grants-in-Aid are not.

That same year the queen removed everyone but her husband and mother from the Civil List. The others now derive their income from other sources. One who had already been doing so was Prince Charles, who became the 24th Duke of Cornwall on his mother's accession and as such, receives the annual net revenues of the Duchy of Cornwall. This comprises 52,250 hectares of land, mostly in the south of England, which is used for commercial purposes. In 1994, it earned the Prince of Wales 4.9 million pounds ($7.5 million) before tax—which he's been paying since 1969. For this reason, Diana, Princess of Wales also didn't receive any money from the state when she was married to Charles.

So, there you have it. Oh yes, and as for that "wealthiest woman in the world," nonsense: The queen's monetary worth has been exaggerated out of all proportion. The royal palaces, royal art treasures, and Crown Jewels do *not* belong to her; they're simply held by her as the sovereign and then passed on to her successor. She does own homes such as Balmoral, Sandringham, and Sunninghill Park (home of the Duke of York), as well as various other properties in the U.K. She doesn't, however, own property anywhere else, and according to the Lord Chamberlain in 1993, estimates that her investment portfolio was worth 100 million pounds ($150 million) and upwards were "grossly overstated."

The Least You Need to Know

➤ With strong Scottish ancestry on her mother's side, Queen Elizabeth II has more British blood running through her veins than many of her predecessors.

➤ The royals are a very sporting family.

➤ Prince Philip, Princess Anne, and the queen lead the royal field in terms of the number of annual engagements that they undertake.

➤ The Civil List covers the annual expenses of the sovereign's household. It is not a salary.

➤ Since 1993, the queen has been paying tax on her income and profits.

Charles—The Man Who Would Be King

In light of the enormous press coverage he's always received, the severe criticisms he's been subjected to with regard to his marital problems, and the fact that he is the heir to the British throne, Prince Charles warrants his own chapter. In it, I describe the childhood that helped create the man and the solo lifestyle that preceded the fairytale wedding. This, I hope, will put the prince into perspective, describing the environment and atmosphere in which he was raised and the resultant attitudes that these both shaped.

As you'll see, Charles endured a far-from-happy childhood and adolescence before coming into his own as a young man. At several stages in his life, he was just settling into a routine that he liked when royal duty intervened and the playing field was changed. One such instance led to the wedding to beat all weddings—something else I describe to you here. In the meantime, let's try to understand the mind of a future monarch.

Little Big Man: Born to Rule

Imagine seeing your mom or dad's face on a postage stamp. Or hearing the nation regularly breaking into song to ask God to save one of them. These thoughts may be particularly amusing, disturbing, or downright peculiar, but they're reality if you're the child of a monarch. As such, you quickly grow accustomed to other strange behavior: seeing people bow and scrape all over the place when you're around, hearing them address you as "Your Royal Highness," and watching thousands of them line the streets and wave little flags when you ride in a carriage on a special occasion. Yes, all part of life's little routine.

At least it has been for the likes of Prince Charles. Which is all well and good, except that in his case, he was also forced to spend a large part of his childhood separated from one or both of his parents. Before and after the queen's accession, she and Philip were always busy doing one royal thing or another. This left young Charles in the hands of his nannies or, later on, his boarding school teachers. Now, compared to those royal predecessors who were raised as the offspring of bloodthirsty, power-hungry tyrants, Charles probably had it pretty easy. Everything's relative, however, so just as said predecessors often (but not always) grew up to be bloodthirsty, power-hungry tyrants themselves, Charles was greatly shaped by his own upbringing.

A Right Royal Tale

November 14, 1948, was a cold and rainy Sunday, yet as word spread that Princess Elizabeth had gone into labor with her first child the crowds started to gather outside Buckingham Palace. Inside, on the other hand, there was an expectant father who wasn't gathering himself next to his wife. By early evening Philip, Duke of Edinburgh, had decided that, instead of waiting around, he'd go swimming and play a game of squash with a friend in another part of the palace. It was, therefore, on the squash court that Philip learned about the birth of his son, the heir to the British throne, who had entered the world around 9:15 p.m.

For about a year after Charles was born on November 14, 1948, Princess Elizabeth was on hand to take care of her baby while Philip pursued his naval career from the London base of the Admiralty. In addition, the failing health of King George VI meant that Elizabeth had to assume some of her father's royal duties. Nevertheless, she and Philip did spend some time together, and on August 15, 1950, Princess Anne was born.

Thereafter, both children saw their mother on a regular basis: half an hour in the mornings and, when possible, a couple of hours in the afternoons! Nannies Mabel Anderson and Helen Lightbody filled in the rest of the time. As Charles began to toddle around, he was also taught the same things that you and I learned as a child: Always stand, unless told otherwise, when you're in the presence of your grandfather (in Charles' case, King George VI), and always bow before you're kissed by your great-grandmother (Queen Mary). It was wise to observe these rules since the young prince saw more of these two people than his own parents.

The monarch's health was steadily declining. By July 1951, Philip had given up his day job to help Princess Elizabeth full-time with the royal duties, and it was while touring Kenya that, on February 6, 1952, they learned about George VI having passed away in his sleep. For Elizabeth, his death meant that, as queen, she and her family moved from London's Clarence House to Buckingham Palace, while her mother and sister moved in the opposite direction. For the four-year-old Prince Charles, on the other hand, it also meant that he was now afforded some of life's necessities: his own private car and chauffeur, a governess to help with his early education, a footman to take care of his requests, and a private detective to watch over him. Oh yes, and he also became the Duke of Cornwall. (The prince, that is, not the detective.)

On June 2, 1953, the day of his mother's coronation, Charles got to see masses of people all waving their little flags as he stood on the front balcony of his home, Buckingham Palace. For the most part, however, the queen wanted to keep this shy and impressionable child out of the limelight and especially away from the nosy media. Her press secretary therefore issued statements asking the reporters and photographers to allow Charles and his governess a little space when the two of them visited public places. For the most part the press complied, but it wouldn't be the last time that such requests were made.

School Days: Lonely Boy

It was customary for the heir to the throne to receive his or her education at home, but Elizabeth II wanted to break with tradition. In the fall of 1956 she enrolled her seven-year-old son at Hill House private school in London's Knightsbridge so that each afternoon he would mix with children other than those of royal or aristocratic stock. Of course, the teachers had to observe the proper protocol by addressing their new pupil as "Prince Charles," but his classmates were allowed to dispense with the formality. Meanwhile, to break Charles in gently, he was tutored initially by his governess, Catherine Peebles, in the mornings; in 1957, he began attending Hill House full-time.

Things were going fine, but then Prince Philip's influence made its mark. This man's man had already asserted his fatherly role by trying—and failing—to teach his sensitive young son to box; Charles was

Royal Rebuttal
It has long been popular for people to poke fun at Prince Charles' protruding and oversized ears. Yet, while you may think that he takes all this ribbing in his stride, it's actually a sensitive subject. When he went to Gordonstoun boarding school in Scotland, Charles' large lugs were the object of non-stop ridicule by the other children—and a source of great upset for him.

much happier reading, painting, fly fishing, swimming, and watching television on his own. Philip, however, felt it would be best if the boy went to Cheam, the same private boarding school that he himself had attended in his youth. The queen was convinced as well: Cheam would provide Charles with an excellent education in a secluded environment well away from the press. *Wrong!*

It had generally been accepted that the news cameras would be on hand to capture the stiff-backed little boy arriving at his new school in the fall of 1957. What the royal parents hadn't counted on, however, was the reporters' subsequent tactic of bribing Charles' fellow pupils in order to glean some tidbits of gossip. ("'Ere sonny, this chocolate bar could be yours if you tell me what 'is Royal Highness has been gettin' up to…") The queen was furious. Her press secretary soon made it clear to the newspaper editors that if they didn't stop making her child's life a misery, she would be forced to have him educated back at Buckingham Palace. Being that this was the late 1950s, the editors relented.

Depressed about being away from home and increasingly withdrawn as a result of the prying camera lenses, Charles was going through one of the most miserable periods of his young life. (He would have to endure a few more when he was older.) Aside from history and geography, he limped through his schoolwork and, at first, he didn't exactly excel at sports either. The prince did eventually become captain of Cheam's soccer team, but the school regretted this decision: The team lost every single game and scored a crowd-pleasing total of four goals all season. When England won the soccer World Cup tournament nearly a decade later, Charles' leadership qualities weren't called upon.

Hear Ye, Hear Ye

"I didn't wake up in my pram one day and say, 'Yippee,' you know. But I think it just dawns on you, slowly, that people are interested in one."

—*Prince Charles card*

Eventually, the prince did begin to get the hang of school life, but he was still depressed about being away from home. Therefore, when it was time to move on to a new school, the queen thought that Eton, located close to Windsor Castle, would be a fair compromise. Her husband, however, didn't agree. It was no good turning the 13-year-old boy into a namby-pamby, Philip believed; he needed to be farther away where he could get some privacy and learn to be a real man. Gordonstoun in Scotland is where Philip had flourished, so Gordonstoun in Scotland was where Charles would go. It's debatable as to whether or not Charles himself had any say in the matter, but, having previously let his father down ("Four goals *all season*?"), he wanted to please him. Big mistake.

After familiarizing himself with life at Gordonstoun, Charles probably wished that he'd defied the duke, thrown a tantrum, and insisted on going to Eton. Cricket had bored him at Cheam, but now he was expected to immerse himself in mountain climbing, fire fighting, life saving, and running assault courses. To the pampered prince it was just like being in the army, except that he wasn't being paid to go through all of the drudgery. What's more, his royal celebrity and the constant shadowing by his private detective only served to alienate many of his classmates. The result was that Mr. Homesick of Cheam was now Mr. Lonely of Gordonstoun, whiling away his free time with solitary walks along Scotland's rugged northeast coastline.

At the same time, when Charles did try to get into the swing of things and do a bit of socializing, the press was ready to knock him down. Sample the idiotic episode in 1963 when headlines and controversy were manufactured because the 14-year-old prince innocently tried to order a cherry brandy at a local bar. The resultant grilling he received only deepened his unhappiness at school, but caused him little joy with his father when he went home for the holidays.

The Duke of Edinburgh's haughty lectures and scathing criticisms of his son often ended in tears—and they weren't the father's tears. There is one story that on one particular occasion Philip pushed his luck too far and Charles came back with a rejoinder that he'd probably been tempted to use for quite some time—one that could simply and efficiently take the wind out of the duke's sails. Charles simply told his father, "You don't talk to a future king of England like that." Prince Philip reportedly left the room.

Still, 1964 was little better than 1963 for plucky Prince Charles. His English essay book went missing at school and extracts from it turned up in the pages of some magazines. To make matters worse, it was also asserted that the prince had sold the essay book to a classmate because he was in need of some cash! (Don't you just love stories like that?)

As it happens, things were about to take a major turn for the better. Charles' efforts in Gordonstoun's music and drama productions won him praise and popularity among his fellow students, and on the academic front, he also passed the necessary "O" level (ordinary level) exams to qualify him for higher education. The year was 1965 and the prince was 16; the following year, his parents allowed him to take a break from Gordonstoun to study at Timbertop in the Australian outback. There, in the remote foothills of the Victorian Alps, Charles took to the outdoor life like a fish takes to water. The boy who once didn't like the idea of rock climbing was now hunting, felling trees, shearing sheep, and panning for gold. What's more, he also got to grips with cooking his own meals and cleaning the hut he shared with other students. Unfortunately, I couldn't find a photo of him wearing an apron and brandishing a feather duster.

Hear Ye, Hear Ye
"It's such hell here, especially at night. I don't get any sleep practically at all nowadays. The people in my dormitory are foul. They throw slippers—or rush across the room and hit me as hard as they can. Last night was hell. Literally hell."
—*Prince Charles, in a letter to his parents from Gordonstoun, 1964*

The prince was one happy camper during his time in Australia, and when he returned to Gordonstoun he was altogether more confident. In 1967, he passed his "A" level (advanced level) exams in French and history. As a result, he qualified for university studies by conventional means—a feat no other heirs to the British throne had ever managed. They didn't need to. After all, they were royal! On July 1, 1969, Charles was invested as

Prince of Wales, and the following year, having completed his history course at Trinity College, Cambridge, he also became the first-ever heir to attain an honors degree.

You see, even though this was the height of the peace-and-love, flower-power era, Charles didn't grow his hair long or smoke dope on the university campus. Instead, the prince studied hard and surrounded himself with members of the landed gentry, not all of whom were male. Lucia Santa Cruz had been his first steady girlfriend. Numerous others were to follow.

Pre-Diana: The Casanova Prince

There were the playmates and confidantes, like Lady "Kanga" Tryon, Camilla Shand, Georgina Russell, Laura Jo Watkins, Jane Ward, Lady Amanda Knatchbull, Lady Sarah Spencer, and Sabrina Guinness, the heiress and former date of Mick Jagger and Ryan O'Neal. There were the famous faces, such as actress Susan George and The Three Degrees' lead singer Sheila Ferguson. And then there were the contenders, who, during Charles' hot-to-trot bachelor years of the 1970s, were considered (by the British press at least) to be not just good friends, but ladies with a serious chance of becoming the Princess of Wales.

A Right Royal Tale

Prince Charles first met Camilla Shand at a polo match during the early 1970s and they instantly hit it off. Although she really liked the Prince of Wales, Miss Shand apparently didn't fancy marrying him and becoming a public figure—a fairly ironic stance in light of subsequent events. What events, you might ask? In 1973 Camilla wed cavalry officer Andrew Parker-Bowles. Sound familiar? If you still don't get the connection, be patient; all will be revealed in Chapter 25. In the meantime, you might be interested to know that Camilla's great-grandmother, Alice Keppel, was one of the more well-known mistresses of Charles' great-great-grandfather, Edward VII.

First, during the early part of the decade, there was Lady Jane Wellesley, the daughter of the 8th Duke of Wellington, who Charles dated for about three years. Then, in 1976, a young lovely by the name of Davina Sheffield raced to the front of the pack. The prince was reportedly crazy about her, his relatives thoroughly approved, and her face was all over the newspapers. Unfortunately, so were the tell-all revelations by one of her former lovers. Goodbye Davina.

More romantic flings followed, aided and abetted by Charles' great-uncle, Lord Louis Mountbatten. For, among the many private trysting places that the Casanova prince was able to make good use of was Broadlands, the residence of "Uncle Dickie" (as Charles fondly referred to Mountbatten). This was all very convenient, but then Charles appeared to be seriously smitten again when he started going out with Anna "Whiplash" Wallace. (Before you get any fanciful ideas, let me explain that she gained her nickname because of her hot temper.)

Both keen hunters, Anna and Charles liked each other at first glance. The prince was subsequently charmed by the way in which Anna appreciated him for who he was rather than what he represented. What she didn't appreciate, however, was being ignored by Charles as he mingled all evening with other guests at the Queen Mother's 78th birthday party at Windsor Castle in June 1978. Now the "Whiplash" went into action, berating the prince for his shoddy behavior and storming out. Before her dramatic exit, she had also warned him never to treat her like that again, but he did only a short while later when they both attended a high society ball in Gloucestershire ("Glosster-shear"). That was it. Anna whipped her lash and walked out for the last time.

Nevertheless, on that occasion Prince Charles hadn't been mingling with other guests all evening, but one guest in particular. Her name was Camilla Parker-Bowles, and it wouldn't be the last time that she would crop up in the middle of one of Charles' relationships.

In the meantime, for about nine months in 1977 and 1978 the prince was seeing someone I mentioned a little earlier: Lady Sarah Spencer. She was the eldest sister of one Lady Diana Spencer, and as I mentioned back in Chapter 5, it was during a pheasant shoot in November 1977 that Charles and Di met for the first time, in the middle of a plowed field on the Althorp estate. Well, it wouldn't be until a full year later that they would get together again, Charles having invited Sarah and Di to his 30th birthday party at Buckingham Palace. By then, the relationship with Sarah was over and the prince's latest companion was Susan George.

Despite all his women, however, now that Charles was in his 30s, the whispering started; he was the oldest-ever bachelor Prince of Wales (the others were all married by his age but most of them just *lived* like bachelors), and it was therefore time for him to settle down and produce an heir. The queen, Prince Philip, and the palace courtiers were all applying pressure, and even though Charles was more than happy to continue playing the field, his sense of royal duty also told him that they were right.

There really was little option. The Prince of Wales had to find himself the right woman.

Fairytale Romance and Wedding of the Century

As a result of the marriage of Lady Diana Spencer's other sister, Jane, to the queen's assistant private secretary, Robert Fellowes, Di found herself being invited to a number of royal get-togethers in 1979 and 1980. During the summer of that year, it became obvious that the Prince of Wales was taking a special interest in the 19-year-old ingénue; dancing extra close to her at a party in July, inviting her to a performance of Verdi's *Requiem* at the Royal Albert Hall. It was when they were spotted together while Charles was salmon fishing in the River Dee at Balmoral, however, that all of the speculation really got underway. And the person responsible for spotting them? James Whitaker, royal correspondent and the writer of the Foreword to this *Complete Idiot's Guide.*

"HE'S IN LOVE, AGAIN" announced *The Sun* on September 8, 1980, and once again the big question was "Could this be the one?" Soon there was a definite sense that the answer was "yes" and at that point all hell broke loose. The daily press attention that Diana attracted wherever she went, often when traveling between her London apartment and the kindergarten where she worked, amounted to out-and-out harassment. It was as if the news media were speeding events towards their inevitable conclusion, while the prince and Lady Diana were still trying to conduct a proper courtship and size each other up—a feat that would prove virtually impossible.

A Right Royal Tale

The marriage of Prince Charles to Lady Diana Spencer marked the first time since 1659 that the heir to the British throne actually married a British subject. The queen gave her assent at a meeting of the Privy Seal, following which an instrument (document) was drawn up for Her Majesty's signature. This instrument was sealed with the Great Seal of England, which dates from late Anglo-Saxon times, weighs more than 8 pounds, and authenticates all important government documents. Only after the queen had formally assented could Charles and Diana's marriage take place. This was in accordance with the Royal Marriage Act passed in 1772 by George III, who disapproved of the marriages of his two brothers.

"It is with the greatest pleasure that the Queen and the Duke of Edinburgh announce the betrothal of their beloved son, the Prince of Wales, to the Lady Diana Spencer, daughter of the Earl Spencer and the Honourable Mrs. Shand Kydd." This announcement was made by Buckingham Palace at 11:00 am on Tuesday, February 24, 1981. Diana had accepted Charles' proposal of marriage in the nursery of Windsor Castle back on February 6—a proposal that had been made after the prince's extensive consultations with his courtiers and confidantes. The big event was now set for Wednesday, July 29. History was in the making. Breaking with tradition, the venue for the service was St. Paul's Cathedral, preferred by Charles for its famous architecture courtesy of Sir Christopher Wren and its superior acoustics. Wedding invitations—2,650 of them—were mailed out. Between the engagement announcement and the wedding day, more than 10,000 gifts were received—not because the guests sent three or four gifts each, but because the general public also got in on the act. In addition, more than 100,000 people sent letters.

Charles' wedding outfit was his Royal Navy commander's uniform. Diana's was the trend-setting Elizabeth and David Emanuel creation, comprised of a boned and fitted bodice of ivory silk paper taffeta and antique lace embroidered with mother-of-pearl sequins, together with billowing sleeves, a V-shaped neckline, and a record-setting royal bridal train measuring 25 feet in length. The ivory silk veil with mother-of-pearl sequins was held in place by the dazzling Spencer family diamond tiara. The dress was "something new"; lace that had belonged to George V's wife, Queen Mary, was "something old"; earrings belonging to Diana's mother, Frances Shand Kydd, were "something borrowed"; and a small blue bow sewn to the bride's waist along with a gold horseshoe was "something blue."

Before the dress was completed, Di rehearsed her walk in the ballroom of St. James' Palace with several yards of paper tissue attached to her head. She also had to rehearse getting in and out of the glass coach that would transport her and her father, Earl Spencer, to St. Paul's, while Lady Susan Hussey coached her in the techniques of the all-important royal wave. Di's engagement ring, which Charles had purchased for 28,500 pounds ($54,150) from the royal jewelers, Garrards, consisted of a large oval sapphire surrounded by 14 diamonds set in white gold. The wedding ring was carved from the same nugget of Welsh gold as that used for the wedding bands of the Queen Mother, the queen, Princess Margaret, and Princess Anne.

Approximately one million people lined the procession route on the big day, while an estimated worldwide TV audience of around one billion tuned in to watch the 70-minute service as well as all of the pageantry both before and after. The excitement culminated in an unscripted act: Standing before the cheering crowds on the balcony of Buckingham Palace, the happy couple actually kissed each other *on the lips*. Eighteen minutes were then spent taking the royal wedding portraits inside the Palace, and then a select list of 118 guests sat down to a three-course meal. The wedding cake, by the way, had five tiers, was five feet high, and weighed 200 pounds. Charles cut it with his ceremonial sword.

The honeymoon commenced at Broadlands, the Hampshire home of Lord and Lady Romsey and former residence of the late "Uncle Dickie" Mountbatten. This was where Princess Elizabeth and Prince Philip had spent their wedding night in 1947, and also where, you might recall, Charles apparently spent many a night during his freewheeling bachelor days. From there, the prince and Di flew to Gibraltar, where they boarded the royal yacht *Britannia* for a Mediterranean cruise around Tunisia, Sardinia, the Greek islands, and Egypt.

Then it was back to Balmoral, where the newlyweds joined the rest of the Royal Family. The couple posed for the press photographers while Charles once again fished in the River Dee and all appeared to be happiness for the Princess of Wales.

"What will my future be?" Charles, Prince of Wales, during a 1992 visit to South Korea. (Photo courtesy of Reuters/ Corbis-Bettmann)

The Least You Need to Know

➤ Charles' parents were away performing royal duties for most of his early childhood.

➤ Despite being homsesick, Charles moved from Cheam boarding school to faraway Gordonstoun in northeast Scotland at the instigation of authoritarian Prince Philip.

➤ Charles graduated from Trinity College, Cambridge with a BA (Honours) degree in history.

➤ When he reached his 30s, royal pressure was applied to Charles so that he would marry and produce an heir.

➤ Charles and Diana got married at St. Paul's Cathedral in London on July 29, 1981.

Chapter 25

The Party's Over: Broken Marriages, Shattered Dreams

In This Chapter

➤ The episodes that have rocked the House of Windsor

➤ Diana's death in Paris

➤ Anger and sorrow following the Princess' demise

➤ What's in store for the future Charles III and William V, as well as Prince Harry

➤ A final chance to prove your royal knowledge

Having worked our way through 67 kings and queens, I have to say that, all things considered, the House of Windsor is one of the best royal dynasties that England or Britain as a whole has ever seen. Obviously, times have changed, the monarchy has been tamed, and these 20th-century figureheads don't have the absolute power that would enable them to behave like tyrants. However, a good number of the Hanoverian monarchs also proved that a lack of constitutional strength can still make for a lousy king.

Of course, some of Britain's most powerful rulers did engineer great social and political changes, and there's no way of knowing how successful Edward VII, George V, George VI, and Elizabeth II would have been in that regard were they given the opportunity. Nevertheless, even without all the murder, torture, treachery, and overt megalomania, the Windsors have managed to provide us with plenty to praise, criticize, admire, and condemn. And there's certainly been no lack of scandal to gossip about. All of these facets are incorporated into this chapter; the "improper" but nonetheless human behavior of the

Royals; the tragic death of Princess Diana: the public's outpouring of love and anger following her demise; and the current situation of Princes Charles, William, and Harry.

Perhaps, however, the greatest ecstasy or agony will be experienced by you when you test your royal knowledge one more time and total up your combined scores!

House of Scandal

I hope this book has taught you that the Windsors are not the only dysfunctional family the British monarchy has known. In fact, by current standards I can't think of one British dynasty that wouldn't qualify for that dubious distinction. Down the centuries, royal relatives would gladly murder one another in their quest for the throne, while those who had possession of it hardly played by the rules, even given the conventions of their day.

Still, while there was plenty to gossip about in centuries past, the advent of television, radio, and mass-market publications have ensured that the stories reach more people more quickly. Furthermore, as censorship has been relaxed and respect for public figures' privacy has decreased, the scandals that would have once been suppressed are now exposed and pored over daily—and participants won't have their heads chopped off as a result!

On Her Majesty's Service

For the record, 15 English kings are known to have sired illegitimate children; James I, Charles II, and William IV had 46 between them. Meanwhile, at least five monarchs, William II (Rufus), Richard I (the Lionheart), Edward II, James I, and Charles I had gay lovers. Most of them were quite open about their alternative lifestyles, even though only William never married, and all except William and Richard had children.

Although Edward VII was an overt and well-known philanderer, the custom since the repressive Victorian era among most other royal seducers has been to sleep with whom they please, but to do so discreetly. During the first half of this century, that approach was largely successful. The press and sometimes even the public would get to know about certain transgressions, but as long as these deeds weren't flung in their faces, citizens would generally turn a blind eye.

For instance, ever since the early days of the queen's marriage, there was plenty of talk about Prince Philip engaging in nocturnal activities with a number of glamorous socialites and actresses. There was even a rumor that he'd already fathered two children by the time he got married. In the beginning, the names associated with him included Greek entertainer Helene Cordet and musical star Pat Kirkwood ("Britain's Betty Grable"). Later, there were actresses Merle Oberon and Anna Massey, the Countess of Westmoreland, and Susie Ferguson, the mother of Prince Andrew's estranged wife Sarah. Phil and Fergie: It has a nice ring to it!

Talk even circulated in society circles about the queen having certain close companions, and gossip about Prince Andrew bearing an uncanny resemblance to one of them. Over the years, hundreds of rumors circulated about the royals. Amazingly, a fair number of the old standbys—many unsubstantiated and most already fairly well known among royal watchers—appeared as new revelations in Kitty Kelly's 1997 exposé *The Royals*. Here's a sampling of some of the speculations that have plagued the House of Windsor:

➤ The Queen Mother was born out of wedlock and had to be artificially inseminated in order to conceive her daughters Elizabeth and Margaret.

➤ Princess Elizabeth was a nymphomaniac when she first married Philip.

➤ Princess Margaret is anti-Semitic.

➤ Prince Philip is bisexual.

➤ Prince Edward is gay.

➤ Prince Harry is not Prince Charles' son.

Not too surprisingly, *The Royals* wasn't published in Britain for fear of the Royal Family taking legal action. Even so, the British are not prudish when it comes to a bit of scandal. Indeed, their tabloid newspapers—sold on regular newsstands as opposed to supermarkets— thrive on it, and from the late-1970s onward they had a field day thanks to the unwitting efforts of the current monarchy.

Hear Ye, Hear Ye
"How do you keep the natives off the booze long enough to get them to pass the test?"
—*Prince Philip speaking to a driving instructor in Scotland*

The first to help the tabloids was Princess Margaret, who went off the rails during the second half of the 1970s when her marriage to Tony Snowdon was disintegrating. Moving over into the jet-set fast lane, the heavy-smoking, hard-drinking, and overeating Princess turned into a tabloid regular as the press photographers captured her out and about with handsome boy-toy Roddy Llewellyn. The telephoto zoom lenses were especially busy when the couple indulged themselves on the Caribbean isle of Mustique. Back at Buckingham Palace, the courtiers were busying deciding what to do. In the end, the personal problems and the pressures caught up with Margaret. As mentioned in Chapter 23, she began canceling public engagements due to ill health, and this move provoked public complaints about what she was doing to earn her keep.

In light of that disturbing trend, Lady Di's arrival on the scene during the early 1980s was a welcome diversion from the royals' perspective, not to mention an agreeable boost to their image. Yet, therein also laid the seeds of disaster, for, initially unknown to the press and therefore the general public, there were problems in the marriage of the Prince and Princess of Wales literally before it had begun. As the world would later learn, these troubles centered around a couple of factors: Charles was still very close to his old flame Camilla Parker-Bowles, and Diana was suffering from the eating disorder bulimia nervosa.

Accounts vary as to how close Charles was to Camilla at this stage of the game, yet according to Andrew Morton's 1992 book, *Diana: Her True Story*, two days before the wedding Di was on the verge of calling it off. She'd apparently discovered a gold-chain bracelet that her fiancée was giving to Camilla and that bore the entwined initials "F" and "G"; Charles and Camilla's pet names for one another are Fred and Gladys! The wedding, of course, went ahead as planned, but then on the honeymoon the new husband wore cufflinks in the shape of two intertwining "Cs" that were a gift from Camilla. He often kept to himself on that trip, reading books, fishing, and generally not paying his wife the kind of attention that she sought. Before the honeymoon was over, it was clear that they had sharply differing personalities and interests; he the loner, she the socialite.

Diana's eating disorder consisted of eating binges interspersed with periods of fasting and induced vomiting, and it accounted for her dramatic weight loss during the early stages of the marriage. This illness, combined with Diana's desperate feelings regarding the state of her relationship with Charles, would reportedly lead to a series of "cry-for-help" suicide attempts: cutting her wrists with a razor blade, throwing herself against a glass cabinet, cutting herself with the serrated edge of a lemon slicer, stabbing herself in the chest and thighs with a penknife, and throwing herself down a flight of stairs when she was three months pregnant with Prince William.

By 1983, there was already heavy press speculation about the state of the Wales' marriage, based on Diana's gaunt appearance and the lack of warmth between the couple when they appeared in public. As the 1980s wore on, there would also be signs that Di was bored with her husband, while he, the heir to the throne, resented playing second fiddle to a very popular princess. Accordingly, the gossip about their marital problems would became more intense, yet it was the 1992 publication of Andrew Morton's book that really blew the cover off the public facade.

At that time, the wily author asserted that the source for his explosive material was Diana's circle of close friends, who wanted to state things from her point of view. Many people suspected, however, that Di herself was behind the project, as so many faithful allies would never have participated without her giving the go-ahead. The suspicions turned out to be closer to the mark than anyone but the author and these allies knew. Shortly after Diana's death, Morton would disclose that the princess herself had granted six lengthy interviews while he was researching the book. She then reviewed the manuscript and provided photographs. The interviews were published in the October 13 and October 20, 1997, issues of *People* magazine, while Di's words also appeared in a revised edition of the book. Naturally, we were told, she would have wanted it that way.

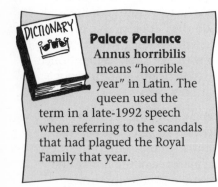

Palace Parlance
Annus horribilis means "horrible year" in Latin. The queen used the term in a late-1992 speech when referring to the scandals that had plagued the Royal Family that year.

Meanwhile, back in 1992, the queen was having her *annus horribilis*. To begin, there was Princess Anne's divorce from Captain Mark Phillips, followed by the separation of the Duke and Duchess of York—otherwise known as Andrew and Fergie—and a fire at Windsor Castle that caused 40 million pounds ($60 million) worth of damage. Still while the queen was reeling from one setback after another, she couldn't have foreseen quite how *horribilis* the next five years would turn out to be.

Bowing to pressure from the queen, Charles and Diana initially put on a show of unity by publicly appearing together and privately, in front of their two young children, behaving cordially. Those lackluster efforts, however, were soon undermined by a series of scandals that rocked the House of Windsor down to its foundations. In August 1992, the British tabloid *The Sun* published a transcript of a phone conversation between Diana and a friend named James Gilbey that had been recorded on New Year's Eve, 1989. This included Gilbey calling the princess "Squidgy" and telling her how much he loved her, while she responded in kind and also referred to her royal relatives as "this f—ing family."

As if that wasn't bad enough, in January 1993, *The Sun*'s rival, *The Daily Mirror*, published a transcript of a taped conversation between Charles and Camilla, also dating back to December 1989. In addition to the routine "I love you" comments, this featured the added bonus of the future king of England telling his sweetheart, "I want to feel my way up and down you and in and out...particularly in and out...I fill up your tank...I need you several times a week. I'll just live in your trousers."

Oh dear. It was all downhill from that point on, even though the marriage was already in the basement. There would be riding instructor James Hewitt going public about his love affair with Di, in the form of a book and a TV movie both modestly entitled *Princess in Love*. There would be a $2^1/_2$-hour TV documentary entitled *Charles: The Private Man, The Public Role*, in which the title character would confess to interviewer Jonathan Dimbleby that he'd embarked on an affair with Camilla Parker-Bowles while he was married, but only after the marriage was "irretrievably broken down." There would be Dimbleby's authorized book, *Prince of Wales: A Biography*, in which Charles would state that he'd never loved Diana but had been pressured into marrying her by his trusty father, Prince Philip. There were numerous tabloid revelations about Diana's romantic involvement with married men. And there was the Princess of Wales' response to her husband's 1994 TV interview in the form of her own, on BBC's *Panorama* in late-1995. In it, she stated "There were three of us in this marriage, so it was a bit crowded," while admitting to her own affair with Captain James Hewitt.

While all of this was going on, Fergie had also been doing her bit for the royal cause, captured sunbathing topless in the South of France by paparazzi photographers, as well as having her toes sucked by wealthy businessman Johnny Bryan. The fact that the Princesses Beatrice and Eugenie were with them on the vacation didn't go down well at all in the mother country.

In 1996, the marriages of both the Prince and Princess of Wales and Duke and Duchess of York were dissolved. Di subsequently threw herself into her charity work and championing of humanitarian causes, while Fergie, a compulsive over-spender, endeavored to bounce back from bankruptcy by becoming a spokesperson for Weight Watchers and Ocean Spray. At last, life appeared to be moving on. Now, perhaps, things would progress on a more even keel for the "Family Firm."

Death of the People's Princess

Stripped of the title Her Royal Highness and endowed with a 17 million pounds ($26 million) divorce settlement, the Princess of Wales was basically a free agent. She could do as she pleased with whom she pleased whenever she pleased. In the summer of 1997, she began a relationship with Dodi Al Fayed, a 42-year-old playboy and eldest son of Mohammed Al Fayed, the extremely wealthy Egyptian-born owner of Harrods department store in London. The father, who has been denied British citizenship for more years than he would care to remember, is notorious in the U.K. for, among other things, paying Conservative MPs to ask questions in the House of Commons. Admitting to this act helped bring down the Tory government in early 1997.

By openly consorting with Dodi and his family, Diana was considered by many people in Britain—as well as a large section of the press—to be thumbing her nose at the establishment. The paparazzi, whom she had always relied on for self-promotion and resented when they intruded on her private life, now had a new highly rewarding topic to photograph: the adventures of Dodi and Di. Unfortunately, this combination would result in tragic consequences.

It was the evening of Saturday, August 30, 1997, and Dodi and Di decided to have dinner at the swank Ritz Hotel in Paris, another property owned by Mohammed Al Fayed. While there, Dodi gave Diana a $205,400 diamond "friendship ring" that had been specially made by Albert Repossi, a Paris jeweler. Repossi would later state that Dodi had told him he wanted to spend the rest of his life with the princess. As things turned out, his wishes came true in untimely fashion.

Royal Rebuttal

True, Diana was a very British princess who helped plenty of good causes. Prior to her death, however, she had planned to reduce her charity work drastically. In addition, in late August she told French newspaper *Le Monde* that she'd considered leaving Britain long ago but had stayed because her sons William and Harry had to remain in the country.

Followed to the Ritz by a legion of press photographers, the couple soon decided to make a swift getaway so that they could find some peace and quiet at Al Fayed's nearby apartment. The plan was for Dodi's chauffeur to act as a decoy by speeding off in a Range Rover, while the Ritz's assistant director of security, Henri Paul, would drive the couple away using a side entrance. As captured by the hotel's video security cameras, Dodi and Diana climbed into the back seat of a Mercedes S 280 at 12:20 a.m., with Al Fayed's Welsh bodyguard, Trevor Rees-Jones, taking the front passenger seat. As the car pulled away, several sharp-eyed photographers on motorbikes immediately tagged it. They kept up with the vehicle as it traveled along an expressway adjacent to the River Seine, but then, according to the lensmen's later testimony, were left behind when the car accelerated from a red light at a tremendous speed.

Precisely what happened next is open to conjecture. Certainly the Mercedes hurtled into a tunnel not far from the Eiffel Tower at an estimated speed of up to 120 mph. At a slight curve in the road it swerved, hit the tunnel's 13th concrete support column, spun around, and slammed into the facing wall, rendering the front half of the vehicle virtually unrecognizable. Had it swerved to avoid a car in front? Had it made contact with a car? Had, as some eye-witnesses would later testify, a paparazzi biker cut in front of the car in order to take photos of the famous passengers? Camera film subsequently impounded by the French police would include shots taken from in front of the vehicle, but did these originate from before it actually reached the tunnel? The investigators had their work cut out, especially as the testimony of eye-witnesses on the scene clashed with that of the paparazzi.

Dodi Al Fayed and driver Henri Paul had died on impact. Trevor Rees-Jones, the only passenger to be wearing a seatbelt, lay unconscious. Diana was semi-conscious. The paparazzi claimed that they had behaved in a proper manner. Several onlookers, however, claim the photographers did anything but behave properly; instead, the onlookers asserted, the photographers gathered around the car like ghouls, shooting pictures of the crash scene and its victims. Some supposedly even got into a tussle with police when they were prevented from getting a few more juicy photos. Either way, it took emergency teams more than an hour to extricate Diana from the wreckage, but, despite the concerted efforts of doctors at one of Paris' best hospitals, La Pitie-Salpatriere, she died from massive internal injuries at 4:00 a.m. local time. Rees-Jones, meanwhile, would miraculously survive.

Press Pressure and a Very Public Funeral

Most of the world went into shock upon hearing the news of Diana's death, especially Britain, where the national grieving was on an unprecedented scale, and also America, where people lined up for hours to lay flowers and sign condolence books at the various British embassies. Meanwhile, the same British tabloid newspapers that had only recently condemned Diana's statements and actions—and which would be cited by her brother, Charles, as being directly responsible for her death—now proceeded to eulogize the "People's Princess." Seeking to shift the blame from themselves, they were blessed with the news that Henri Paul had been driving with a blood-alcohol level more than three times the legal French limit. His employer, Mohammed Al Fayed, would initially—and wrongly—dispute that claim; it would soon emerge that Paul had also been taking a drug prescribed for the withdrawal symptoms suffered by a recovering (or, evidently, errant) alcoholic.

In the meantime, while that controversy raged, the British tabloids next vented their anger on another vulnerable party: the Royal Family! That's right, those heartless individuals who had done Diana wrong! They were to blame: Charles the unfaithful husband, Her Majesty the uncaring mother-in-law, the royal courtiers who had conspired from the beginning to make Diana's life pure misery. Public opinion largely mirrored the opinions in the tabloids. The Palace duly announced that Diana would be accorded a "unique funeral for a unique person," but that wasn't enough for the irate public or, more

265

On Her Majesty's Service

To compare how television portrayed Charles and Diana's marriage during the optimistic early days and scandal-ridden later years, here are four films to look out for: *Charles and Diana: A Royal Love Story* (1982); *The Royal Romance of Charles and Diana* (1982); *Charles and Diana: Unhappily Ever After* (1992, released on video as *Charles and Diana: A Palace Divided*); and *Diana: Her True Story* (1993).

especially, the conniving press. "Not one word has come from a royal lip," hissed *The Sun*, "not one tear has been shed in public from a royal eye." *The Mirror* put it more succinctly: "Your people are suffering. Speak to us Ma'am."

So the queen did, in an unprecedented live TV broadcast to the nation—and watched around the world—at 6:00 p.m. local time on September 5, 1997. Talking in her capacity as the sovereign "and as a grandmother," the monarch fully praised the late lamented Princess of Wales, while assuring people that William and Harry would be properly cared for. Diana's brother, however, would have something more to say about William and Harry's upbringing.

The following day, an estimated worldwide television audience of 2.1 billion people tuned in to the funeral and saw not only a procession route that had been tripled in length to accommodate several million mourners, but also numerous other departures from royal tradition. Concessions made to public demand and in recognition of the fact that the monarchy's very future was on the line included:

➤ The British flag, the Union Jack, flying at half-mast atop Buckingham Palace. Because Diana was no longer a member of the Royal Family, traditionally the flag would not have been lowered.

➤ The cortege passing through London's Wellington Arch, a privilege normally only reserved for monarchs.

➤ The queen bowing to the coffin as it passed in front of the palace.

At Westminster Abbey, dignitaries, heads of state, and celebrity friends were among the 2,000-strong congregation, yet notable for their absence were the members of the press. They'd originally been invited, only for Diana's brother, Earl Charles Spencer, to pointedly uninvite them the day before the service. This act was only one of several points he'd be making on this unforgettable occasion.

Shortly after Elton John performed "Candle In The Wind 1997," comprising the tune of his Marilyn Monroe tribute with new Diana-inspired lyrics written by Bernie Taupin, the aggravated Earl spoke his mind. Praising his sister as "a symbol of selfless humanity," he quickly turned on the press for making her "the most hunted person of the modern age." Then it was the turn of the Royals, as the Earl made a promise to Diana:

> On behalf of your mother and sisters I pledge that we, your blood family, will do all we can to continue the imaginative and loving way in which you were steering these two exceptional young men, so that their souls are not simply immersed by duty and tradition, but can sing openly as you planned.

His words were a direct challenge to the Royal Family, issued in front of the largest ever number of public witnesses.

What the Earl could do to stay true to his pledge would remain to be seen. In the meantime, the queen and her fellow royals were actually turning the situation to their own advantage—very quickly. The sovereign's speech to the nation had won over quite a few people, and so did the meet-and-greet that she, Philip, their three sons, and two grandsons indulged in with the London crowds on that same day before the funeral. (Anne was conspicuous by her absence.) Shortly after the funeral, Charles made a public speech in which he expressed his own sorrow and thanked the people for their tremendous outpouring of love for his late wife.

That was it! As if by magic, Charles was suddenly well on his way to recovery in the eyes of many of his now-former critics! Which all goes to prove one thing: The majority of British people still want to retain the monarchy. In order to survive, therefore, the Royal Family must show sensitivity to public opinion and, if it isn't too much bother, behave with discretion.

Royal Rebuttal

"Cold," "uncaring," and "unemotional" were the main criticisms aired about the Royal Family immediately following Diana's death. The queen, however, cried during the funeral service, while Charles was clearly close to tears both there and when he fetched his ex-wife's body back from Paris. Incidentally, at the funeral he broke with convention and wore a navy suit, Di's favorite, which she'd selected for him.

Charles, William, and Little Hen

You know what's going to happen: Prince William, 15 at the time of his mother's death, is destined to become the world's most eligible bachelor. He's (thankfully) inherited Diana's good looks and charm, but will he be plagued by the press as much as the late princess? The likely answer is yes, in which case he'll have to temper his aversion to the tabloid terrors: When he was just 11 he nearly got into a fight with photographers on the ski slopes in Austria.

Still, it also appears that Prince Charles is more sensitive to both of his sons' needs than he's often given credit for. He and Diana may not have agreed on the style of the princes' upbringing, but they were in accordance with one another regarding many of the fundamentals. Don't forget, Charles may have been shaped by his upbringing, but he didn't like it. Consequently, both parents agreed to send William to Eton, the school near Windsor Castle that, you may remember, the Prince of Wales wanted to attend after Cheam, but which his father rejected in favor of spartan, far-away Gordonstoun. Prince Harry will probably attend Eton too.

Diana was a best friend and an emotional support for her boys, even though she often relied on William for support as much as he relied on her. Now Charles will have to fill that role as best he can for both his children, while grandma the queen can also lend a helping hand. He may not be cut out to hang around in jeans and a baseball cap while digging into burgers and fries, but Charles can go a long way toward helping his kids by making them a high priority in his life. If he learned anything from his childhood—and it appears he did—then William and Harry will even take precedence over his royal duties, and certainly, for now, over his relationship with Camilla Parker-Bowles. According to press reports, immediately after Diana's death Charles told his aides that the children must come first and ordered his staff to clear his schedule when they are at home. Whether his plan pans out remains to be seen.

Before the fall—Diana and Charles wave to the adoring crowds after their wedding at St. Paul's Cathedral. (Photo courtesy of UPI/Corbis-Bettmann)

As for Charles' own future, although it initially looked as if Diana's untimely end would turn her ex-husband into the most vilified royal since Edward VIII, it has instead enabled him to emerge out of her shadow. Charles could never win while Diana was around—her popularity and charm would beat him hands-down. Now, however, he has the chance to reinvent himself.

Are You a Complete Royal Idiot? Quiz #4

Okay, here goes. One last chance to leave your friends impressed or yourself depressed.

1. What nicknames were given to the crop-haired Parliamentarians and long-haired royal courtiers during the reign of Charles I?

2. In what year did England become a short-lived republic?

3. What disasters hit London in 1665 and 1666?

4. What was the name of the plan to kill Charles II and his brother James in 1683?

5. What significant act, apart from dying, did Charles II perform on his deathbed?

6. Who took over the English throne when James II went into exile?

7. Who were the Jacobites?

8. In whose reign did the Act of Union unify the thrones of England and Scotland?

9. What were the nicknames of George I's two Hanoverian mistresses?

10. Who became Britain's first Prime Minister during the reign of George I?

11. Which king purchased Buckingham Palace?

12. Which style of architecture dates back to the reign of George IV?

13. Who, to date, is England's longest-reigning monarch?

14. What was the name of the 1904 pact between Britain and France that Edward VII facilitated?

15. Which monarch changed the Royal Family name to Windsor?

16. What momentous royal event took place on December 11, 1936?

17. What was George VI's proper first name?

18. Who was Princess Margaret prevented from marrying during the mid-1950s?

19. What was Prince Philip's surname before he married Princess Elizabeth?

20. Which Royal Family member competed for Britain in the 1976 Montreal Olympics?

21. How did Prince Charles' teachers have to address him when he attended school?

22. With what degree did Charles graduate from Trinity College, Cambridge in 1970?

23. In what year did the Prince of Wales marry Lady Diana Spencer?

24. Who was Princess Margaret's boy-toy at the time of her marriage break-up?

25. What is an *annus* in Latin?

Once again, the answers appear in Appendix G. Here's how to rate your performance:

➤ 20 or more—You're a natural born ruler.

➤ 13-19—You could become a figurehead monarch.

➤ 6-12—Maybe it's time to consider abdication.

➤ 5 or fewer—It's a shame, isn't it?

Now total up your combined scores from all four quizzes to see how you rate overall:

➤ 90-100—You are, without doubt, a right royal expert.

➤ 70-89—Excellent. You deserve a telegram from the queen. (You won't get one, but you deserve one.)

➤ 50-69—Good. You're certainly no royal idiot.

➤ 30-49—Mmm. It's a close call.

➤ Less than 30—For once, I have nothing to say.

The Least You Need to Know

➤ The Windsors have generally been better behaved than most of their predecessors.

➤ Prince Charles' relationship with Camilla Parker-Bowles was a significant contributor to his marital problems with Princess Diana.

➤ During her marriage, Diana suffered from bulimia nervosa and attempted suicide on five different occasions.

➤ Diana, Princess of Wales, died in Paris on August 31, 1997 and was buried in her native England on September 6, 1997.

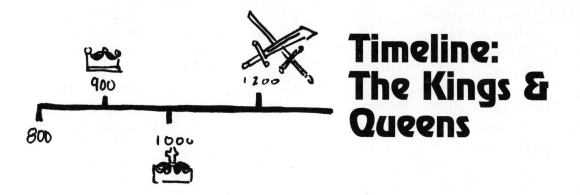

Timeline: The Kings & Queens

Here's a list of the kings and queens who have sat on the English throne, and that of Great Britain and the United Kingdom, since 802 AD.

Note that in some instances, a monarch was deposed only to return later, while other monarchs ruled simultaneously. If no "Born" date appears, the date of this monarch's birth is not known. A "c." indicates "circa" or "around," meaning no one knows exactly when the monarch was born, but he or she was born at approximately the given date or within the given date span.

Saxons and Danes

Monarch	Born	Reigned
Egbert, King of Wessex		802-839
Ethelwulf		839-855
Ethelbald		855-860
Ethelbert		860-866
Ethelred		866-871
Alfred the Great	849	871-899
Edward the Elder	870	899-925
Athelstan	895	925-939
Edmund I	921	939-946
Edred		946-955
Edwy	before 943	955-959
Edgar	943	959-975

continues

continued

Monarch	Born	Reigned
Edward II the Martyr	c.962	975-979
Ethelred II the Unready (deposed)	968/969	979-1013 and 1014-1016
Sweyn		1013-1014
Edmund II Ironside	before 993	Apr-Nov 1016
Canute the Great	c.995	1016-1035
Harold Harefoot	c.1016/7	(jointly with)
Hardicanute	c.1018	1035-1037
Harold Harefoot (alone)		1037-1040
Hardicanute (alone)		1040-1042
Edward III the Confessor	c.1002-5	1042-1066
Harold II	c.1020	Jan-Oct 1066
Edgar Atheling		Oct-Dec 1066

House of Normandy

Monarch	Born	Reigned
William I the Conqueror	c.1027-8	1066-1087
William II Rufus	c.1056-60	1087-1100
Henry I Beauclerc	1068	1100-1135
Stephen	by 1100	1135-1154

House of Angevin

Monarch	Born	Reigned
Henry II Curtmantle	1133	1154-1189
Richard I Coeur de Lion (the Lionheart)	1157	1189-1199
John Lackland	1167	1199-1216

House of Plantaganet

Monarch	Born	Reigned
Henry III	1207	1216-1272
Edward I Longshanks	1239	1272-1307
Edward II	1284	1307-1327
Edward III	1312	1327-1377
Richard II	1367	1377-1399

House of Lancaster

Monarch	Born	Reigned
Henry IV	1366	1399-1433
Henry V	1387	1413-1422
Henry VI	1421	1422-1461
(deposed)		and 1470-1471

House of York

Monarch	Born	Reigned
Edward IV	1442	1461-1470
(deposed)		and 1471-1483
Edward V	1470	Apr-Jun 1483
Richard III	1452	1483-1485

House of Tudor

Monarch	Born	Reigned
Henry VII	1457	1485-1509
Henry VIII	1491	1509-1547
Edward VI	1537	1547-1553
Jane		Jul 10-19, 1553
Mary I	1516	1553-1558
Elizabeth I	1533	1558-1603

House of Stuart

Monarch	Born	Reigned
James I	1566	1603-1625
Charles I	1600	1625-1649
Charles II	1630	1649
(interregnum)		and 1660-1685
James II	1633	1685-1689
Mary II	1662	(jointly with)
William III	1650	1689-1694
William III (alone)		1694-1702
Anne	1665	1702-1714

House of Hanover

Monarch	Born	Reigned
George I	1660	1714-1727
George II	1683	1727-1760
George III	1738	1760-1820
George IV	1762	1820-1830
William IV	1765	1830-1837
Victoria	1819	1837-1901

House of Saxe-Coburg and Gotha

Monarch	Born	Reigned
Edward VII	1841	1901-1910

House of Windsor

Monarch	Born	Reigned
George V	1865	1910-1936
Edward VIII	1894	Jan-Dec 1936
George VI	1895	1936-1952
Elizabeth II	1926	1952 -

Royal Family Trees

This appendix provides family trees for nine royal dynasties. These don't include the Anglo-Saxon kings, who didn't belong to an official royal House, while Edward VII, whose surname was Saxe-Coburg-Gotha, is included with the Hanoverians. That's because he really was classified as such. Only when his son George V changed the family name to Windsor did the dynasty effectively change.

Please note: With the exception of the final family tree, each one features, at the bottom, the king who commenced the next dynasty. A dotted line (----) separates him from his predecessors. (For example, Henry II appears at the bottom of the Norman family tree in order to show his ancestry, but he was, in fact, the first Angevin monarch. He therefore also appears at the top of the Angevin family tree.)

THE NORMANS

1066–1154

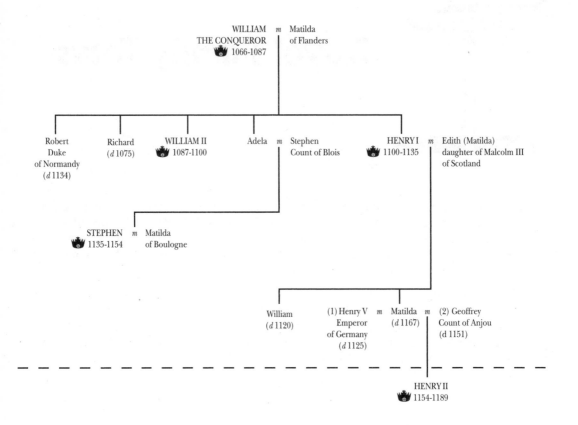

THE ANGEVINS
1154–1216

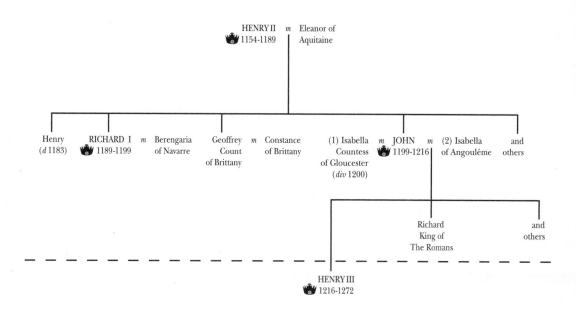

HENRY II *m* Eleanor of
1154-1189   Aquitaine

Henry — RICHARD I *m* Berengaria — Geoffrey *m* Constance — (1) Isabella *m* JOHN *m* (2) Isabella — and
(*d* 1183) 1189-1199   of Navarre   Count   of Brittany   Countess   1199-1216 of Angouléme   others
                                        of Brittany   of Gloucester
                                                                 (*div* 1200)

Richard   and
King of   others
The Romans

HENRY III
1216-1272

THE PLANTAGANETS

1216–1399

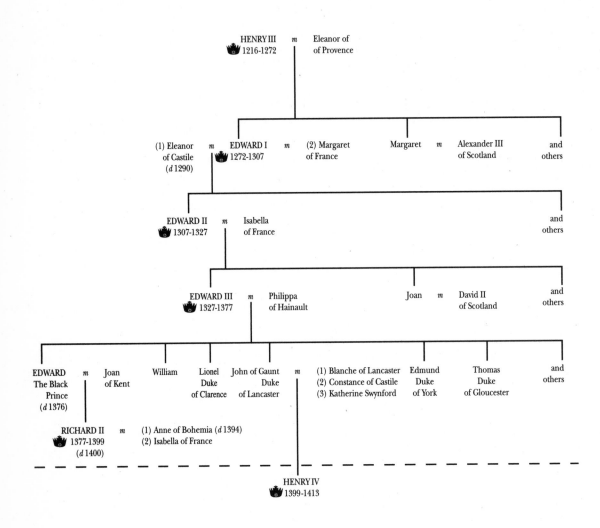

THE HOUSE OF LANCASTER
1399–1461

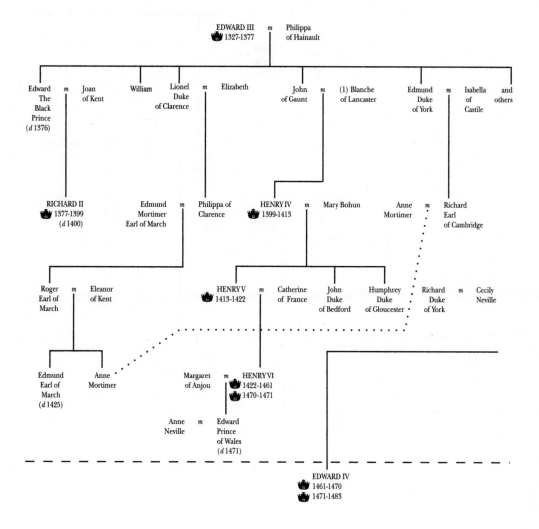

THE HOUSE OF YORK
1461–1485

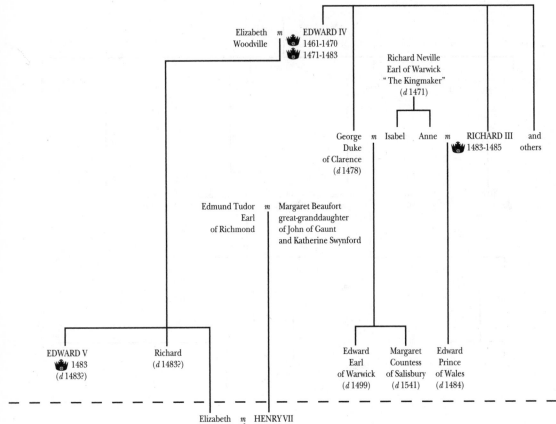

THE TUDORS

1485–1603

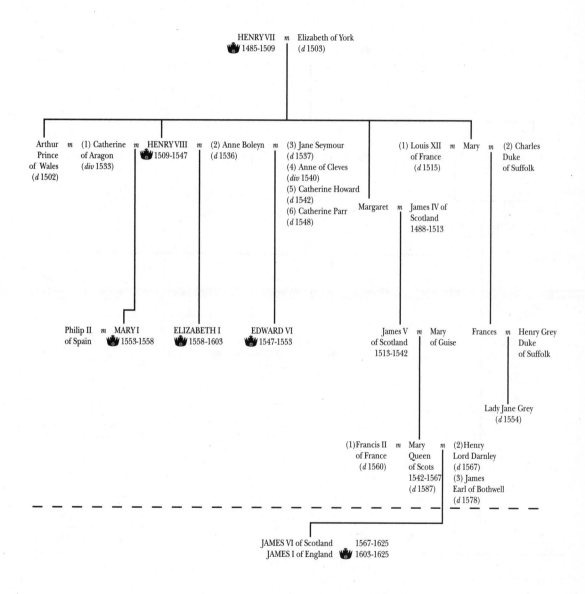

THE STUARTS
1603–1714

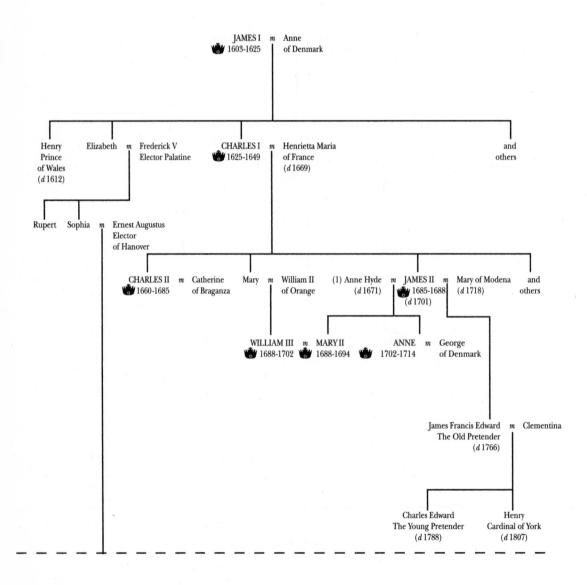

THE HANOVERIANS
1714–1910

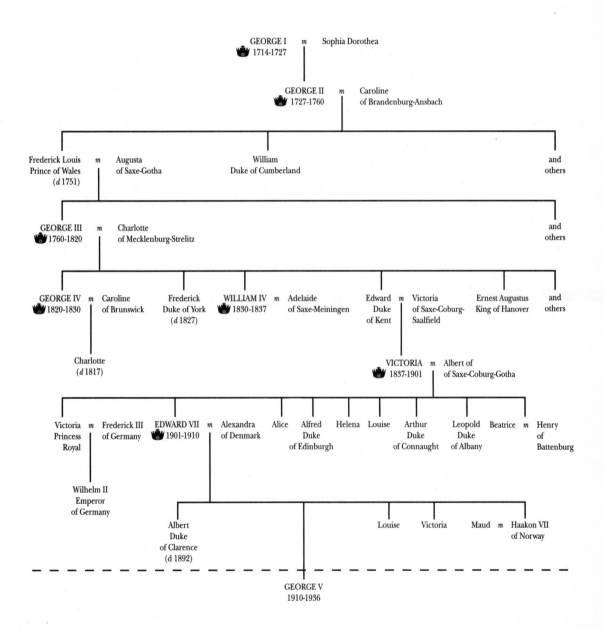

THE HOUSE OF WINDSOR
1910–

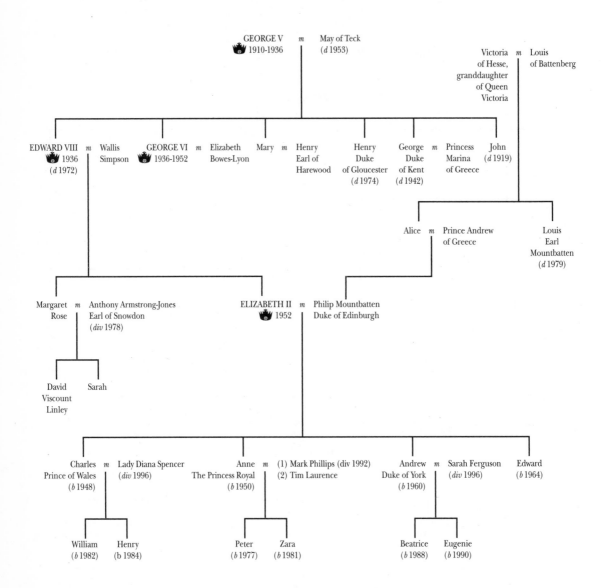

Recommended Reading: A Selective Bibliography

Many of the following books were used in the writing of this *Complete Idiot's Guide to British Royalty*:

Allison, Ronald & Sarah Riddell (eds.), *The Royal Encyclopedia* (Macmillan Press, 1991).

Buskin, Richard, *Princess Diana: Her Life Story 1961-1997* (Publications International/ Signet, 1997).

Campbell, Lady Colin, *Diana in Private: The Princess Nobody Knows* (Smith Gryphon, 1992).

Cannadine, David, *The Context, Performance and Meaning of Ritual: The British Monarchy and the 'Invention of Tradition', c.1820-1977*—in Hobsbawm, Eric and Ranger, Terence, *The Invention of Tradition* (Cambridge University Press, 1983).

Cannon, John & Ralph Griffiths (eds.), *The Oxford Illustrated History of the British Monarchy* (Oxford University Press, 1988).

Crookston, Peter (ed.), Kenyon, John (consultant), *The Ages of Britain* (St. Martin's Press, 1983).

Cross, F.L, and E.A. Livingstone (eds.), *The Oxford Dictionary of the Christian Church* (Oxford University Press, 2nd edition, 1974).

Delderfield, Eric R., *Kings & Queens of England & Great Britain* (David & Carles, 1990).

Dimbleby, Jonathon, *The Prince of Wales: A Biography* (William Morrow and Company, 1994).

Edgar, Donald, *Britain's Royal Family in the Twentieth Century* (Crescent Books, 1979).

Frazier, Antonia (ed.), *The Lives of the Kings and Queens of England* (Alfred A. Knopf, Inc., 1975).

Fry, Plantaganet Somerset, *The Kings & Queens of England & Scotland* (Grove Press, 1990).

Holden, Anthony, *King Charles III: A Biography* (Grove Press, 1988).

Lee, Min (ed.), *Dictionary of British History* (Larousse, 1994).

Longford, Elizabeth (ed.), *The Oxford Book of Royal Anecdotes* (Oxford University Press, 1989).

Morgan, Kenneth O., (ed.), *The Oxford History of Britain* (Oxford University Press, 1993).

Morton, Andrew, *Diana: Her New Life* (Pocket Books, 1994).

Morton, Andrew, *Diana: In Her Own Words* (Simon and Schuster, 1997).

Murray, Jane, *The Kings and Queens of England - A Tourist Guide* (Charles Scribner's Songs, 1974).

Shenkman, Richard, *Legends, Lies & Cherished Myths of World History* (Harper Perennial, 1993).

Unstead, R.J., Illustrated by Victor Ambrus, *The Story of Britain* (Thomas Nelson, Inc., 1969)

Usherwood, Stephen, Illustrated by Anthony & Geoffrey Harper, *Reign by Reign* (London, Michael Joseph, 1960).

Whitaker, James, *Diana vs. Charles: Royal Blood Feud* (New American Library, 1993)

Notable Battles

Following is a selective list of some of the more notable battles in English/British history, not all of them victories. Once upon a time the kings led their forces in armed conflicts, but all of that ended during the mid-18th century when the monarchs became figureheads and Parliament decided that there was no need for them to risk their lives in such a fashion. Here are some choice samples from the days when they did, even though in some cases they weren't actually participating on the front line.

- ➤ **Hastings**, October 14, 1066: The English army is defeated by the invasion force of William of Normandy, and King Harold is killed.

- ➤ **Bannockburn**, June 24, 1314: The routing of Edward II's army by the much smaller forces of Robert the Bruce secure Scottish independence.

- ➤ **Crecy**, August 26, 1346: Edward III's army scores one of the great English military victories, losing less than 200 men while crushing the French, of whom more than 10,000 died.

- ➤ **Agincourt**, October 25, 1415: Henry V masterminds a strategically brilliant victory against the superior French forces, losing less than 400 Englishmen while killing around 9,000 Frenchmen.

- ➤ **Bosworth Field**, August 22, 1485: Richard III's army is defeated—and he is killed—by the forces of Henry Tudor, thus transferring power from the House of York to the House of Tudor.

➤ **Flodden Field**, September 9, 1513: After invading England in response to Henry VIII's invasion of France, James IV of Scotland is slaughtered together with most of his nobles and members of the Scottish clergy.

➤ **Gravelines**, August 9, 1588: English ships batter the infinitely superior Spanish Armada, sending it into a hasty and ultimately disastrous retreat.

➤ **Marston Moor**, July 2, 1644: In what proves to be a turning point in the Civil War, Charles I's Royalist army is defeated by the Parliamentary forces.

➤ **Naseby**, June 14, 1645: Parliament's New Model Army, led by Oliver Cromwell and Thomas Fairfax, crushes the Royalist forces, effectively ending the first part of the Civil War.

➤ **The Boyne**, July 1, 1690: The Protestant army of William III defeats the Irish Catholics who are supporting the claim to the throne of the deposed James II.

➤ **Blenheim**, August 13, 1704: In a dashing move, British, Dutch, Bavarian, and Austrian troops under the Duke of Marlborough intercept the French and save Austria from invasion.

➤ **Dettingen**, June 27, 1743: In driving the French out of Bavaria, George II, at nearly 60 years of age, becomes the last British monarch to lead his troops into battle.

Royal Residencies

There have been plenty of royal residencies down the centuries, some of which no longer exist, others of which are barely recognizable from when they were used in this capacity. The following are some of the most recognizable ones that are still standing today:

➤ **Audley End, Essex**   Built in 1603 and purchased by Charles II in 1669, this palace was passed on to the Earl of Suffolk after Charles' death, as the King had never actually paid the full purchase price to the Earl's ancestor. It was remodelled in the 18th and 19th centuries.

➤ **Balmoral, Grampian**   After renting a small castle named Balmoral in 1848, Queen Victoria and Prince Albert purchased the Scottish estate four years later. The original granite castle was replaced by a much larger white granite building that Albert himself co-designed. Today it remains a favorite holiday home of the Royal Family.

➤ **Brighton Pavilion, Sussex**   In 1786, when the future George IV was still Prince Regent, he bought a farmhouse and converted it into a villa for his secret wife, Mrs. Fitzherbert, to live in. Then, from 1815 to 1822, it was transformed into an exotic palace that the Prince and his friends could use as a getaway on England's south coast. Eventually, after he'd become King, George lost interest in the building, and it was sold to the Town Council in 1848. Today, it's open to the public.

➤ **Buckingham Palace, London**   Originally built between 1702 and 1705 for John Sheffield, the Duke of Buckingham, the Palace was sold by his son to George III in 1761. The King moved there from St. James' Palace the following year. During the reign of George IV, Buckingham Palace underwent rebuilding and extension work, and this continued through the reign of William IV until 1837, shortly after Queen Victoria had ascended to the throne. She, however, didn't live there after Prince Albert's death, and so it's only since the reign of Edward VII that the Palace has served as the main London residence of the sovereign.

➤ **Clarence House, London**   This extension to St. James' Palace was originally built for William IV when he was still the Duke of Clarence. This is where Princess Elizabeth and Philip Mountbatten lived after they were married in 1947, and where the Queen Mother has resided since her daughter's accession in 1952.

➤ **Hampton Court, Middlesex**   An enormous palace built for Cardinal Wolsey amid 2,000 acres of magnificent gardens and parkland, it was handed over to Henry VIII in 1525 when Wolsey wanted to curry favor with the volatile king. Henry actually took possession four years later, and thereafter it would be a favorite royal residence up to and including the reign of George II. George III didn't like it, and so after his ascension it was no longer used by the monarch. Today, it is England's most lavish non-royal residence.

➤ **Hatfield House, Hertfordshire**   Once the home of Elizabeth, Henry VIII's daughter by Anne Boleyn, this was sold off in 1607 and today belongs to romance novelist Barbara Cartland. Incidentally, the oak tree under which Elizabeth was reportedly sitting when she learned that she had become Queen still exists.

➤ **Holyroodhouse, Edinburgh**   James IV of Scotland originally converted an abbey on this site into a royal residence, yet after it was destroyed by fire in 1543 it was rebuilt by James V of Scotland and then Charles II. Today it's still in use for certain ceremonial occasions.

➤ **Kensington Palace, London**   Purchased during the joint reign of William III and Mary II, "KP," as it has come to be known, has gone through several rebuilding programs down the years and been favored by successive monarchs. Queen Victoria was born there and Princess Diana lived there following her split from Prince Charles. It is also the home of Princess Margaret.

➤ **Kew Palace, London**   Built by a merchant in 1631 and then known as the Dutch House, this red-brick mansion was for a while the residence of George III and Queen Charlotte. Today it stilll stands in Kew Gardens.

➤ **Marlborough House, London**   Designed by Sir Christopher Wren and built between 1709 and 1711, this red-brick house was the home of successive Dukes of Marlborough until it was taken over by George IV's daughter, Princess Charlotte, in 1817. Numerous other royals lived there, the last of them being George V's widow, Queen Mary. She died in 1953, and six years later it became a government building known as the Commonwealth Centre.

➤ **Osborne House, Isle of Wight**   Queen Victoria's husband, Prince Albert, designed the residence that was completed here in 1851. Their son, Edward VII, didn't like it, however, and so he gifted it to the nation in 1902 and it subsequently became an officers' convalescent home. Today it's open to the public.

➤ **Palace of Westminster, London**   Once the residence of kings from Edward the Confessor to Henry VIII, it was largely rebuilt during the Victorian era and is now the meeting place for Parliament and a location of government offices.

➤ **St. James' Palace, London**   Built by Henry VIII on the site of a former leper hospital for women, this originally had St. James' Park and Hyde Park as its privately enclosed surrounding areas. During the reign of George III it ceased to be a royal residence but today it's still used in that capacity, serving as the London base of Prince Charles and the place that ambassadors are accredited to.

➤ **Sandringham, Norfolk**   Originally purchased for Edward, Prince of Wales, in 1861, this estate is where Princess Diana was raised and where there's a home that the Royal Family utilizes each Christmas. During the rest of the year the estate is often open to the public.

➤ **The Tower of London**   Originally constructed as a timber-and-earth castle by William the Conqueror in 1066 to celebrate his victory at the Battle of Hastings, the Tower would be rebuilt and added to up until Victorian times. Since its inception it has served as a fortress, a palace, a prison, a place of torture and execution, a royal mint, a menagerie, and an arsenal. Today this classic castle structure with the surrounding dry moat houses the Crown Jewels and is one of London's most popular tourist attractions.

➤ **Windsor Castle, Berkshire**   Like the Tower of London, this was originally built as a wood-and-earth military stronghold by William the Conqueror soon after the Norman invasion of 1066. Henry I converted the wooden tower into stone, Henry II made comprehensive additions, and by the early 14th century the castle was being primarily used as a residence. Extensive rebuilding then took place during the reigns of Charles II, George III, and George IV, and today, as one of the principal homes of the Queen and her family, it is the oldest royal residence still in regular use.

Those Big-Screen Royals

As you should be able to tell by the stories that have appeared in these pages, England's kings and queens are prime material for colorful, incident-filled movies, and, right from the start, moviemakers were quick to latch onto this. Here now is a selective list of some of those celluloid efforts, together with brief credits and plot synopses. At the end I'm also providing you with a short list of some of the TV productions that have dealt with the same subject matter.

The Private Life of Henry VIII (1933)

Starring: Charles Laughton, Binnie Barnes, Robert Donat, Elsa Lanchester, Merle Oberon.

Directed by: Alexander Korda.

The acclaimed British production featuring Charles Laughton's flamboyant, Oscar-winning portrayal of England's tyrannical and much-married monarch. Laughton's wife, Elsa Lanchester, plays Anne of Cleves ("The Mare of Flanders").

Tudor Rose (a.k.a. *Nine Days a Queen, Lady Jane Grey*—1936)

Starring: Nora Pillbeam, John Mills, Felix Aylmer, Frank Cellier, Gwen Ffrangcon Davies, Cedric Hardwicke.

Directed by: Robert Stevenson.

The story of Lady Jane Grey, England's first and shortest-reigning queen, with Nora Pillbeam in the title role.

Tower of London (1939)

Starring: Basil Rathbone, Boris Karloff, Barbara O'Neil, Ian Hunter, Vincent Price.

Directed by: Rowland V. Lee.

Rathbone plays evil Richard III; Karloff's his murderous sidekick, Mord; and Price is the Duke of Clarence in this meandering and uninspired production about some of the misdeeds of an out-of-control monarch.

The Private Lives of Elizabeth and Essex (1939)

Starring: Bette Davis, Errol Flynn, Olivia de Havilland, Donald Crisp, Alan Hale, Vincent Price.

Directed by: Michael Curtiz.

Bette Davis and Errol Flynn are on the top of their form in the title roles, pledging their love for one another while putting personal power first. Colorful, campy, and a lot of fun, although this is Hollywood's version of British history rather than the real thing.

Henry V (1945)

Starring: Laurence Olivier, Robert Newton, Leslie Banks, Renee Asherson, Esmond Knight, Leo Genn.

Directed by: Laurence Olivier.

Olivier won a special Academy Award "for his outstanding achievement as actor, producer and director" in bringing this Shakespeare classic to the big screen. Beautifully filmed and wonderfully acted, it also utilized Henry's rousing leadership of his men at the Battle of Agincourt to serve as stirring World War II propaganda.

The Mudlark (1950)

Starring: Irene Dunne, Alec Guinness, Finlay Currie, Anthony Steel, Wilfred Hyde-White.

Directed by: Jean Negulesco.

Fictional account of Queen Victoria, in mourning since the death of Prince Albert, being brought out of herself by way of her friendship with a homeless young boy who breaks into her castle.

King Richard and the Crusaders (1954)

Starring: Rex Harrison, Virginia Mayo, George Sanders, Laurence Harvey.

Directed by: David Butler.

Wooden acting and cardboard sets are the main feature of this daft costumer in which George Sanders plays Richard the Lionheart!

Richard III (1955)

Starring: Laurence Olivier, John Gielgud, Ralph Richardson, Claire Bloom, Alec Clunes, Cedric Hardwicke, Stanley Baker.

Directed by: Laurence Olivier.

A slightly stiff British filmization of Shakespeare's play sees actor/director Olivier delivering the definitive portrayal of England's most vilified king, complete with the hunchback he never had in real life.

The Virgin Queen (1955)

Starring: Bette Davis, Richard Todd, Joan Collins, Herbert Marshall, Jay Robinson, Dan O'Herlihy, Rod Taylor.

Directed by: Henry Koster.

Bette gives the full treatment to her second wonderful portrayal of the aging Queen Bess, as this time the romantic sparks fly with Sir Walter Raleigh.

The King's Thief (1955)

Starring: David Niven, Ann Blyth, George Sanders, Edmond Purdom, Roger Moore, Alan Mowbray.

Directed by: Robert Z. Leonard.

Colorful but routine costume drama centering on intrigue in the court of Charles II and a nobleman's attempt to steal the Crown Jewels.

Tower of London (1962)

Starring: Vincent Price, Michael Pate, Joan Freeman, Robert Brown.

Directed by: Roger Corman.

Vincent Price takes over the role of Richard III in a cheapo remake that makes the 1939 original look pretty decent by comparison.

A Man For All Seasons (1966)

Starring: Paul Scofield, Wendy Hiller, Leo Mckern, Robert Shaw, Orson Welles, Susannah York, John Hurt, Nigel Davenport, Vanessa Redgrave.

Directed by: Fred Zinnemann.

A multi-Oscar-winner centering on the conflict arising between Henry VIII and Sir Thomas More when the king's request to divorce Catherine of Aragon is denied by the Pope, and he asks More to support him in his break from the Church of Rome. Reworked by Robert Bolt from his stage play, and remade as a TV movie in 1988.

Camelot (1967)

Starring: Richard Harris, Vanessa Redgrave, Franco Nero, David Hemmings, Lionel Jeffries.

Directed by: Joshua Logan.

Horrible screen adaption of the Lerner & Loewe stage musical about the King Arthur legend. Poorly directed and badly sung, it nevertheless won Oscars for the costumes, scoring, and art direction.

The Lion in Winter (1968)

Starring: Peter O'Toole, Katherine Hepburn, Jane Merrow, Anthony Hopkins, Nigel Terry, Timothy Dalton.

Directed by: Anthony Harvey.

Tremendous British-made drama concerning the deliberations of Henry II (O'Toole) as to who should be his successor. Katherine Hepburn won an Oscar for her portrayal of the King's wife, Eleanor of Aquitaine, while Hopkins and Dalton both made their big-screen debuts.

Anne of the Thousand Days (1969)

Starring: Richard Burton, Genevieve Bujold, Irene Papas, Anthony Quayle, Peter Jeffrey.

Directed by: Charles Jarrott.

Compelling, wonderfully acted, if historically inaccurate account of the troubled relationship between Henry VIII and his second wife, Anne Boleyn.

Cromwell (1970)

Starring: Richard Harris, Alec Guinness, Robert Morley, Dorothy Tutin, Frank Finlay, Timothy Dalton, Patrick Wymark, Patric Magee.

Directed by: Ken Hughes.

Well photographed but overlong and uneven account of the the rise to power of England's Lord Protector, Oliver Cromwell (Harris), at the expense of Charles I (Guinness).

Don't Lose Your Head (a.k.a. *Carry On Henry VIII*—1972)

Starring: Sid James, Kenneth Williams, Joan Sims, Charles Hawtrey, Barbara Windsor.

Directed by: Gerald Thomas.

Part of the British series of *Carry On* farces, this focusses on Henry VIII's lecherous escapades and exposes the "untold story" of his two extra wives!

Henry VIII and His Six Wives (1973)

Starring: Keith Michell, Donald Pleasence, Charlotte Rampling, Jane Asher, Lynne Frederick.

Directed by: Waris Hussein.

Adapted from a 1972 BBC-TV series, this straightforward retelling of the out-of-control king's marital problems derives much of its power from Michell's outstanding performance as the man at the center of all the controversy.

Excalibur (1981)

Starring: Nicol Williamson, Nigel Terry, Helen Mirren, Nicholas Clay, Cherie Lunghi, Patrick Stewart, Gabriel Byrne, Liam Neeson.

Directed by: John Boorman.

Everything that *Camelot* should have been but wasn't. A highly stylized, visually sumptious, and brilliantly directed telling of the King Arthur legend, full of offbeat imagery and sexual innuendo.

Lady Jane (1985)

Starring: Helena Bonham Carter, Cary Elwes, John Wood, Michael Hordern, Jill Bennett, Jane Lapotaire, Patrick Stewart, Joss Ackland.

Directed by: Trevor Nunn.

Well-acted, wonderfully directed retelling of the political maneuvering and in-fighting that surrounded Lady Jane Grey's ascension to the English throne and her swift downfall.

Henry V (1989)

Starring: Kenneth Branagh, Derek Jacobi, Brian Blessed, Alec McCowen, Ian Holm, Richard Briers, Robert Stephens, Robbie Coltrane, Judi Dench, Paul Scofield, Emma Thompson.

Directed by: Kenneth Branagh.

Branagh makes a stunning directorial debut with this adaption of Shakespeare's play, altogether different from Laurence Olivier's interpretation but every bit as good.

The Madness of King George (1994)

Starring: Nigel Hawthorne, Helen Mirren, Ian Holm.

Directed by: Nicholas Hytner.

Alan Bennett's highly amusing adaption of his own sharp-witted tragi-comic stageplay about George III's struggle with porphyria, the uninformed doctors who attempted to "treat" him, and the Prince of Wales who wanted to usurp him.

Braveheart (1995)

Starring: Mel Gibson, Sophie Marceau, Patrick McGoohan, Catherine McCormick.

Directed by: Mel Gibson.

Gibson's multi-Oscar-winning epic about Scottish patriot William Wallace's valiant but ultimately fatal attempts to overthrow English rule of his homeland by waging war against the forces of Edward I.

First Knight (1995)

Starring: Sean Connery, Richard Gere, Julia Ormond, Ben Cross.

Directed by: Jerry Zucker.

The worst of the movies dealing with the King Arthur legend—not that the story is even recognizable, thanks to the scriptwriters. Plenty of action but no substance means that a good cast is totally wasted. As for Richard Gere as Sir Lancelot, well…

Mrs. Brown (a.k.a. *Her Majesty, Mrs. Brown*—1997)

Starring: Judi Dench, Billy Connolly, Geoffrey Palmer, Antony Sher.

Directed by: John Madden.

An entertaining account of the controversial and much-gossipped-about relationship between old Queen Victoria and her Scottish servant, John Brown.

Here now is a select list of some of TV's royal dramas:

➤ *The Six Wives of Henry VIII*   1972 series starring Keith Michell.

➤ *Elizabeth R*   1972 series starring Glenda Jackson as Elizabeth I.

➤ *Edward VII*   1977 series starring Timothy West.

➤ *Edward and Mrs. Simpson*   1981 series starring Edward Fox as Edward VIII.

➤ *Charles and Diana: A Royal Love Story*   1982 movie starring David Robb and Caroline Bliss.

➤ *The Royal Romance of Charles and Diana*   1982 movie starring Christopher Baines and Catherine Oxenburg in the title roles, together with Dana Wynter as the Queen, Stewart Granger as Prince Philip, and Olivia de Havilland as the Queen Mother!

➤ *Charles and Diana: Unhappily Ever After*   1992 movie starring Roger Rees and Catherine Oxenburg (again). Released on video as *Charles and Diana: A Palace Divided*.

➤ *Fergie & Andrew: Behind the Palace Doors*   1993 movie starring Pippa Hinchley and Sam Miller.

➤ *Diana: Her True Story*   1993 movie starring Serena Scott Thomas and David Threlfall.

Palace Parlance Glossary

annus horribilis   Means "horrible year" in Latin, a dead language that was used by the ancient Romans before evolving into French, Spanish, and some English. The queen used the term in a late-1992 speech.

armada   A term that describes a fleet of warships. The most famous use of it relates to the Spanish Armada that was dispatched by King Philip II to invade England in 1588.

Assize courts   Courts dating back to the reign of Henry II, that were presided over by judges who traveled on circuit to hear criminal and civil cases. The Courts Act of 1971 abolished this system in Britain.

Bloody Assizes   The name accorded to the trials presided over by Judge Jeffries in 1685 after the Battle of Sedgemoor. Three-hundred and twenty of Monmouth's supporters, mostly poor laborers, were executed, and 800 transported to America as slaves.

burh   The Anglo-Saxon word for fortress (or fort); over the years it has evolved into the place-name suffix, "-bury." In England, examples of this are towns such as Shrewsbury and Canterbury.

chivalry   Presently associated with such attributes as bravery, honor, courtesy, and the fearless protection of women, yet during the Middle Ages the word originally referred to the knightly class.

The Civil List   Comprises the annual allowance by Parliament for the official expenses of the sovereign's household, so that royal duties can be carried out. It's set for a period of up to 10 years.

Constitutional monarch   Describes a sovereign who has to adhere to the laws and principles of the State. The 1689 Bill of Rights comprised a cornerstone of the British Constitution regarding Parliament's control over the monarchy.

Dauphin   The title given to the eldest son of the king of France. The Dauphin's wife was the Dauphine.

Equerry   An officer of the royal household who attends to members of the royal family. An equerry may also be charged with supervision of the horses belonging to a royal or noble household.

fief   The territory controlled by a vassal.

heir presumptive   The title accorded a successor whose claim may be set aside by the birth of another heir. An heir apparent, on the other hand, cannot be displaced in this way.

Jacobites   The people who supported the claim to the English throne of James II, as well as that of his son and grandson. The word derives from Jacobus, which is Latin for James.

Lollards   The derisive title accorded followers of English theologian John Wycliffe, who translated the Bible into English and preached against the formality of the Church. Although suppressed, his movement anticipated the Reformation.

morganatic marriage   A union between a man of high rank and a woman of lower rank, whereby the wife and children can't claim his title or possessions. A king's wife would have no royal status.

primogeniture   Refers to the right of succession or inheritance that belongs to either a first-born child or eldest son. This is why reigning monarchs are always desperate to sire offspring who will succeed them.

Protestants   Reformers, during the 16th century, who attacked the principles of the Roman Catholic Church and demanded separation from it. Inspired by revolutionary theologians John Calvin and Martin Luther, they largely divided into Calvinists and Lutherans.

Puritan   The historic name given to a member of that group of English Protestants who regarded the work of the Reformation as incomplete, and still sought to simplify the forms of church service.

the queen's subjects   Refers to the citizens of Great Britain as well as the British Commonwealth. These even include the members of the Royal Family. The only exception is the sovereign herself.

regalia   Refers to the royal items that are employed at a coronation ceremony. The word derives from "regal," which means of or by a king or kings, or even fit for a king.

roundheads   The nickname given to the mostly Puritan Parliamentarians who sported cropped hair at the time of the Long Parliament. This distinguished them from the king's swaggering, longhaired courtiers, who they dubbed Cavaliers.

serfdom   A form of slavery whereby workers aren't allowed to leave the land on which they work. In England, the Statute of Labourers of 1351 prevented workers from changing jobs in search of higher pay.

the Short Parliament   The term Charles I used in April, 1640 when he needed supplies for his battles with the Scots. Parliament refused to comply, and so the King dissolved it within three weeks.

the Stone of Scone   The coronation seat of early Scottish kings. Captured by Edward I, it was installed under the English Coronation Chair that was constructed in 1301. It was returned to Scotland in 1996.

Tory   An Irish term for a royalist outlaw, whereas Whigs had been Scottish Presbyterians who opposed royal power. During the late 17th century, England's chief political parties therefore applied these names derisively to each other.

vassals   People who took possession of land in return for allegiance and service to the monarch. This was known as the feudal system.

The Witan   The council of the Anglo-Saxon kings, once considered to be the first English parliament. In Old English, witan means "meeting of wise men."

Are You a Complete Royal Idiot? Quiz Answers

Quiz #1

1. Charles II
2. Edward VIII
3. Ten
4. President Ronald Reagan
5. "Randy Andy"
6. Seven
7. Alfred
8. 1066
9. William III and Mary II
10. The House of Hanover
11. "Between reigns"
12. Oliver Cromwell
13. The Act of Settlement
14. 1953

15. Edward VII
16. The Star of Africa
17. The Jewel House at the Tower of London
18. April 21, 1926
19. Trooping the Colour
20. Decoration, the Peerage, and Knighthood
21. The Central Chancery
22. The sovereign's official birthday and New Year's Day
23. Twenty-two
24. A Russian cannon
25. The accolade

Quiz #2

1. Johnnie and Frances
2. Earl Spencer
3. Elizabeth and David Emanuel
4. Fortress of fort
5. Athelstan
6. Eric Bloodaxe
7. The council/parliament of the Anglo-Saxon kings
8. Lady Godiva
9. The feudal system
10. The Domesday Book
11. Beauclerc
12. Plantaganet
13. Thomas a Beckett
14. Richard I (the Lionheart)
15. King John
16. The eldest son of the king of France
17. Edward I
18. The coronation seat of early Scottish kings
19. Isabella, wife of Edward II
20. The 100 Years' War
21. The Peasants' Revolt
22. Henry V
23. The House of York
24. He had him drowned in a cask of malmsey wine
25. The Bloody Tower at the Tower of London

Quiz #3

1. Henry VII
2. The Court of the Star Chamber
3. Newfoundland
4. Elizabeth of York, the eldest daughter of Edward IV
5. Thomas Wolsey
6. The Field of the Cloth of Gold
7. Catherine of Aragon, Anne Boleyn, Jane Seymour, Anne of Cleves, Catherine Howard, and Katherine Parr
8. The divorce of Henry VIII and Catherine of Aragon
9. Anne Boleyn and Catherine Howard
10. "The Mare of Flanders"
11. His sisters Mary and Elizabeth
12. Nine days
13. Philip of Spain
14. Thomas Cranmer
15. Calais
16. Elizabeth I
17. Sir Walter Raleigh
18. Sir Francis Drake
19. Mary, Queen of Scots
20. 1588
21. James VI of Scotland
22. Rex or Regina, Latin for, respectively, King or Queen
23. Sir Robert Catesby
24. November 5, 1605
25. El Dorado

Quiz #4

1. Roundheads and Cavaliers
2. 1649
3. The Great Plague and The Great Fire
4. The Rye House Plot
5. He converted to Catholicism
6. William III (William of Orange) and Mary II
7. The people who supported the claim to the throne of James II and his descendants
8. Queen Anne
9. "The Elephant" and "The Maypole"
10. Sir Robert Walpole
11. George III
12. Regency
13. Queen Victoria
14. The Entente Cordiale
15. George V
16. Edward VIII announced his abdication
17. Albert
18. Group Captain Peter Townsend
19. Mountbatten
20. Princess Anne
21. Prince Charles!
22. BA (Honours) in History
23. 1981
24. Roddy Llewellyn
25. A year

Index

E

K

M